Praise for *Semantic Modeling for Data*

Not only for Semantic Web and ML practitioners, this book illuminates the critical subject of how our clarity and precision in our language and thinking interoperate to make a tremendous impact on the fitness of our software. Highly recommended for analysts, architects, programmers—anyone in software development.

—*Eben Hewitt, CTO and author of* Semantic Software Design *and* Technology Strategy Patterns

Panos's clear-sighted text offers practical guidance and pragmatic advice to help you avoid the traps of vague, misleading, and just plain wrong semantic modeling.

—*Helen Lippell, taxonomy and semantics consultant, UK*

Among the attempts to bring logic, ontology, and semiotics in information engineering, this book is probably one of the best and more complete sources.

—*Guido Vetere, CEO and cofounder at Isagog*

Semantic Modeling for Data
Avoiding Pitfalls and Breaking Dilemmas

Panos Alexopoulos

Beijing · Boston · Farnham · Sebastopol · Tokyo

Semantic Modeling for Data

by Panos Alexopoulos

Copyright © 2020 Panos Alexopoulos. All rights reserved.

Published by O'Reilly Media, Inc., 1005 Gravenstein Highway North, Sebastopol, CA 95472.

O'Reilly books may be purchased for educational, business, or sales promotional use. Online editions are also available for most titles (*http://oreilly.com*). For more information, contact our corporate/institutional sales department: 800-998-9938 or *corporate@oreilly.com*.

Acquisitions Editor: Jonathan Hassell
Development Editor: Michele Cronin
Production Editor: Kate Galloway
Copyeditor: Kim Cofer
Proofreader: Piper Editorial, LLC

Indexer: Ellen Troutman Zaig
Interior Designer: David Futato
Cover Designer: Karen Montgomery
Illustrator: O'Reilly Media, Inc.

September 2020:   First Edition

Revision History for the First Edition
2020-08-19:   First Release

See *http://oreilly.com/catalog/errata.csp?isbn=9781492054276* for release details.

978-1-492-05427-6

[LSI]

Table of Contents

Part III. The Dilemmas

Preface

Knowledge graphs, ontologies, taxonomies, and other types of semantic data models have been developed and used in the data and artificial intelligence (AI) world for several decades. Their use captures the meaning of data in an explicit and shareable way, and enhances the effectiveness of data-driven applications. In the past decade, the popularity of such models has particularly increased. For example, the market intelligence company Gartner included knowledge graphs in its 2018 hype cycle for emerging technologies; and several prominent organizations like Amazon, LinkedIn, BBC, and IBM have been developing and using semantic data models within their products and services.

Behind this trend, there are two main driving forces:

- Data-rich organizations increasingly realize that it's not enough to have huge amounts of data. In order to derive value from it, you actually need this data to be clean, consistent, interconnected, and with clear semantics. This enables data scientists and business analysts to focus on what they do best: extracting useful insights from it. Semantic data modeling focuses exactly on tackling this challenge.

- Developers and providers of AI applications increasingly realize that machine learning and statistical reasoning techniques are not always enough to build the intelligent behavior they need; complementing them with explicit symbolic knowledge can be necessary and beneficial. Semantic data modeling focuses exactly on building and providing such knowledge.

Several languages, methodologies, platforms, and tools are available for building semantic models, coming from different communities and focusing on different model aspects (e.g., representation, reasoning, storage, querying, etc.). However, the overall task of specifying, developing, putting in use, and evolving a semantic model is not as straightforward as one might think, especially as the model's scope and scale increases. The reason is that human language and thinking is full of ambiguity, vagueness, imprecision, and other phenomena that make the formal and universally accepted representation of data semantics quite a difficult task.

This book shows you what semantic data modeling entails, and what challenges you have to face as a creator or user of semantic models. More importantly, it provides you with concrete advice on how to avoid dangers (*pitfalls*) and overcome obstacles (*dilemmas*). It teaches you some fundamental and enduring semantic modeling principles that remain true, no matter which particular framework or technology you are using, and shows you how you can apply these in your specific context.

After reading this book, you will be able to critically evaluate and make better use of existing semantic models and technologies, make informed decisions, and improve the quality and usability of the models you build.

Who Should Read This Book

This book is for data practitioners who develop or use semantic representations of data in their everyday jobs (knowledge engineers, information architects, data engineers, data scientists, etc.), and for whom the explicitness, accuracy, and common understandability of the data's meaning is an important dimension of their work.

You will find this book particularly useful if you recognize yourself in one or more of the following situations:

- You are a taxonomist, ontologist, or other type of data modeler who knows a lot about semantic data modeling, though mostly from an academic and research perspective. You probably have a PhD or MSc in the field and excellent knowledge of modeling languages and frameworks, but you have had little chance to apply this knowledge in an industrial setting. You are now in the early stages of an industrial role and you have the opportunity to apply your knowledge to real-world problems. You have started realizing, though, that things are very different from what the academic papers and textbooks describe; the methods and techniques you've learned are not as applicable or effective as you thought. You face difficult situations for which there is no obvious decision to be made and, ultimately, the semantic models you develop are misunderstood, misapplied, or provide little added value. This book will help you put your valuable and hard-earned knowledge into practice and improve the quality of your work.

- You are a data or information architect, tasked with developing semantic models that can solve the problem of semantic heterogeneity between the many disparate data sources and applications or products that your organization has. For that, you have already applied several out-of-the-box semantic data management solutions that promised seamless integration, but the results you got were mostly unsatisfactory. This book will help you to better understand the not so obvious dimensions and challenges you need to address in order to achieve the semantic interoperability you want.

- You are a data scientist, expert in machine learning and statistical data analysis, and part of a multidisciplinary team that builds semantic models for AI applications (e.g., knowledge graphs for virtual assistants). You interact daily with ontologists, linguists, and other semantic professionals, but you struggle to understand their lingo and how your skills can be combined with theirs. This book will introduce you to the basics of semantic data modeling and will help you identify the aspects of it where your expertise can have the biggest impact.

- You are a data scientist, expert in machine learning and statistical data analysis, working with data that has been created and semantically described by other people, teams, and organizations. Often, you are unsure about what these semantic data models really represent and whether they are appropriate for the kind of analysis you want to make or solution you want to build. Even worse, you make incorrect assumptions about the data's semantics, ending up with machine learning models and data science solutions that do not work as you had expected. This book will show you how to be more critical toward the semantic models you work with and anticipate/tackle problems that may occur.

In a nutshell, this is a book for a broad range of data professionals who want to learn how to "talk semantics" in order to work more effectively together and increase the quality, usability, and value of their data.

What to Expect in This Book

In this book I will not attempt to give you detailed instructions on how to develop a semantic data model from scratch, or how to use specific semantic modeling languages and frameworks. There is already plenty of documentation for that purpose that I'll point you to. Instead, I will take a helicopter view of the semantic modeling life cycle, discuss fundamental principles and challenges, present relevant technologies and resources, and zoom in on particular issues and situations that deserve your attention and require careful treatment.

My goal is not to completely cover the field or present recent trends, but to provide you with practical and pragmatic knowledge that will help you to do your job better, both as a creator and a user of semantic models. For that, the book will focus on:

Semantic thinking, not just languages or tools
　　Most textbooks and tutorials on semantic modeling assume that producing good semantic models is primarily a matter of using the right language or tool. This book, instead, will teach you the necessary principles and techniques to use the available modeling language or framework correctly, in an effort to avoid the *Garbage In, Garbage Out effect*.

What doesn't work

Knowing what doesn't work and why can be a more effective way to improve the quality of a system or process than knowing only what does work, in theory or in only some cases. This book applies this principle to the task of semantic data modeling by focusing on a) identifying as many ways as possible in which things can go wrong, b) what would be the consequences of that, and c) what could be done to avoid such situations.

Non-Boolean phenomena

Most semantic modeling methodologies and frameworks assume that all human knowledge can be separated into false and true statements, and provide little support for tackling "noisy" phenomena like vagueness or uncertainty. The real world, however, is full of such phenomena, and this book will help you not merely handle them, but actually use them to your advantage.

Decisions in context

Semantic data modeling is challenging, and modelers face many types of dilemmas for which they need to make decisions. Describing successful yet isolated experiments, or "success stories," rarely helps break these dilemmas. This book focuses on identifying as many difficult situations as possible and showing you how to break through them in your own context.

Organizational and strategic aspects

A semantic data modeling initiative is rarely a one-off engineering project; instead, it's a continuous effort of fueling an organization with up-to-date and useful semantic knowledge that serves its business and data strategy. As such, it requires considering not only technical, but also organizational and strategic aspects, including how to productively work with a broad range of stakeholders (executives, technical teams, end users, salespeople, etc.).

Throughout the book, I will make reference to and draw lessons from personal experiences from organizations and semantic-related projects I have worked for, and particularly Textkernel, the company I work for as I am writing this book. Textkernel is a Dutch company that develops software for semantically analyzing and matching people's résumés and job vacancies and, for that purpose, develops and utilizes a knowledge graph about the HR, recruitment, and labor market domain. Many of the pitfalls and dilemmas you will find in the book are derived from my experience there as the main person responsible for the knowledge graph's development, application, and evolution.

Also, to illustrate many of the book's arguments, I will draw examples from semantic languages, frameworks, standards, and data models developed by the *Semantic Web* community, without suggesting that these are the only or the best means to develop semantic data models. The Semantic Web has been an ambitious collaborative effort to enable the publishing of semantic machine-readable and shareable data on the web. In its effort to achieve that goal, it has produced methods, technologies, and data that exemplify both good and bad practices of data modeling that you should be aware of.

Finally, be aware that this book is about modeling data at the conceptual level of abstraction and, as such, does not cover the tasks and challenges of efficiently storing and processing data in data-intensive applications. For that purpose, Martin Kleppman's *Designing Data-Intensive Applications* (O'Reilly) and other similar books are great resources to peruse.

Book Outline

This book is arranged in three parts.

In Part I, we discuss fundamental concepts, phenomena, and processes related to semantic data modeling, setting the tone for the rest of the book and establishing a common ground and terminology. In Chapter 1, we discuss in more detail how semantic modeling can contribute to doing better data science and AI, and demonstrate how bad modeling practices might undermine this effort. Chapter 2 provides an overview of the most general and common semantic modeling elements that are found in different data modeling frameworks, while Chapter 3 describes some important semantic and linguistic phenomena that characterize human language and thinking, and play an important role in a semantic model's quality. Chapter 4 describes the quality dimensions that should be considered when evaluating a semantic model, along with basic metrics and measurement methods for each dimension. Finally, Chapter 5, focuses on the development process of a semantic model, looking at the challenges, steps, and activities it involves, and the methodological and technological support that is available for each of them.

In Part II, we take a close look at the most common pitfalls we fall into when we develop and apply semantic data models, and discuss concrete methods and techniques to effectively avoid them. In Chapter 6, we see how we might compromise the human-interpretability of a semantic model by describing its elements in inaccurate and incomplete ways. In Chapter 7, we look at how we might do the same for a model's machine-interpretability by using, in unintended ways, the elements the modeling languages and frameworks provide. In Chapter 8, we examine the circumstances under which we might end up building a semantic model that nobody ever asked for, as well as how the model's development and quality may suffer from not using the right knowledge acquisition mechanisms. In Chapter 9, we see how a model's quality is not only affected by mistakes made during its specification and development, but also by bad practices followed when measuring and managing it. Chapter 10 challenges the assumption that just because a semantic model has been designed for the same domain or data an application operates in, its semantics are directly applicable and beneficial to it. Finally, Chapter 11 looks at the broader strategic and organizational context where semantic data modeling takes place, and identifies relevant pitfalls and bad practices that may prevent an organization from successfully executing semantic data initiatives.

In Part III, we switch from semantic modeling pitfalls to dilemmas, examining how to effectively deal with situations where we need to choose between alternative courses of action, each with its own advantages and disadvantages. In Chapter 12, the dilemmas that concern us are related to choosing between different ways of representing the same meaning, even within the same modeling language. In Chapter 13, we deal with dilemmas about what should be included in a semantic model and what can (or should) be left out, so that the model has the right balance of expressivity and content it needs. Chapter 14, in turn, considers the challenges of evolving and governing a semantic model and describes how to craft a proper strategy to tackle them. Finally, Chapter 15 brings together some of the recurring themes of this book, and builds on them to envisage the future.

Conventions Used in This Book

The following typographical conventions are used in this book:

Italic
> Indicates new terms, URLs, email addresses, filenames, and file extensions.

`Constant width`
> Used for program listings, as well as within paragraphs to refer to program elements such as variable or function names, databases, data types, environment variables, statements, and keywords.

> This element signifies a tip or suggestion.

> This element signifies a general note.

> This element indicates a warning or caution.

O'Reilly Online Learning

O'REILLY®   For more than 40 years, *O'Reilly Media* has provided technology and business training, knowledge, and insight to help companies succeed.

Our unique network of experts and innovators share their knowledge and expertise through books, articles, and our online learning platform. O'Reilly's online learning platform gives you on-demand access to live training courses, in-depth learning paths, interactive coding environments, and a vast collection of text and video from O'Reilly and 200+ other publishers. For more information, visit *http://oreilly.com*.

How to Contact Us

Please address comments and questions concerning this book to the publisher:

O'Reilly Media, Inc.
1005 Gravenstein Highway North
Sebastopol, CA 95472
800-998-9938 (in the United States or Canada)
707-829-0515 (international or local)
707-829-0104 (fax)

We have a web page for this book, where we list errata, examples, and any additional information. You can access this page at *https://oreil.ly/semantic-modeling-4-data*.

Email *bookquestions@oreilly.com* to comment or ask technical questions about this book.

For more information about our books, courses, conferences, and news, see our website at *http://www.oreilly.com*.

Find us on Facebook: *http://facebook.com/oreilly*

Follow us on Twitter: *http://twitter.com/oreillymedia*

Watch us on YouTube: *http://www.youtube.com/oreillymedia*

Acknowledgments

There are many people I would like to thank for the role they played in the realization of this book.

First, George Anadiotis, Paco Nathan, and Mike Loukides, who believed in this project and set the wheels in motion.

Second, my reviewers and beta readers who provided meticulous and constructive feedback about the book: Helen Lippell, Thomas Frisendal, Eben Hewitt, Patrick Harrison, George Sigletos, Guido Vetere, Jelle Jan Bankert, Artemis Parvizi, Boris Villazon Terrazas, Ghislain Atemezing, and Miika Alonen. Of course, all opinions and mistakes in the book are my own.

Third, the editorial, design, and production teams at O'Reilly who supported me throughout the development process, put up with my long sentences and sloppy writing, and helped me produce a high-quality book: Michele Cronin, Jonathan Hassell, Kate Galloway, Kim Cofer, David Futato, and Karen Montgomery.

Finally, I am infinitely grateful to my beloved Spyretta for her patience and support throughout the writing process that has taken almost two years.

PART I

The Basics

CHAPTER 1

Mind the Semantic Gap

Our agreement or disagreement is at times based on a misunderstanding.
—Mokokoma Mokhonoana

In the era of the big data and AI frenzy, data is considered a gold mine that awaits organizations and businesses that will find and extract their gold. Whether you call this data science, data analytics, business intelligence, or something else, you can't deny that data-related investments have increased significantly, and the demand for data professionals (engineers, analysts, scientists, etc.) has skyrocketed.

Do these professionals manage to find gold? Well, not always. Sometimes, the large ocean of data that an organization claims to have proves to be a small pond. Other times, the data is there but it contains no gold, or at least not the kind of gold that the organization can use. Often it is also the case that both data and gold are there, but the infrastructure or technology needed for the gold's extraction are not yet available or mature enough. But it can also be that data professionals have all they wish (abundance of the right data, gold to be found, and state-of-the-art technology) and still fail. The reason? The *semantic gap* between the data supply and the data exploitation side.

Let me explain. As data practitioners, many of us work mainly on the data supply side: we collect and generate data, we represent, integrate, store, and make it accessible through data models, and we get it ready for usage and exploitation. Others of us work mainly on the data exploitation side: we use data to build predictive, descriptive, or other types of analytics solutions, as well as build and power AI applications. And many of us wear both hats. We all have the same mission, though: to derive value from data.

This mission is often compromised by what I like to call the semantic gap—the situation that arises when the data models of the supply side are misunderstood and misused by the exploitation side, and/or when the data requirements of the exploitation side are misunderstood by the supply side. In both cases, the problem is caused by insufficient or problematic modeling of the data's semantics. This book is about helping practitioners of both sides work better with semantic data models and narrow (if not close) the semantic gap.

What Is Semantic Data Modeling?

Semantics is the study of meaning, concerned with the relationship between signifiers that people use when interacting with the world (words, phrases, signs, and symbols), and the things in that world that these signifiers denote (entities, concepts, ideas). The goal is the creation of a common understanding of the meaning of things, helping people understand each other despite different experiences or points of view. When applied in computer science, semantics helps computer systems interpret more accurately what people and the data they produce mean, as well as interface more efficiently and productively with other disparate computer systems.

In that sense, semantic data modeling can be defined as the development of descriptions and representations of data in such a way that the latter's meaning is *explicit*, *accurate*, and *commonly understood* by both humans and computer systems. This definition encompasses a wide range of data artifacts, including metadata schemas, controlled vocabularies, taxonomies, ontologies, knowledge graphs, entity-relationship (E-R) models, property graphs, and other conceptual models for data representation.

As an example, in Figure 1-1 you can see part of the SNOMED CT Standard Ontology, a semantic model that describes the meaning of core medical terms (such as clinical findings, symptoms, diagnoses, medical procedures, and others) by grouping them into concepts, providing them with synonyms and definitions, and relating them to each other through hierarchical and other types of relations [1].

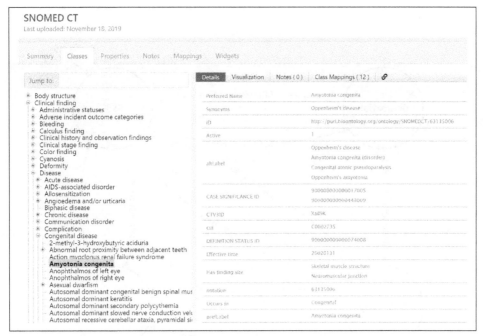

Figure 1-1. View of the SNOMED CT ontology

Similarly, Figure 1-2 shows (part of) the schema of the European Skills, Competences, Qualifications and Occupations (ESCO) classification, a multilingual semantic model that defines and interrelates concepts about occupations, skills, and qualifications, for the European Union labor market domain [2].

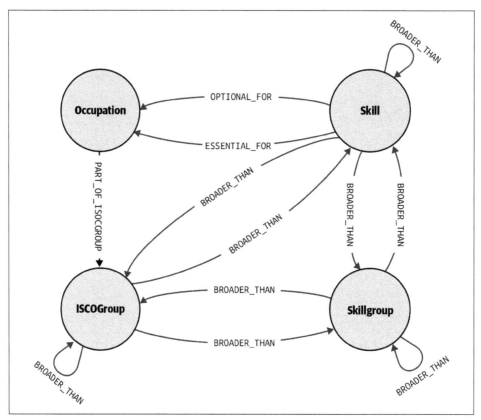

Figure 1-2. ESCO classification schema

In general, defining the necessary and sufficient criteria for a data model to be semantic in a clear way is not a straightforward task, and there are several debates within the data community about this [3] [4]. It can be similarly difficult and controversial to clearly define the exact nature and defining characteristics of particular types of semantic data models (e.g., what exactly is a knowledge graph, what is an ontology, and what are their differences) [5] [6].

In this book I am not going to engage in such debates. Instead, I will use the term *semantic model* to refer to any representation of data whose goal is to make the meaning of data explicit and commonly understood among humans and machines, and focus on the challenge of achieving this goal.

What I won't consider as semantic models, at least for the purposes of this book, are machine learning models, and the reason is that their goal is not the explicitness of meaning. Semantic models consist of symbolic representations of knowledge and reasoning behavior, while machine learning models consist of latent representations at the subsymbolic level that do not have any obvious human interpretation. The latter excel at capturing knowledge that is not crisp (e.g., statistical regularities and similarities) while the former capture discrete facts and record precise identities. For example, a machine learning model might learn the typical features that can separate a cat from a dog, but would not be able to keep track of the fact that Leika was a Soviet dog that went into space.

This does not mean that semantic modeling is an inherently better or worse approach to working with data than machine learning; it merely means that the two approaches are different. And it's exactly because of these differences that they should be seen as complementary approaches for AI and data science rather than competing ones.

Machine learning can help automate the development of semantic models, and semantic modeling can help accelerate and enhance the development of machine learning models. And while this book is primarily about semantic modeling, it explores and supports this synergy by showing semantic modelers how to make good use of machine learning methods and tools, and machine learning practitioners how to make good use of semantic models.

Why Develop and Use a Semantic Data Model?

Ontologies, knowledge graphs, and other types of semantic models have been around for several decades; their popularity, however, has particularly increased in the last few years, with Google announcing in 2012 that "their knowledge graph allowed searching for things, not strings" [7] and Gartner including knowledge graphs in its 2018 hype cycle for emerging technologies [8]. Currently, apart from Google, many prominent organizations like Amazon [9], LinkedIn [10], Thomson Reuters [11], BBC (*https://oreil.ly/Td—d*), and IBM [12] are developing and using semantic data models within their products and services.

One reason why an organization would want to invest in a semantic data model is to enhance the functionality of its AI and data science applications and services. Even though such applications nowadays are (rightly) based on machine learning and statistical techniques, there are several tasks for which having access to explicit symbolic knowledge can be necessary and beneficial.

As an example, consider Watson, IBM's famous question-answering system that competed in the popular quiz show *Jeopardy!* in 2011 against human champions, and managed to win the first-place prize of $1 million [13]. As Watson's creators report, even though the majority of evidence analysis the system performed to find the answer to questions relied on unstructured information, several of its components used knowledge bases and ontologies to tackle specific knowledge and reasoning challenges [14].

One of these challenges was that, because many questions expressed temporal or geo-spatial relations, Watson needed to determine whether candidate answers for a given question were temporally compatible with it, or contained the same geospatial relation as the one expressed in the question. Also, in order to rule out candidate answers whose types were incompatible with what the question asked (e.g., ruling out persons when the question asked for countries), the system required to know which types were mutually exclusive (e.g., that a person cannot also be a country). This kind of knowledge was provided to Watson via semantic data models.

Another important reason organizations would want a semantic model is to standardize and align the meaning of typically heterogeneous and managed-in-silos data, provide it with context, and make it more discoverable, interoperable, and usable for analytics and other purposes [15].

For example, Thomson Reuters, a news and information services company, launched a knowledge graph in 2017 that integrated data about organizations, people, financial instruments, quotes, deals, and other entities, coming from more than 20,000 different sources (content analysts, content partners, and news sources) [16]. The graph's purpose was to enable data discovery and analytics services that could help the company's clients assemble the data and information they needed faster and more reliably.

In all cases, if you are building a semantic data model for a given application scenario, it's very important that the model effectively conveys to its users those aspects of the data's meaning that are important for its effective interpretation and usage within that scenario. If that's not the case, there is a substantial risk that your model will not be used or, even worse, be used in wrong ways and with undesired consequences. Conversely, if for a given application scenario you are using a semantic model that you haven't yourself developed, it's very important to ensure that the semantics of its data are the ones your scenario actually needs. If that doesn't happen, you might also have undesired consequences. Let's see why.

Bad Semantic Modeling

To see how a semantic model can be problematic, let's take a closer look at the ESCO classification in Figure 1-2. This model was released in 2017 by the European Commission, after six years of development, with the ambition to provide standardized conceptual knowledge about occupations, skills, and qualifications, that could be used by data scientists and software developers for the following purposes:

- Semantically analyze labor market data (CVs, job vacancies, educational programs, etc.) in a consistent, standardized, and commonly understood way, across languages.

- Develop intelligent software that could automatically match job seekers to job providers.

- Derive labor market analytics that could provide actionable insights to job seekers, employers, governments, and policy makers (e.g., a country predicting future skill needs in a particular industry and adapting its educational policy accordingly).

Now, ESCO provides several semantic "goodies" to achieve this ambition. For example, it identifies and groups together all terms that may refer to the same occupation, skill, or qualification concept. This is a very useful piece of knowledge because it can be used to identify job vacancies for the same occupation, even if the latter may be expressed in many different ways. Equally useful is the knowledge the model provides about the skills that are most relevant to a given occupation (see `essential_for` and `optional_for` relations in Figure 1-2). Such knowledge can be used, for example, by education providers to identify gaps in the demand and supply of particular skills in the market, and update their curricula accordingly. Table 1-1 shows some examples of essential skills for three occupations.

Table 1-1. Examples of skills and competences for particular occupations found in ESCO

Occupation	Essential skills
Data scientist	Data mining, data models, information categorization, information extraction, online analytical processing, query languages, resource description framework query language, statistics, visual presentation techniques
Knowledge engineer	Business intelligence, business process modeling, database development tools, information extraction, natural language processing, principles of artificial intelligence, resource description framework query language, systems development life cycle, systems theory, task algorithmization, web programming
Data entry supervisor	LDAP, LINQ, MDX, N1QL, SPARQL, XQuery, company policies, database, documentation types, information confidentiality, query languages, resource description framework query language

Now, the modelers of this latter piece of knowledge in ESCO have fallen into one of the many semantic modeling pitfalls I describe in this book, namely presenting subjective knowledge as objective, and not adequately informing the model's users about *vagueness*.

Here is the problem: If you ask one hundred different professionals which skills are most important for their profession, you will most likely get one hundred different answers. If, even worse, you attempt to distinguish between essential and optional skills, as ESCO does, then you should prepare for a lot of debate and disagreement. Just take a look at Table 1-1 and see how many essential skills you agree with.

The issue is that the notion of essentiality of a skill for a profession is (in the majority of the cases) vague; i.e., it lacks crisp applicability criteria that clearly separate the essential from the nonessential skills. And without such criteria, it's wrong (and potentially harmful) to present the `essential_for` relation as objective and valid in all contexts.

Imagine, for example, that you are building some career advice software that takes as input someone's desired profession (e.g., data scientist) and tells them what skills they need to obtain and/or enhance in order to find a job in that profession. For that purpose, you could directly use ESCO's data and tell your users, for instance, that in order to become knowledge engineers they must learn web programming. This might indeed be the case in some contexts, but do you think presenting it as an indisputable fact applicable in all contexts is a sound practice?

To be fair to ESCO, similar problems appear in many semantic data models. And to be fair to data modelers, semantic modeling is hard, because human language and perception is full of ambiguity, vagueness, imprecision, and other phenomena, that make the formal and universally accepted representation of data semantics quite a difficult task.

In practice, the key challenge in building a good semantic model is to find the right level of semantic expressiveness and clarity that will be beneficial to its users and applications, without excessive development and maintenance costs. From my experience, software developers and data engineers tend to under-specify meaning when building data models, while ontologists, linguists, and domain experts tend to over-specify it and debate about semantic distinctions for which the model's users may not care at all. The job of a semantic modeler is to strike the right balance of meaning explicitness and shareability that their data, domains, applications, and users need. This job is threatened by *pitfalls* and *dilemmas*.

Avoiding Pitfalls

A pitfall in semantic modeling is a situation in which the model's creators take a decision or action that is clearly wrong with respect to the data's semantics, the model's requirements, or other aspects of the model's development process, and leads to undesired consequences when the model is put to use. A pitfall can also be the omission of an action that is necessary to avoid such consequences. The latter's probability or severity may vary, but that doesn't mean that a pitfall is not a mistake that we should strive to avoid when possible. ESCO's nontreatment of vagueness that I described earlier may not seem like a big problem at first, but it's undeniably a risk whose consequences remain to be seen.

Falling into a pitfall is not always a result of the modeler's incompetence or inexperience. More often than we would like to admit, the academic and industry communities that develop semantic modeling languages, methodologies, and tools, contribute to the problem in at least three ways:

- We use contradictory or even completely wrong terminology when describing and teaching semantic modeling

- We ignore or dismiss some of the pitfalls as nonexistent or unimportant

- We fall into these pitfalls ourselves and produce technology, literature, and actual models that contain them

To see how this actually happens, consider the following two excerpts from two different semantic modeling resources:

> "...OWL classes are interpreted as sets that contain individuals... The word concept is sometimes used in place of class. Classes are a concrete representation of concepts..."

> "A [SKOS] concept can be viewed as an idea or notion; a unit of thought...the concepts of a thesaurus or classification scheme are modeled as individuals in the SKOS data model..."

The first excerpt is found in a popular tutorial about Protégé [17], a tool that enables you to build semantic models according to the Ontology Web Language (OWL) [18]. The second one is derived from the specification of the Simple Knowledge Organization System (SKOS) [19], a World Wide Web Consortium (W3C) recommendation designed for representation of thesauri, classification schemes, taxonomies, and other types of structured controlled vocabularies.

Based on these definitions, what do you understand to be a concept in a semantic model? Is it a set of things as the Protégé tutorial suggests, or some unit of thought as SKOS claims? And what should you do if you need to model a concept in OWL that is not really a set of things? Should you still have to make it a class? The answer, as we will see in the rest of the book, is that the SKOS definition is more accurate and useful, and that the "concept = class" claim of the OWL tutorial is at best misleading, causing several semantic modeling errors that we will see later in the book.

In any case, my goal in this book is not to assign blame to people and communities for bad semantic modeling advice, but to help you navigate this not-so-smooth landscape and show you how to recognize and avoid pitfalls, both as a model creator and user.

Breaking Dilemmas

Contrary to a pitfall, a semantic modeling dilemma is a situation in which the model's creators have to choose between different courses of action, each of which comes with its own pros and cons, and for which there's no clear decision process and criteria to be applied.

As an example, consider the options that the developers of ESCO have to treat the vague `essential_for` relation between occupations and skills. One option is to flag the relation as "vague" so that the users know what to expect, but that won't reduce the potential disagreements that may occur. Another option is to try to create different versions of the relation that are applicable to different contexts (e.g., different countries, industries, user groups, etc.) so that the level of potential disagreement is lower. Doing this, however, is costlier and more difficult. So, what would you advise ESCO to do?

In this book, I will describe several dilemmas related to a semantic model's development and usage, but I won't give you a definite and "expert" solution for them simply because there's no such thing. To tackle a semantic modeling dilemma you need to treat it as a decision-making problem; i.e., you need to formulate the alternative options and find a way to evaluate them from a feasibility, cost-benefit, strategic, or other perspective that makes sense for your goals and context. For that, I will show you how to frame each dilemma as a decision-making problem, and show you what information you should look for in order to reach a decision.

CHAPTER 2

Semantic Modeling Elements

Take advantage of the ambiguity in the world. Look at something and think what else it might be.
—Roger von Oech

A difficulty you might face when talking with other data professionals about semantic models is understanding and agreeing on what these models might look like and what elements they might consist of. If you ask a database developer who has been working all their life with relational database systems, their answer will most likely include tables, fields, and primary and foreign keys. If, on the other hand, you ask an ontology engineer with a background in Semantic Web technologies, they will mention classes, object properties, datatype properties, and individuals. And if your interlocutor's origins are traced back in linguistics, it's quite probable that they will refer to synsets, lemmas, synonyms, and hyponyms.

In practice, all these people refer to similar types of semantic modeling elements, yet they are accustomed to different terminologies that make it hard to immediately comprehend one another. At the same time, different people and communities use the same terms for different elements, making common understanding even more difficult.

Such a common understanding, though, is crucial for building data models that are semantically interoperable to each other. Until we all have at our hands a universal semantic modeling language that everyone uses (which I don't think will ever happen), we need to be able to draw conceptual mappings between models consisting of different element types without introducing semantic errors.

For example, as we briefly mentioned in Chapter 1 and will explain in more detail later in this chapter, a concept in SKOS is not really the same as a class in OWL. This means that if you try to merge a SKOS model with an OWL one by transforming all concepts into classes, the resulting model has a high chance of being semantically inaccurate.

With that in mind, this chapter provides an overview of the most general and common semantic modeling elements that are found in different data modeling languages, frameworks, and communities, including:

- Semantic Web languages, specifications, and standards like Resource Description Framework (Schema) a.k.a. RDF(S) [20] [21], OWL, and SKOS
- Description Logics [22], a family of formal knowledge representation languages that provide the logical formalisms for Semantic Web languages
- National and international standards for controlled vocabularies, thesauri, and taxonomies like ANSI/NISO Z39.19 [23] and ISO25964 (*https://oreil.ly/ZTKmK*)
- Lexical databases like WordNet (*https://oreil.ly/nK5O0*), VerbNet (*https://oreil.ly/Wvvp-*), FrameNet (*https://oreil.ly/JaZuE*), or PropBank (*https://oreil.ly/gJpKt*)
- Conceptual models for database design like the E-R model [24] for relational databases or the labeled property graph model for graph databases [25]

The goal is not a complete, textbook-like description of all these frameworks, but rather the establishment of a common and unambiguous terminology for the modeling elements that will be the protagonists of this book and its pitfalls and dilemmas. Reading this chapter will help you better understand what a semantic model can consist of, analyze and compare different models expressed in different ways, and more effectively communicate your own model to all its relevant stakeholders.

General Elements

Let's start our overview with the elements that we find in the vast majority of semantic modeling languages and frameworks: *entities*, *relations*, *classes*, *attributes*, *terms*, and *axioms*.

Entities

Without being too philosophical, an entity is something that may exist concretely or abstractly, outside or within our mind. An entity is concrete when it has a physical manifestation by which it can be sensed and identified. A particular person, organization, document, or event are all examples of concrete entities. In philosophy and metaphysics, concrete entities are known as *particulars* and their key characteristic is that they can exist over time but they can only be in one place at a time, i.e., they are "nonrepeatable" entities. Linguistically, concrete entities are usually described via proper nouns.

An abstract entity, on the other hand, does not exist in a particular time or place, but rather as an idea, category, or concept. For example, the concept of Person as "a being that has certain capacities or attributes such as reason, morality, consciousness or self-consciousness" [26] is abstract, while you and me as particular persons are concrete. Similarly, a film genre like Film Noir, a field of science like Biology, or a sport like Soccer are all examples of abstract entities. Table 2-1 juxtaposes examples of concrete and abstract entities in different domains.

Table 2-1. Concrete and abstract entities

Concrete	Abstract
The 2018 Champions League Final Game	Soccer
Socrates' Trial	Justice
Nelson Mandela	Politician
Empire State Building	Architecture
C++	Object-oriented programming
Volkswagen AG	Car manufacturing
Mick Jagger	Rock music

Entities are core elements in a semantic model and should be unique and unambiguous within it. The same entity may have multiple names (e.g., the city of Rome in Italy is also known as "the Eternal City"), and the same name may refer to multiple entities (e.g., Rome is also a town in the state of Georgia in the United States), yet an entity's meaning is unique. This is what the "Things Not Strings" slogan of Google's Knowledge Graph is all about, namely that the search engine can actually identify the entities that the keywords imply.

A semantic model may contain both abstract and concrete entities, in any proportion. For example, the LinkedIn knowledge graph contains concrete entities like people, jobs, companies, and schools, but also abstract ones like job titles and skills. Similarly, the English version of DBpedia (*https://wiki.dbpedia.org*) (a large knowledge graph that is automatically derived from Wikipedia) contains more than six million concrete entities like persons, places, works, and organizations, but also more than a million abstract categories.

In general, modeling abstract entities is more difficult than modeling concrete ones. One reason is that, as humans, we often do not have a clear understanding of such entities. Try, for example, to agree with your peers on a universal definition of love, success, freedom, or racism. But even defining concepts within your domain of expertise can be a challenge. Try providing a definition of data scientist that is globally accepted and covers all cases.

To make things worse, the meaning of abstract entities changes more frequently than that of concrete ones. Concepts like masculinity and femininity, for example, are not currently interpreted in the same way as two hundred years ago, while the Battle of Waterloo that took place around that time remains more or less the same event. For these two reasons, you need to be extra careful when dealing with abstract entities, not only as a creator of semantic models, but also as a consumer.

For example, let's say that you are building a supervised machine learning classifier to determine the genres a film belongs to (e.g., Comedy or Science Fiction) and you query a film knowledge graph to derive concrete films for each genre to use as training data. If your classifier's users and the knowledge graph's creators do not share the same interpretation of these genres, then the precision of your classifier will be pretty low.

Relations

The second key element of semantic models is relations. A relation expresses a particular way that two or more entities can be related to one another. For example, the entity Lionel Messi can be related to the entity soccer via the relation plays, as well as via the relation likes (assuming Messi actually likes soccer). These are both binary relations in the sense that they link exactly two entities. If, however, we say that "Lionel Messi married Antonella Roccuzzo in Argentina," then we have a ternary relation as there are three related entities.

Terminology-wise, things can get pretty confusing when talking about relations. If you have worked with relational databases you will know that the term *relation* is equivalent to a set of tuples (or table). That's the reason in entity-relationship modeling, the term *relationship* is used instead of relation. On the other hand, if you are a Semantic Web expert, you will know that in RDF(S) relations are called *properties*, and in OWL they are called *object properties*.

To make things worse, in Description Logics relations are known as *roles*, a term used also in the field of formal ontology to denote a certain kind of abstract entity like Student or Customer [27]. I am not going to argue here which terminology is correct and which is not, and to avoid confusion I will stick with the term *relation* throughout the book.

Relations are important modeling elements that contribute to the explicitness and machine-interpretability of the meaning of entities by describing characteristics of them and providing knowledge and context that could be used for reasoning. An isolated entity that is not linked to any other entities can be (usually) human interpretable through its name and some natural language definition, yet for a machine none of these elements are directly usable.

For example, if someone applies to a vacancy for a software developer position, writing in their résumé that they are a Java developer, the hiring manager will automatically know that the application is relevant, since a Java Developer is a kind of

`Software Developer`. However, a machine cannot do the same if it doesn't know (or has no means to derive) this relation.

Classes and Individuals

Classes are abstract entities that represent kinds of things in the world that may serve as semantic types of other entities, concrete or abstract. For example, the entity Song can be used as a type of the entity `Stairway to Heaven` and the entity `Team Sport` as the type of the entity `Basketball`. Equivalently, we say that `Stairway to Heaven` is an instance of the class `Song`, and `Basketball` an instance of the class `Team Sport`. Figure 2-1 shows additional examples of class-instance pairs. The instances of a class are also known as individuals.

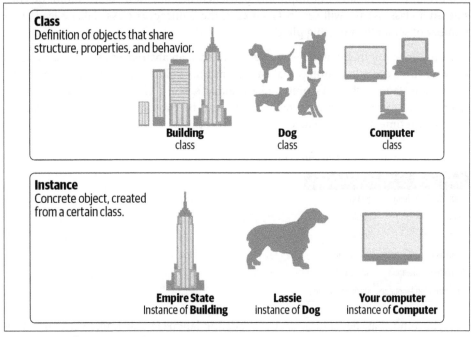

Figure 2-1. Class versus instances

Classes are useful semantic modeling elements because they provide an abstraction mechanism for grouping together entities that share the same structure, characteristics, and behavior (and thus meaning). This mechanism enables us to state facts or define rules that are applicable to all the entities that belong to the same class. For example, we can use the class `United States Lawyer` to say that all lawyers in the United States have passed the bar examination, without stating this fact for every individual lawyer in the country.

Now, as we have already seen, in certain semantic modeling languages (like Description Logics and OWL), the term *concept* is used interchangeably with the term *class*. That, however, is only partially correct; a concept can indeed play the role of a class if its definition implies a set of entities that instantiate it, but this is not always the case.

For example, the definition of the concept Song as "a single (and often standalone) work of music that is typically intended to be sung by the human voice with distinct and fixed pitches and patterns using sound and silence and a variety of forms that often include the repetition of sections" [28] explicitly states that its instances are particular pieces of music. On the other hand, the concept Biology defined as "the natural science that studies life and living organisms, including their physical structure, chemical processes, molecular interactions, physiological mechanisms, development and evolution" [29] does not imply any particular instantiations, so it cannot be considered a class. As we will see in Chapter 7, the "concept = class" fallacy leads to a number of semantic modeling pitfalls.

The only criterion that matters when determining if an abstract entity can be a class is whether there are other entities that can be instances of it. If you can't find any (convincing) instances, then it's pretty likely that it's not a class. Table 2-2 juxtaposes abstract entities that I am personally certain can be classes, and entities for which I have a hard time finding instances. What do you think?

Table 2-2. Clear and doubtful class entities

Clear classes	Doubtful classes
Supreme Court judge	Justice
Song	Music
Soccer game	Soccer
Politician	Communism
Marketing software	Advertising
Programming language	Machine learning

Keep in mind that, depending on the modeling language and framework, an entity can be potentially a class, yet not necessarily explicitly modeled as such. In property graphs, for example, there is no formal distinction between a class and an instance since everything is a node (node labels can play the role of a class but not exclusively). In SKOS, you can define an entity as an instance of the class Concept but you can't create instances of it. And in OWL, entities that can be classes are often modeled as individuals because, otherwise, they cannot be related to other entities. This means that you should not assume that across different semantic models the same entities will be modeled in the same way.

Furthermore, sometimes the modeling language you use obliges you to decide whether an entity should be modeled as a class or as an instance. This is the case, for example, in E-R modeling where its creator Peter Chen proposes that proper nouns should be modeled as individual entities (e.g., "John Kennedy," "London," etc.) and common nouns as classes (e.g., "dog," "city," etc.) [30]. Similarly, certain variations of OWL, like OWL-Lite and OWL-DL, explicitly prohibit an entity from being both a class and an individual. This is also reflected in corresponding ontology engineering methodologies and tutorials, like METHONTOLOGY [31], that include as an obligatory step of the modeling process the classification of domain terms as classes or individuals.

The main problem with having to do such a selection is that there are several entities that can be legitimately modeled as both a class and an individual. For example, the entity `Eagle` can be modeled as a class, representing the set of all individual eagles on Earth, as well as an individual belonging to the class `Animal Species`. The same can be said for the entity `Data Scientist`, which can be modeled as the class of all persons who work as data scientists but also as an instance of the class `Occupation`. In Chapter 12 I describe how you can tackle this class or individual modeling dilemma.

Classes in Semantic Models Versus Classes in Machine Learning

The notion of class exists also in machine learning where it denotes the different categories a classification model is trained to assign to data. A classifier, for example, that is trained to detect spam emails would have two classes, namely `spam` and `nonspam`. The difference between such classes, and classes in a semantic model, is that the latter have a stricter meaning and must have other entities as (potential) instances of them.

For example, in a machine learning classification model that determines if an image depicts the Eiffel Tower or the Parthenon, the two monuments are the model's classes. In a semantic model, however, these can't be classes as they represent concrete individual entities with no meaningful instances (the images that depict the monuments are not actually instances of the monuments themselves but of the class `Image`).

This means that if you are developing such a classifier and you use a knowledge graph as a source of training data, your target classes and their examples are not necessarily available in the graph as class-instance pairs, but they may have some other representation. Conversely, if you want to incorporate the output of the classifier within a semantic model, you should first decide if the target classes are best represented as semantic classes or individuals.

Attributes

An entity attribute is used to represent a characteristic of an entity that we cannot (or choose not to) represent as a relation with another entity, and instead we use literal values (i.e., numbers, strings, dates, etc.). We usually use an attribute to represent:

- Characteristics with values that don't make much sense as distinct entities (e.g., age, height, weight, salary, etc.)
- Characteristics not really related to the domain but useful for administration or other purposes (e.g., the person who added the entity in the model or the method used for its discovery)

In Table 2-3 you can see the attributes and the relations that DBpedia defines for films and educational institutes. Notice that the conceptual distinction between a relation and an attribute is not always clear and ends up being a matter of representation choice. For example, `filmAudioType` and `campusType` are not so conceptually different to justify representing the first as relation and the second as an attribute. In Chapter 12, I discuss ways to tackle the attribute-relation modeling dilemma.

Table 2-3. Attributes and relations in DBpedia for films

Entity type	Relations	Attributes
Film	Director, originalLanguage, musicComposer, producedBy, starring	originalTitle, filmAudioType, completionDate, subjectTerm, filmColourType
Educational Institute	Administrator, dean, actingHeadteacher, alumni	brinCode, campusType, facultySize, endowment

Terminology-wise, in RDF(S) entity attributes are called *properties* (so there is no distinction between them and relations) and in OWL they are called *datatype properties*. Again, for the sake of clarity, I will stick with the term *attribute* throughout the book.

Similarly to entity attributes, a relation attribute is used to represent a characteristic of the relation between two or more entities. This happens when this characteristic does not characterize just one of the related entities, but the relation itself. For example, if I say that "John is friends with Sally since 2013," the year `2013` is not an attribute of John's or Sally's but of their friendship. Figure 2-2 shows an example of a model with both entity and relation attributes.

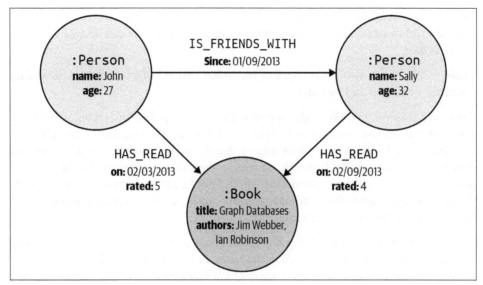

Figure 2-2. Example of entity and relation attributes

Complex Axioms, Constraints, and Rules

Besides entities, classes, attributes, and relations, certain frameworks provide more complex elements that allow the modeling of more elaborate data semantics and enable reasoning: namely, the derivation of facts that are not explicitly expressed in the model.

For example, in E-R models, we can define cardinality constraints about relations, namely the minimum and maximum number of objects and subjects they can have (e.g., the relation wasBornIn can link an entity of type Person to exactly one entity of type Location). Also in OWL, we are able to define a class by specifying the range of the relation objects of another class (e.g., we can define the class Parent as the set of entities that are instances of the class Person and are related to at least one other instance of the same class via the relation hasChild). And if we use the Semantic Web Rule Language (SWRL) [32] we can define a rule that says that if a person A is the parent of person B, and person C is the brother of person A, then C is the uncle of B.

In general, similar axioms can behave very differently in different modeling frameworks, and that often leads to undesired reasoning behavior. A characteristic case is when inference rules are mistaken for constraints, and vice versa. This and other such cases are described in more detail in Chapter 7.

It's important to note that when we talk about reasoning in ontologies and other types of semantic models we mainly refer to *deductive* reasoning, namely the process of reasoning from one or more statements (premises) to reach a logically certain conclusion. If all premises are true and the rules of deductive logic are followed, then the conclusion reached is *necessarily true*. If, for example, we know that drinking hemlock (always) causes death and that Socrates drank hemlock, we can deduce that Socrates has died.

There are, however, two other types of reasoning that we often come across as data scientists: *abduction* and *induction*.

Abductive reasoning works in the opposite direction of deduction, trying to infer the premises that led to a conclusion by reverse-engineering known deduction rules. For example, if we know that hemlock causes death and that Socrates is dead, we can *abduce* that Socrates drank hemlock. Of course, there can be other causes for Socrates' death, and that's exactly why abductions should not be always considered as necessarily true. In data science this kind of reasoning can be used to explain the results and behavior of machine learning models [33].

Inductive reasoning, in turn, takes a premise and a conclusion and attempts to infer the rules by which the former leads to the latter. For example, if we know that Socrates drank hemlock and that he died, we might *induce* that hemlock causes death. This is essentially what we do when we train supervised machine learning models; i.e., we infer rules by generalizing and extrapolating from (multiple) premise-conclusion pairs. Just as with abduction, these rules are not always true.

When you design a semantic model to be used for reasoning, it's important to clarify the kind of reasoning that is really required. Conversely, if you have at your disposal a semantic model that provides inference capabilities, you need to understand the exact nature of these inferences.

Terms

Last but not least, we have terms. A *term* is a string of characters (word or phrase) that can be used to lexically describe an entity, a relation, an attribute, or any other modeling element. It doesn't have a meaning on its own but it's used to express (part of) the element's meaning. This is evident from the fact that one term can have multiple meanings (e.g., the term *bank*) but also from the fact that an entity doesn't change its meaning if you describe it in another way (e.g., referring to the entity Rome as "the Eternal City" does not alter the entity's identity). This lexical nature of terms means that you can't have a semantic model consisting only of terms because, in such a case, you wouldn't really be representing any meaning.

Now, if you are an expert in taxonomies and controlled vocabularies, you might argue that a taxonomy contains terms, not entities. Well, not exactly. The terms you put in a taxonomy have an implied meaning, so in reality they are entities and concepts, just not formally defined as such. For example, when you say that a bank is a kind of financial institution, you use the term *bank* with a specific meaning in mind, that of "a financial institution that accepts deposits from the public and creates credit." If you had to include bank in the same taxonomy also with its geographical meaning, you wouldn't use exactly the same term because you would have ambiguity.

You can see this principle in action in WordNet, a lexical database for the English language that groups English words (nouns, verbs, adjectives, and adverbs) into units of meanings called *synsets*. Each synset represents a particular meaning (called *sense*) of one or more words. For example, as you can see in Figure 2-3, the word *code* has three different senses as a noun and two as a verb.

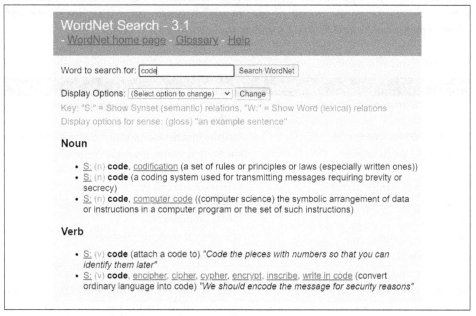

Figure 2-3. Senses of the term code *in WordNet*

In essence, semantic modeling is about linking words and terms to their senses, and that is your main challenge when you develop a semantic model. On the other hand, by exploiting such links in your data science applications you help the latter interpret the data more accurately and produce more meaningful results.

Common and Standardized Elements

While in theory we can use the preceding generic semantic modeling elements to define any specific element we like, in practice there are some pretty common and standardized elements that we find in most modeling frameworks and languages. Unfortunately, just as it happens with the basic modeling elements, these elements have many different names. Let's take a look at them.

Lexicalization and Synonymy

Lexicalization is the process by which new words are added to a language in order to express a concept. In the context of semantic modeling, a lexicalization relation links a model element (entity, relation, attribute, etc.) to one or more terms that can be used to express it in natural language. These terms are basically either synonyms or lexical variants to each other.

Two terms are synonyms when their meanings are regarded as the same or nearly the same in a wide range of contexts. I say "nearly" because true synonymy is rare and often depends on context. Table 2-4 shows some common synonym types.

Table 2-4. Types of synonyms

Type	Examples
Synonyms of different linguistic origin	Cats/felines, freedom/liberty, sodium/natrium, sweat/perspiration
Popular and scientific name synonyms	Aspirin/acetylsalicylic acid, gulls/Laridae, salt/sodium chloride
Generic and trade name synonyms	Petroleum jelly/Vaseline, photocopies/Xeroxes, refrigerators/Frigidaires, tissues/Kleenex
Variant names for emergent concepts	Hovercraft/air cushion vehicle
Current or favored terms replacing outdated or deprecated terms	Poliomyelitis/infantile paralysis, developing countries/underdeveloped countries
Slang or jargon synonyms	Helicopters/whirlybirds, psychiatrists/shrinks
Dialectical variants	Elevators/lifts, subways/undergrounds

Lexical variants differ from synonyms in that synonyms are different terms for the same entity, while lexical variants are different word forms for the same term. These forms may derive from spelling or grammatical variation or from abbreviated formats. Table 2-5 shows some common variant categories for the English language.

Table 2-5. Types of lexical variants in English

Type	Examples
Direct versus inverted order	Radar antennas/antennas, radar
Orthographic variants	Romania/Rumania/Roumania, ground water/ground-water/groundwater
Stem variants	Pediatrics/paediatrics
Irregular plurals	Mice/mouse
Full name and abbreviation variants	International Federation for Documentation/FID, pi mesons/pions, polyvinyl chloride/PVC

Again, in different modeling frameworks and languages, lexicalization relations take different names and forms. For example, in RDF(S) and OWL, lexicalization is facilitated via the `rdfs:label` relation that relates a modeling element with a string-language pair called a *lexical label*. In SKOS, the modeler is able to make a distinction between the `preferred`, `alternative`, and `hidden` lexical labels for any given element. The preferred and alternative labels are meant to be used for generating or creating human-readable representations of elements, while the hidden labels are intended for labels that may be useful for an application but not appropriate or necessary for human consumption (e.g., lexical variants).

Also, in WordNet, the words belonging to a synset are found using the `lemma` relation, whereas in the worlds of (non-SKOS) taxonomies, thesauri, and controlled vocabularies (see the ANSI/NISO Z39-19 or ISO 25964 standards) terms with the same meaning are designated as *preferred terms* and *nonpreferred terms*. The former are also called *descriptors* and the latter *alternate descriptors*.

Lexicalizations and synonyms are very important in a semantic model for a couple of reasons. First, they clarify further the meaning of entities and other elements; no matter how clear and unambiguous an element's name may be, complementing it with some of its most common synonyms helps make its meaning clearer and more explicit. Second, as I mentioned earlier, they help data science applications handle the linguistic variety of data better and interpret it more accurately.

As an example of the latter, imagine that you are building a labor market analytics system that analyzes a large number of job vacancies in order to observe the changes in the demand of certain professions. Because different vacancies may be using different terms to refer to the same profession (e.g., "software developer" and "software programmer"), the system needs to know that these terms are synonyms in order to count together their vacancies and calculate a single (and more accurate) demand for them. A semantic model (like ESCO that we saw in Chapter 1) can provide this knowledge.

Nevertheless, pretty often, semantic models contain synonym terms that do not really have the same meaning, and that may cause several problems in applications that use them. In Chapter 7 you will learn how to recognize and avoid this pitfall, both when developing and using a semantic model. Moreover, as we will see later in the book, striving to include all the possible lexicalizations its elements may have in a semantic model is not always a good idea. In Chapter 13 you will learn how to select and use those lexicalizations that are most beneficial for your applications.

Instantiation

An instantiation relation links an entity to one or more classes it is an instance of (e.g., `Stairway to Heaven` to `Song` and `Basketball` to `Team Sport` as we saw earlier). In RDF(S) and OWL, this relation is known as `rdf:type` while in the ANSI/NISO Standard it is indicated by the abbreviation BTI (standing for "Broader term (instance)") or NTI (standing for "Narrower term (instance)").

From a *meaning construction* point of view, instantiation is pretty useful as it lets humans and machines know what characteristics and behavior an entity is expected to have, based on the classes it belongs to. Conversely, it complements and clarifies the meaning of a class by directly providing the entities the latter is meant to contain.

Meaning Inclusion and Class/Relation Subsumption

A *meaning inclusion* relation between two modeling elements (entities, relations, or attributes) indicates that the meaning of the one is included in the meaning of the other. For example, the meaning of the entity Screwdriver is included in that of Tool in the sense that a screwdriver is a specific kind of tool. The same can be said for the concepts Supervised Machine Learning and Machine Learning or the relations has Father and hasParent. In linguistics, the meaning inclusion relation is known as *hyponymy/hypernymy*, where hypernym is the more generic element and hyponym the more specific.

When meaning inclusion is applied to classes, it is called *class subsumption* or *subclassing* and has the following logical implication: If class A is a subclass of class B then all entities that instantiate A are also instances of B. Thus, for example, if we say that Soccer Game is a subclass of Sports Event, then a reasoner will infer that the 2019 Champions League Final is also an instance of Sports Event (and of all its superclasses for that matter). Similarly, if the meaning inclusion is about relations, then it has the logical implication that if relation A is subsumed by relation B then all entities related via A are also related via B.

Class and *relation subsumption* are typically found in languages like RDF(S) and OWL where they are known as rdfs:subClassOf and rdfs:subPropertyOf, respectively; you will also probably have seen them in (Enhanced) Entity-Relationship models [34]. In any case, class subsumption relations are very often modeled in a wrong way and lead to problematic inferences. In Chapter 7 I describe several such pitfalls and ways to avoid them.

Part-Whole Relation

The *part-whole relation* is a semantic relation that we typically express in natural language with the *part-of* predicate. For example, we say that "A wheel is part of a car," or that "Germany is part of the European Union." In linguistics, this relation is known as *meronymy/holonymy* with a meronym being the part and holonym the whole. In the ANSI/NISO Standard it is indicated by the abbreviation BTP (standing for "Broader term (partitive)") or NTP (standing for "Narrower term (partitive)").

Even though from a logical perspective *part-of* is typically treated as one relation, from a semantic and linguistic perspective there are at least six variations of it [35]:

Component-integral object

This relation models the relation between components and the objects they belong to. For example, "A brain is part of a human," "A wheel is part of a car," "A handle is part of a cup," etc.

Member-collection

This relation is similar to the *component-integral* relation but with the difference that the parts are not required to perform a particular function or possess a particular position with respect to each other and to their wholes. For example, "A person is part of a crowd," "A judge is part of a judgment committee," etc.

Portion-mass

This parthood relation applies when the parts and the whole are similar to each other and to the whole which they comprise. For example, "A slice of cake is part of a cake," "A meter is part of a kilometer," etc.

Stuff-object

This is a relation that is most often expressed using the "is partly" expression. For example, "This building is partly steel," "Table salt is partly natrium," etc.

Feature-activity

This is a relation that designates the features or phases of activities and processes. For example, "Testing is part of software development," "Thesis writing is part of getting a PhD," etc.

Place-area

This is the relation between areas and places or locations within them. For example, "Yosemite National Park is part of California," "Manhattan is part of New York City," etc.

In Chapter 7, we will see how part-whole relations are often modeled in a wrong way, also resulting in wrong inferences.

Hierarchical Relations

In taxonomies, a hierarchical relation between entities indicates that one is in some way more general (broader) than the other (narrower). This covers three different relation types we've seen already, namely instantiation, meaning inclusion, and part-whole relations.

In SKOS, hierarchical relations are represented via the `skos:broader` and `skos:narrower` elements, whereas in the ANSI/NISO Standard they are designated as `BT` (broader term) or `NT` (narrower term).

Semantic Relatedness

A *semantic relatedness* relation between two model elements indicates that the latter's meanings are somehow related, without specifying the exact nature of this relation, either because we don't know it or we don't care. For example, "A thermostat is related to temperature control," "Apache Tomcat is related to Java," etc. In taxonomies, this relation is known as *associative*, represented in SKOS via `skos:related`, and in the ANSI/NISO standard via `RT` (`related term`). What we usually care about when we define and use such a semantic relatedness relation is that the elements it connects are considered sufficiently similar by the model's users (that's why it is also known as *semantic similarity*).

As we will see in Chapter 10, it is relatively easy to get humans to agree that two concepts are semantically similar outside of any context, but hard within one. This means that when you are developing a semantic model in a specific context, you need to be extra careful that the relatedness you define and populate is appropriate for that context. The same applies if you are using a model's relatedness relation in a different context than the one it has been created for.

Mapping and Interlinking Relations

Mapping relations are used to link elements that belong to different semantic models. Such links enable the semantic interoperability between data applications that are based on different underlying semantic models.

OWL provides the relation `owl:sameAs` to denote that two individual entities between different models have the same meaning. For example, the entity `Machine Learning` in English DBpedia [36] is stated to be the same as the entity `Apprentissage_automatique` in the French one [37].

Also, for interlinking between classes, OWL offers the relation `owl:equivalentClass` which is very different from `owl:sameAs`: the equivalence it expresses is extensional, i.e., two classes are equivalent if they always have the same instances. SKOS, on the other hand, provides five different relations for the same purpose [38]:

`skos:exactMatch`
> Given two entities in different models, this indicates a high degree of confidence that the two entities can be used interchangeably across a wide range of applications

`skos:closeMatch`
> Given two entities in different models, this indicates that the entities are sufficiently similar that they can be used interchangeably in some applications

`skos:broadMatch`
> Given two entities in different models, this states that one entity's meaning is broader than the other's

`skos:narrowMatch`
> Given two entities in different models, this states that one entity's meaning is narrower than the other's

`skos:relatedMatch`
> Given two entities in different models, this states that the two entities are semantically related, though not in a narrower or broader way

As we will see in Chapter 7, interlinking heterogeneous semantic models is a quite challenging and error-prone task, with `owl:sameAs` and other mapping relations often linking the wrong elements. That's why, if you have to use interlinked semantic models, you should take extra care to check the quality of the interlinking. For the same reason, developing and maintaining mappings between your models and third-party ones can be such a demanding and costly task that you need to decide if it's worthwhile. Chapter 13 discusses this dilemma in more detail.

Documentation Elements

All the elements I've described are already generally considered core components of semantic models, mainly because they are easily machine-processable and can be used for automated reasoning. Nevertheless, next to their formal definitions, these elements need to also be defined using human-readable descriptions, like natural language definitions, provenance information, or scope notes. This documentation, though informal, can be extremely useful for the common understanding of a model by humans and its proper maintenance and usage, therefore you shouldn't automatically discard it as useless. In Chapter 6 I describe in more detail the risks of not including such documentation in your model.

Definitions and examples

A natural language definition describes the meaning of an element in a natural language form, just as in a glossary or dictionary. Thus, for example, according to DBpedia the concept of `Machine Learning` can be defined as "the subfield of computer science that gives computers the ability to learn without being explicitly programmed (Arthur Samuel, 1959)" [36]. Or, according to WordNet, the philosophical concept of `Ontology` can be defined as "the metaphysical study of the nature of being and existence" [39]. Apart from definitions (which are called *glosses*), WordNet also provides for most of its synsets one or more short sentences illustrating their use.

In general, natural language definitions come in four main flavors:

Extensional definitions

These formulate an element's meaning by specifying its extension, that is, every object that falls under its definition. For example, an extensional definition of the class European Country might be given by listing all of the countries that are located in Europe, or by giving some other means of recognizing the members of the corresponding class. Such an explicit listing of the extension is only possible for finite sets, and only practical for relatively small sets. Thus, extensional definitions should be used when listing examples that would give more applicable information than other types of definitions, and where listing the members of a set tells the questioner enough about the nature of that set.

Intensional definitions

These give the meaning of an element by specifying necessary and sufficient conditions for when the element should be used. For example, an intensional definition of the class Bachelor is "unmarried man." This definition is valid because being an unmarried man is both a necessary condition and a sufficient condition for being a bachelor: it is necessary because one cannot be a bachelor without being an unmarried man, and it is sufficient because any unmarried man is a bachelor [40]. Intensional definitions are best used when something has a clearly defined set of properties, and they work well for elements that have too many referents to list in an extensional definition. It is impossible to give an extensional definition for an element with an infinite set of referents, but an intensional one can often be stated concisely. For example, there are infinitely many even numbers that are impossible to list, but the term "even numbers" can be defined easily by saying that even numbers are integer multiples of two.

Definitions by genus and difference

These give the meaning of an element by first stating the broad category it belongs to and then distinguishing it by specific properties. As an example, consider the definition of miniskirt as "a skirt with a hemline above the knee." In this, first we assign a genus (by saying that the entity is a type of skirt) and then we describe the specific properties that make it its own subtype, namely that it has a hemline above the knee.

Ostensive definitions

These give the meaning of an element by pointing out examples. This type of definition is often used where the term is difficult to define verbally, either because the words will not be understood (as with children and new speakers of a language) or because of the nature of the term (such as colors or sensations). Compared to extensional definitions, ostensive definitions are risky as they provide only part of the extension of a term. However, some elements are so complex that extensional definitions are extremely difficult to formulate.

In RDF(S) and OWL, definitions and examples are usually expressed via the `rdfs:comment` attribute, while in SKOS there are dedicated elements for this purpose (`skos:definition` and `skos:example`).

Scope and usage

Scope and usage elements are used to provide additional information about the intended meaning and application of a semantic model and its elements, especially when this information is not directly obvious from the elements' names or definitions. Cases when this may be needed include:

- Some of the model's elements have other meanings, which have been deliberately excluded from the model.

- The model or some of its elements are not applicable in a particular context. For example, the profession of `License Plate Obscurer` exists only in Iran, so it makes no sense to have it as an entity in a model applied in the United States. Similarly, there are 21 countries in the world with no minimum drinking age, so having such an attribute for them will be redundant.

- The model or some of its elements may have been optimized for a particular task or application (e.g., for semantic search) that makes it less useful or even inappropriate for other tasks.

- The model or some of its elements have some known bias that its users need to be aware of.

History and provenance

Provenance elements are used to track the development of entities, relations, and other modeling elements over time, by representing information about changes (who, when, what), versions, compatibility, sources, etc. These can be simple attributes or relations, like those shown in Table 2-6, or more complex models like the PROV Ontology [41] (see Figure 2-4).

Table 2-6. History and provenance elements in OWL and SKOS

Element	Framework	Meaning
`skos:historyNote`	SKOS	Describes significant changes to the meaning or the form of a concept
`skos:editorialNote`	SKOS	Supplies information that is an aid to administrative housekeeping, such as reminders of editorial work still to be done, or warnings in the event that future editorial changes might be made
`skos:changeNote`	SKOS	Documents fine-grained changes to a concept, for the purposes of administration and maintenance
`owl:versionInfo`	OWL	Provides information about the particular version of the model
`owl:priorVersion`	OWL	Identifies a model as a previous version of the given model

Element	Framework	Meaning
`owl:backwardCompatibleWith`	OWL	Identifies a model as a previous version of the given model to which the latter is compatible
`owl:incompatibleWith`	OWL	Identifies a model as a previous version of the given model to which the latter is incompatible
`owl:DeprecatedClass` and `owl:DeprecatedProperty`	OWL	Indicates that a particular class or relation/attribute is not valid anymore but preserved for backward-compatibility purposes

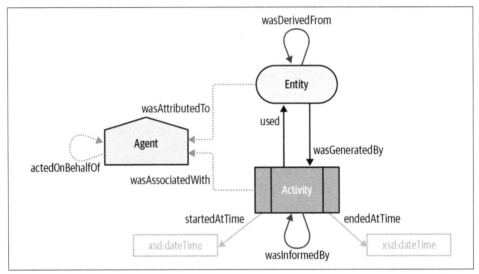

Figure 2-4. Basic classes and relations of the PROV-O ontology

Summary

In this chapter we took a high-level overview of the most general and common semantic modeling elements that are found in data modeling frameworks and languages, describing their intended meaning and usage. We saw how semantic data modeling is quite a rich and diverse field with, ironically, not a standard way of referring to different types of models and modeling elements. Different communities and frameworks use the same terms for different elements, and different terms for the same (or very similar) ones. What some people call *concept*, others call *class*. What you expect to see in a model when you are told that it contains "roles" can be pretty different than what is actually there.

Knowing these similarities and differences can help you make better sense of semantic models that are expressed in different modeling languages, and draw conceptual links between them. This is particularly useful if your job is to merge or map such heterogeneous models, but also if you need to decide what modeling language covers best your model's representation requirements.

Important things to remember:

- Do not assume you understand what a semantic modeling element is about just from its name; always read the fine print of the modeling language's documentation.
- Be extra careful and meticulous when working with abstract entities; they are more difficult to rigorously define, more likely to be misinterpreted, and more likely to be used in unintended ways.
- A semantic model class is not the same as a machine learning class; the latter can also be an individual entity in a semantic model.
- A class is not the same thing as a concept, nor is a subclass hierarchy the same thing as a broader/narrower concept hierarchy. Don't automatically merge them, nor model the one as the other.
- Semantic models are mainly about deductive reasoning; they can help with abduction and induction but they are not inherently designed for these.

In the next chapter we move our discussion from semantic modeling elements to semantic and linguistic phenomena that we should be aware of when developing and using a semantic model.

CHAPTER 3

Semantic and Linguistic Phenomena

*Do you wish me a good morning, or mean that it is a good morning whether I want it or not;
or that you feel good this morning; or that it is a morning to be good on?*
—J.R.R. Tolkien, *The Hobbit, or There and Back Again*

Many of the semantic modeling pitfalls and dilemmas that we'll see in this book are
related to certain semantic and linguistic phenomena that characterize human lan‐
guage and thinking, such as ambiguity, vagueness, and semantic change. Understand‐
ing the exact nature and characteristics of these phenomena, as well as their role and
impact in the development and application of a semantic model, is the first step
toward understanding these pitfalls and dilemmas, and finding ways to tackle them.
This chapter is about helping you make this first step.

Ambiguity

Ambiguity is the situation that arises when a piece of information can be interpreted
in more than one plausible way. For example, if I told you that "I was born in Tripoli,"
and you knew nothing else about me, then you could not possibly determine whether
"Tripoli" refers to the capital of Libya [42], the city of Tripoli in Lebanon [43], or the
capital of Arcadia in Greece [44].

In general, in human language and communication, we observe the following types of
ambiguity:

Phonological ambiguity
This ambiguity arises when there is more than one way to compose a set of
sounds into words. For example, "ice cream" and "I scream" sound more or less
the same.

Syntactic ambiguity

This ambiguity arises when a sentence can have two or more different meanings because of its structure. For example, the sentence "John ate the cookies on the couch" could mean either that there were some cookies on a couch and John ate them, or that John ate some cookies while sitting on a couch.

Anaphoric ambiguity

This ambiguity arises when a phrase or word refers to something previously mentioned, but there is more than one possibility. For example, in the sentence "Margaret invited Susan for a visit, and she gave her a good lunch," the pronoun *she* may refer to Margaret or Susan.

Term-level semantic ambiguity

This ambiguity is also known as lexical ambiguity and arises when a term (single-word or compound) can have more than one meaning. For example, similarly to the aforementioned Tripoli, the term *Kashmir* may refer to the song by the band Led Zeppelin or to the geographical region in India and Pakistan (see Figure 3-1).

Sentence-level semantic ambiguity

This ambiguity arises when even after the syntax and the meanings of the individual words in a sentence have been resolved, the sentence can still be interpreted in more than one way. For example, the sentence "John and Jane are married" can mean either that John and Jane are married to each other or that they are both married but to different people.

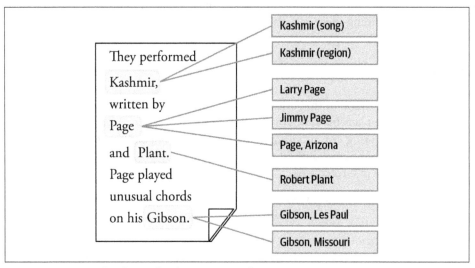

Figure 3-1. Example of term-level semantic ambiguity

Ambiguity and semantic models are usually mentioned together in two situations. The first is when we develop a semantic model from information and data sources that contain ambiguity. The second is when we use a semantic model, usually as part of a larger system, to resolve ambiguity in data. An example of such a system is Accurate Online Disambiguation of Entities (AIDA) [45], a tool that performs named entity recognition (NER) and disambiguation using the YAGO2 knowledge graph [46].

In the first situation, your primary task is to ensure that every element you define within your model has the correct meaning that is actually expressed in your input data, and that this meaning is represented in the model in an unambiguous way, at least with respect to the target domain and context. For example, if you need to incorporate the statement "John and Jane are married" into your model, you need to do the following:

- Determine the exact identities of "John" and "Jane," in case there are more people in the same domain with the same names, and make them clear in the model. This means, for instance, using their full names or some other unique feature of them as an identifier.

- Determine whether the statement's meaning is that John and Jane are married to each other or that each of them is married to someone else, and represent that clearly in the model. For instance, if the intended meaning is the first one, then a relation isMarriedTo between the entities John and Jane should do the trick, whereas if it's the second one, then an attribute marital status with value married for each entity would be a good modeling solution.

In general, describing entities, relations, and other semantic elements in an ambiguity-free way is more difficult than you might think. Chapter 6 discusses this challenge in more detail and provides tips and guidelines for tackling it.

In the second situation, where you use a semantic model as part of a data disambiguation system, your primary concern is to make sure that the model actually helps the system rather than being a hindrance. Unfortunately, the latter can easily happen if the model's content and semantics are not properly optimized for the disambiguation task at hand. Chapter 10 describes this pitfall in more detail and provides a structured methodology for avoiding it.

Uncertainty

In natural language, uncertainty is the phenomenon in which a statement's truth cannot be determined due to complete or partial lack of required knowledge. For example, if I say "It's probably raining right now in Stockholm," then I am referring to a fact that I'm not sure is actually happening right now.

In a semantic model, uncertainty can be manifested in two ways: an explicit one and an implicit one. Explicit uncertainty is when the statement contains keywords like *probably, might, perhaps, apparently*, etc., that clearly communicate the lack of absolute certainty. On the other hand, a statement is implicitly uncertain when it is expressed in a certain way, yet we have reasons to still doubt its truth.

The latter usually happens when we have legitimate reasons not to completely trust the source or the acquisition method of the statement. For example, if we know that some knowledge source contains a substantial percentage of false statements, then we are naturally suspicious for every statement that comes from it. Similarly, when a statement is the result of some automatic knowledge extraction system that has less than 100% precision, then, again, we can't confidently say that it is definitely true.

When you develop a semantic model that you know contains uncertainty, your primary responsibility is to make known the nature, provenance, and level of this uncertainty to the model's users. You might do that for the model as a whole (e.g., by saying that there is a 50% chance for any statement in the model to be true), for parts of it, or even for individual statements. On the other hand, when you use a semantic model for some application, and it's unclear if its statements are certain or not, you should seek to learn the conditions under which the model has been developed, and estimate the extent to which you can trust it.

Vagueness

The best way to understand the phenomenon of vagueness is through the *Sorites Paradox*, an ancient puzzle that can be expressed in the form of the following argument:

- 1 grain of wheat does not make a heap.
- If 1 grain doesn't make a heap, then 2 grains don't.
- If 2 grains don't make a heap, then 3 grains don't.
- …
- If 999,999 grains don't make a heap, then 1 million grains don't.
- Therefore, 1 million grains don't make a heap!

The argument is a paradox because it uses a perfectly fine line of reasoning to reach an obviously false conclusion, namely that a million grains of wheat do not make a heap. The problem lies not on the reasoning but rather on the definition of the concept *heap* which, according to WordNet, is "a collection of objects laid on top of each other" [47]. This definition does not define the minimum number of objects such a collection needs to have in order to be considered a heap and, without such a number, it is very difficult to determine at which point exactly the set of wheat grains becomes a heap. Equally difficult, however, is determining such a number, and this difficulty is what vagueness is all about.

More specifically, vagueness is manifested through predicates that admit borderline cases [48] [49], namely cases where it is unclear whether or not the predicate applies. For example, some people are borderline tall: not clearly tall and not clearly not tall. Alternatively, vagueness is related to the absence of sharp boundaries. For example, on a scale of heights, there appears to be no sharp boundary between the tall people and the rest. Therefore, two equivalent ways of drawing the distinction between vague and nonvague predicates are to say that (i) vague predicates can possibly have borderline cases, while crisp predicates do not or that (ii) vague predicates lack sharp boundaries. Table 3-1 shows ten examples of vague and nonvague adjective senses, collected from WordNet.

Table 3-1. Vague and crisp adjectives

Vague	Crisp
Abnormal: not normal, not typical or usual or regular or conforming to a norm	*Compound*: composed of more than one part
Impenitent: not feeling shame or regret about one's actions or attitudes	*Biweekly*: occurring every two weeks
Notorious: known widely and usually unfavorably	*Unarmed*: not having or using arms
Aroused: emotionally aroused	*Outermost*: situated at the farthest possible
Yellowish: of the color intermediate between green and orange in the color spectrum, of something resembling the color of an egg yolk	*Unfeathered*: having no feathers

In the relevant literature, two basic kinds of vagueness are identified: degree-vagueness (or quantitative) and combinatory vagueness (or qualitative) [48]. A predicate has degree-vagueness if the existence of borderline cases stems from the (apparent) lack of precise boundaries between application and nonapplication of the predicate along some dimension. For example, *bald* fails to draw any sharp boundaries along the dimension of hair quantity and *tall* along the dimension of height. Of course, it might be that a predicate has degree-vagueness in more than one dimension (e.g., *red* can be vague along the dimensions of brightness and saturation).

On the other hand, a predicate has combinatory vagueness if there is a variety of conditions, all of which have something to do with the application of the predicate, yet it is not possible to make any sharp discrimination between those combinations that are sufficient and/or necessary for application and those that are not. A classical example of this type is `Religion`, because there are certain features that all religions share (e.g., beliefs in supernatural beings, ritual acts, etc.), yet it is not clear which of these features are able to classify something as a religion.

It is important that you don't confuse vagueness with the phenomena of inexactness, ambiguity, and uncertainty. For example, stating that someone is between 170 and 180 cm is an inexact statement, but it is not vague as its limits of application are precise. Similarly, the truth of an uncertain statement, such as "Tomorrow the temperature might rise to 27 degrees," cannot be determined due to lack of adequate information about it, not because the measurement of temperature lacks sharp boundaries. Finally, the truth of a statement might not be determinable due to the ambiguity of some term (e.g., in statement "Yesterday we went to the bank" the term *bank* is ambiguous), yet, again, this does not make the statement vague.

Moreover, vagueness is context-dependent as the interpretation of a vague predicate may vary depending on the context to which it is being applied. For example, a person can be tall with respect to the average population height, and not tall with respect to professional basketball players. Similarly, a person can be wealthy with respect to their local community, but poor with respect to their boss.

In a semantic model, vagueness can appear in classes, relations, attributes, and attribute values. A class is vague if, in the given domain, context, or application scenario, it admits borderline cases; namely, if there are (or could be) entities for which it is indeterminate whether they instantiate the class. Primary candidates for being vague are classes that denote some phase or state (e.g., `Adult`, `Child`) as well as attributions, namely classes that reflect qualitative states of entities (e.g., `TallPerson`, `ExperiencedResearcher`, etc.). A relation, in turn, is vague if there are (or could be) pairs of entities for which it is indeterminate whether or not the entities are actually related (e.g., `hasGenre`, `hasIdeology`, etc.). The same applies for attributes and pairs of entities and literal values.

Finally, vagueness can appear in the values of attributes; for example, the attribute `prices` of a restaurant could take as values the vague terms `cheap`, `moderate`, and `expensive`. Primary candidates for generating such terms are gradable attributes such as `size` or `height`, which give rise to terms such as `large`, `tall`, `short`, etc. Table 3-2 shows vague and nonvague relations from the Citation Typing Ontology (CiTO), a publicly available ontology that enables characterization of the nature or type of citations [50].

Table 3-2. Vague and nonvague relations in CiTO

Vague relations	Crisp relations
`plagiarizes`: A property indicating that the author of the citing entity plagiarizes the cited entity, by including textual or other elements from the cited entity without formal acknowledgment of their source	`sharesAuthorInstitutionWith`: Each entity has at least one author that shares a common institutional affiliation with an author of the other entity
`citesAsAuthority`: The citing entity cites the cited entity as one that provides an authoritative description or definition of the subject under discussion	`providesDataFor`: The cited entity presents data that is used in work described in the citing entity

Vague relations	Crisp relations
`speculatesOn`: The citing entity speculates on something within or related to the cited entity, without firm evidence	`retracts`: The citing entity constitutes a formal retraction of the cited entity
`supports`: The citing entity provides intellectual or factual support for statements, ideas, or conclusions presented in the cited entity	`includesExcerptFrom`: The citing entity includes one or more excerpts from the cited entity
`refutes`: The citing entity refutes statements, ideas, or conclusions presented in the cited entity.	`citesAsSourceDocument`: The citing entity cites the cited entity as being the entity from which the citing entity is derived, or about which the citing entity contains metadata.

As we saw in Chapter 1, with the example of ESCO and its "essential" relation between professions and skills, having vague elements in a semantic model, and treating them as crisp, can harm the model's quality and usability. In Chapters 6, 7, and 13 we will see a number of complementary ways to handle vagueness when building a semantic model, but also turn it from a liability to an asset.

Rigidity, Identity, Unity, and Dependence

Rigidity, identity, unity, and dependence are four ontological notions that we find in OntoClean [51] [52], a methodology for validating the semantic correctness of class subsumption relations.

Rigidity is based on the notion of essence. A class is essential for an instance if the latter could not exist if it wasn't an instance of that class, in all worlds and at all times. For example, all humans are necessarily humans and there are no entities that could be a human but aren't. Such classes are called *rigid*. On the other hand, instances of the class `Student` can stop being students (e.g., when they graduate), yet they don't stop existing. A similar argument can be made for things that we currently consider as `Food` and may at some point stop being eaten by some or all people. In these cases, the classes `Student` and `Food` are considered to be *anti-rigid* as they are not essential to any of their instances. A third category are classes that are essential to some of their instances and nonessential to others. For example, the class `HardThing` is essential to hammers but not to sponges. These classes are called *semi-rigid*.

Identity refers to the problem of determining whether or not two entities are the same. A class with identity is one where all instances can be identified as themselves, based on some identity criterion provided either by the class or a superclass of it. For example, the class `Person` has identity because we are typically able to identify whether or not two individuals are the same person (e.g., via their DNA). On the other hand, the class `RedThing` has no identity because any two entities can share the property of being red without being identical. You should note here that an identity criterion is not the same as a membership criterion; the latter gives us information to decide whether an entity belongs to a class or not, but cannot help us distinguish entities from each other.

Unity tells us whether, and under what conditions, instances of a class are considered whole entities or not. For example, the entity one gallon of water cannot be considered a whole object, while the entity Pacific Ocean can. That is because the class AmountOfWater does not have a unity criterion, while the class Ocean does. As with rigidity, there are classes that carry *unity* (i.e., all their instances are wholes with the same unity criteria), classes that carry *non-unity* (i.e., all their instances are wholes but possibly with different unity criteria), and classes that carry *anti-unity* (i.e., not all entities are required to be wholes). An example of a class with non-unity is "LegalAgent," because this can include both people and organizations that have different unity criteria.

Finally, we say that a class C1 is dependent on a class C2 if for every instance of C1 an instance of C2 must exist. An example of a dependent class is Food, because instances of food can only exist if there is something for which these instances are food. For example, if tomorrow we all stop eating bananas, then the concept of Banana will no longer be considered an instance of Food. This does not mean that bananas cease to exist the moment we stop eating them—they just stop having the role of food.

In Chapter 7 we will see how the application of these four notions can help us avoid semantic mistakes when defining subsumption relations and, thus, build models with higher semantic accuracy.

Symmetry, Inversion, and Transitivity

In semantic modeling, *symmetry*, *inversion*, and *transitivity* are phenomena that pertain to relations.

When an entity A is related to entity B via a symmetric relation R, then we can infer that B is related to A via the same relation. For example, if "John is a cousin of Jane," then "Jane is also a cousin of John." On the other hand, when a relation R is transitive, then if R links entity A to entity B, and entity B to entity C, then it also links A to C. For example, if "Paris is located in France" and "France is located in Europe," then it's also the case that "Paris is located in Europe." Finally, we say that a relation R1 is the inverse of a relation R2 if for every entity A related to entity B through R1 we can infer that B is related to A via R2. For example, if "John is the brother of Jane," then "Jane is the sister of John."

All of these phenomena are critical when building systems that reason; therefore, as a semantic modeler, you need to correctly recognize them and include them in your model when it requires them. Unfortunately, as we will see in Chapter 7 there are cases when relations that seemingly have these properties do not really have them.

Closed- and Open-World Assumptions

The closed-world assumption (CWA) states that if we don't know whether a given statement is true or not in our model, then we can infer that it's false. For example, in an airline database, if a traveler has not been assigned a seat, then it can be inferred that they have not checked in. Intuitively, this assumption makes sense when we have complete control over the information that goes into the model and can enforce consistency rules and constraints (in this case that check-in cannot be completed without a seat assignment).

On the other hand, the *open-world assumption* (OWA) states that if we don't know whether a given statement is true or not in our model, then we simply cannot draw any conclusion about its validity. For example, just because a patient's medical record does not mention a particular allergy, we cannot necessarily infer that they do not actually suffer from it. OWA limits us to inference and deductions that follow only from statements that are explicitly true or false in our model. Heuristically, this makes sense when you cannot guarantee that your model is complete at any given moment.

When you develop a semantic model, you need to clarify which assumption it is expected to support, so that you use a modeling framework that supports this assumption. RDF(S) and OWL, for example, are designed to support the OWA, one consequence of which is that axioms that in other languages behave as constraints, actually behave as inference rules. If you are not aware of that, both as a developer and user of RDF(S) models, you risk getting undesired reasoning behavior. Chapter 7 describes this pitfall in more detail.

Semantic Change

Semantic change, also known as semantic drift, is the phenomenon where a term's meaning and usage change over time, often in such a way that its new meaning is radically different than the initial one. For example, the term *awful* was originally used to refer to something that inspired awe, admiration, or wonder, rather than its definition nowadays as something exceptionally bad or displeasing for which we use it nowadays. Table 3-3 shows several examples of such changes.

Table 3-3. Words that changed their meaning over time

Word	Old meaning	Modern meaning
Demagogue	Popular leader	Politician who panders to emotions and prejudice
Egregious	Something remarkably good	Something that is remarkably bad or flagrant
Meat	Solid food	The flesh of animals
Sly	Skillful, clever, knowing, and wise	Sneaky and deceitful
Prestigious	Involving trickery, illusion, or conjuring	Esteemed, honored
Matrix	Female breeding animal	Pattern of lines and spaces

Semantic change typically occurs due to linguistic, psychological, and sociocultural forces (see [53] for a more detailed analysis) and, according to Leonard Bloomfield [54] and Andreas Blank [55], can take several forms:

Specialization
  The new meaning is narrower than the original one. For example, *skyline* used to refer to any horizon, but now in the United States it mostly denotes a horizon decorated by skyscrapers.

Generalization
  The new meaning is more general than the original one. A common example of this is that there are many specific brand names that end up being used for the general product or action, such as *hoover* for cleaning with a vacuum cleaner, or *Google* for searching in the web.

Metaphor
  Change based on similarity. For example, broadcast originally meant "to cast seeds out," but with the advent of radio and television it was extended to indicate the transmission of audio and video signals.

Metonymy
  Change based on contiguity between concepts. For example, because animal horns were used to make musical instruments during the old English period, the term *horn* became the name of the musical instrument itself.

Synecdoche
  Change based on whole-part relation. The convention of using capital cities to represent countries or their governments is an example of this.

Hyperbole
  Change from weaker to stronger meaning (e.g., "torment" meaning "slaughter").

Meiosis

Change from stronger to weaker meaning (e.g., "strike with thunder" meaning "surprise strongly").

Auto-antonymy

Change of a word's sense and concept to the complementary opposite (e.g., the word cleave can mean "to cut apart" or "to bind together").

Folk-etymology

Semantic change based on the similarity of names (e.g., the French term *contre-danse* originates from the English "country dance").

Antiphrasis

Semantic change based on a contrastive aspect of the concepts (e.g., "perfect lady" in the sense of "prostitute").

Beware of Disputable and Potentially Offensive Semantic Changes

Word meaning can also shift meaning over time because of the advocacy of certain groups or communities. For example, *gay* no longer means "colorful and jolly," and *bipolar disorder* is the more modern way of talking about what used to be called "manic depression." These shifts matter even more than the other types of change because they can cause offense, confusion, and dispute when embedded into models or applications.

In the semantic data modeling literature, semantic change is usually modeled (and measured) with respect to three aspects of an entity's representation: a) its labels, i.e., the terms used to express the entity, b) its intension, i.e., the entity's characteristics as expressed via its attributes and relations, and c) its extension, i.e., the set of the entity's instances (when it's a class) [56] [57].

The default role of an entity's extension in semantic drift is disputed by Fokkens et al. [58], suggesting that it depends on the kind of entity. Indeed, some entities have extensions that can change without altering their core meaning. For example, the extension of the concept "Person" changes every time a specific person is born or dies, yet this does not really change our understanding of what a person is. On the other hand, there are concepts whose extension is closely connected to their intension. For example, the concept of "European Union" is partially defined by its member countries.

Terminology Clash

In the semantic modeling world, semantic change is also known as *concept drift*. The latter is a term also found in machine learning, but there it refers to the change over time in the statistical properties of the target variable that the machine learning model is trying to predict.

Semantic drift is typically detected and quantified by measuring the difference in meaning between two or more different versions of the same entity in different points in time [57] [59] [60] [61]. The more dissimilar the two versions are to each other, the greater the drift is.

As a user of a semantic model, semantic change should be your concern when you use the latter to process data, as you need to ensure that the entities' meanings in the model are aligned with the ones in the data. For example, you wouldn't want to analyze historical texts of the 15th century using a contemporary ontology.

On the other hand, as a creator and maintainer of semantic models, you should care about semantic change when the elements in your model change meaning at a high pace. In such a case you need to have mechanisms in place that allow your model to always be up to date. This is quite a challenging task that I will cover in detail in Chapter 14.

Summary

In this chapter we have seen some common semantic and linguistic phenomena that characterize human language and thinking, and which play an important role in the development and application of a semantic model. Some of these, like ambiguity, vagueness, and uncertainty are the main enemies of a model's accuracy. Others, like the open-world assumption or transitivity, can cause reasoning problems if not handled correctly. And the last phenomenon we saw, namely semantic change, can cause a perfectly fine model to gradually lose its quality and usefulness. Understanding the exact nature, characteristics, and impact of these phenomena can help you craft more effective strategies to tackle them, and minimize the negative effects they may have in the models you develop or use.

Important things to remember:

- Vagueness, inexactness, ambiguity, and uncertainty are different phenomena that need to be treated by different means.
- When you create a semantic model you need to ensure that every element you define is described in an unambiguous way.

- Semantic models can be really useful for data disambiguation. More on that in Chapter 10.

- When you develop an uncertain semantic model, make known the nature, provenance, and level of this uncertainty to the model's users. When you use such a model, seek to learn all this information.

- When you develop or use a semantic model, know whether it implements the closed- or the open-world assumption, so that you avoid reasoning surprises.

- When you maintain or use a semantic model, know the nature and pace of its semantic change, to estimate how often it needs to be updated.

The next chapter will help you appreciate better the importance of these phenomena by introducing the main dimensions and methods by which we typically evaluate the quality of semantic data models.

CHAPTER 4

Semantic Model Quality

Come, give us a taste of your quality.
—William Shakespeare, *Hamlet*

The whole goal of this book is to help you build and use high-quality semantic models, so a question that naturally arises is how you can measure this quality. For that, in this chapter, I describe the main quality dimensions that you should consider when evaluating a semantic data model, along with basic metrics and measurement methods for each dimension.

Before we dive into the concrete dimensions and metrics, it's important to understand that there are two different approaches of measuring the quality of a semantic model. The first approach is called *application-centered* and measures the improvement (if any) that the usage of a semantic model brings into a particular application, such as a semantic search engine [62] or a question-answering system [63]. In doing that, it typically compares the application's effectiveness before and after the incorporation of the semantic model.

The advantage of this approach is that we can immediately see if the usage of the model has a visible benefit to the application, and thus assess directly its *fitness for use*. There are some drawbacks, though. First, the observed absence of a such a benefit does not necessarily that the semantic model is low quality; the problem can be with the way the application uses the model as well. Second, even if the problem lies in the model, the end-to-end quality score does not really tell us what is wrong on the model side. Third, if the model is used by multiple different applications at the same time, then trying to improve it for one might make it worse for another.

The second approach to evaluating a semantic model is called *application-neutral* and focuses on measuring the quality of a model with respect to the domain(s) and data it is meant to describe. The advantage of this approach is that the measured quality is consistent and transferable across applications that use the same data. It doesn't mean that the model will have the same effect on all the applications it will be applied to, though.

All the quality dimensions in this chapter concern application-neutral quality, apart from relevancy, which is highly dependent on the application and task a model is used for.

Semantic Accuracy

Semantic accuracy is defined as the degree to which the semantic assertions of a model are accepted to be true. For example, as I am writing these lines, the former country of Yugoslavia appears in DBpedia to be an entity of type Musical Artist [64], which is obviously wrong. On the other hand, Serbia is correctly stated to have Belgrade as its capital [65]. Thus, if DBpedia contained just these two assertions, we could say that it's 50% accurate.

Now, there are several reasons why a semantic model may contain wrong assertions:

Inaccuracy of automatic information extraction (IE) methods
This is by far the most common reason and has to do with the less than 100% accuracy of the algorithms that are typically used to extract semantic assertions from data sources in an automatic way (see Chapter 5). To get an idea of how (in-)accurate such methods can be, consider that the best performing system in the hypernym discovery task from text of the 2018 International Workshop on Semantic Evaluation competition, achieved a precision of 36% for the medical domain and 44% for the music one [66].

Inaccuracy of the data source from which assertions are extracted
In many cases the data from which we get our assertions (either automatically or manually) can contain errors. In "Quantifying the Accuracy of Relational Statements in Wikipedia" [67], for example, it is estimated that 2.8% of Wikipedia's statements are wrong, while in a survey done by *Public Relations Journal* in 2012, 60% of respondents indicated that their company's or client's Wikipedia article contained factual errors or misleading information [68]. These errors vary from small mistakes to intentional alteration of an article's text; the latter case is known as "wiki vandalism" [69].

Misunderstanding of modeling elements' semantics and intended usage
Just because a semantic modeling language defines its elements with a specific meaning and behavior in mind, it does not necessarily mean that people will follow this meaning when using the language in the real world. Thus, for example, as we will see in Chapter 7, we may end up with synonyms in our model that are not really synonyms, classes that are actually instances, and logical inferences that don't make sense.

Lack of domain knowledge and expertise

This is the case when we build a semantic model for a specialized domain and we can't (or don't) involve in the process the right people with the right kind of knowledge. And I say "right" because, as we will see in Chapter 8, domain experts are not necessarily the best choice.

Vagueness

As we saw in Chapter 3, vague assertions can be considered true by one group of users and false by another, without any of them being necessarily wrong. Still, however, if we build a model with input from the one group but have it used by the other group, then we should expect that the latter is pretty likely to treat the model as inaccurate.

The typical way to measure a model's accuracy is to give a sample of its statements to one or more human judges and ask them to decide if they are true or false. The human judges can be domain experts, users of the model (direct or through some application), or even a *crowd*, namely a large number of people that you engage via a crowdsourcing platform [70]. In all cases, you should strive to use multiple judges per statement and accompany your accuracy scores with some inter-agreement measure, especially for statements that are vague.

To accelerate this purely manual approach to measuring accuracy, researchers have developed methods for automatically detecting potential accuracy errors in semantic models. One group of such methods involves using statistical techniques to detect outliers, namely elements that, due to low frequency, low inter-connectivity, or other characteristics, are likely to be wrong [71] [72] [73].

A second group of methods uses reasoning to detect assertions that violate logical consistency rules and axioms already defined in the model [74] [75] [76]. For example, if a model contains the constraint that the relation `capitalOf` can only connect entities of types `City` to entities of type `Country`, then any assertion linking other types of entities through this relation will be flagged as wrong. Of course, for such reasoning to be feasible the model has to be adequately axiomatized and not contain too many errors already; this may not always be possible.

 Beware of Inferred Inaccuracy

An important thing to have in mind when measuring the accuracy of a semantic model is that one wrong statement may result in multiple ones when reasoning is applied. If, for example, you incorrectly state that "class A is a subclass of class B" and A has ten thousand instances, then, after reasoning, you will end up with ten thousand incorrect statements saying that each instance of A is also an instance of B.

Completeness

Completeness of a semantic model can be defined as the degree to which elements that should be contained in the model are indeed there. For example, if a model should contain as entities all European countries but contains only half of them, then its completeness for this particular entity type is 50%.

In the relevant literature, a distinction is usually made between *schema completeness* and *population completeness*. The first refers to the degree to which the model defines all the necessary classes, relations, attributes, and axioms, while the second implies the completeness of individual entities (class instances), relation assertions, and attribute values. For example, if a labor market ontology does not contain the class `Profession` or the class `Skill`, then its schema is definitely incomplete. It can be the case that the ontology does define these classes, yet it contains only a small subset of all the individual professions and skills that are available in the market. In such a case its population completeness is small.

Now, there are several reasons why a semantic model might be incomplete:

Size and complexity
> While, for example, European countries are few and one can model them pretty easily, the number of tagged species on Earth is estimated at 8.7 million [77]. In other words, there are domains that are so large or complex that they require a large amount of resources and effort to complete.

Inaccuracy of automatic IE methods
> The less accurate the automatic model construction methods we have at our disposal, the more manual work we need in order to ensure an acceptable level of accuracy. That obviously slows us down in the effort to complete a model.

Lack of appropriate data sources from which to derive the model
> Sometimes we may have good automatic model construction methods, but not the right amount or type of data we need to use them on (see Chapter 8). This again works against completeness.

Vagueness
> The presence of vagueness in a domain (and hence the model) means dedicating more resources for tackling disagreements and accommodating multiple truths and perspectives.

Domain volatility and dynamics
> The faster a domain evolves, the harder it is to catch up and stay in sync with it. For example, assume that you want to include in your labor market semantic model the relation between professions and the skills they require. Not only will you need to populate this relation for thousands of professions and skills but, most likely, when you are finished, many of these relations will not be valid

anymore because some skills will no longer be required by certain professions. This is the semantic change phenomenon we saw in Chapter 3 and that we will discuss in more detail in Chapter 14.

To measure the completeness of a semantic model, we need to compare the content it currently has with the content it should ideally have. In other words, we need a gold standard that can tell us at any given time how close the model is to completion. In practice, gold standards are extremely hard to find (especially for population completeness), so instead, we usually use *partial gold standards* or *silver standards*.

A partial gold standard contains a subset of the knowledge the model needs to contain. For example, in Färber et al. [78] the authors created a partial gold standard with 41 classes and 22 relations for 5 domains (`People`, `Media`, `Organizations`, `Geography`, and `Biology`) in order to measure and compare the completeness of DBpedia, YAGO, and other publicly available semantic models. Similarly, at Textkernel, my team used ESCO as a partial gold standard to get an idea of the coverage of the company's knowledge graph. Obviously, such an approach cannot tell you whether your model is complete but it can reveal incompleteness.

A silver standard is also a subset of the knowledge the model needs to contain but, contrary to a gold standard, it's (knowingly) not completely accurate. Instead, it is assumed to have a reasonable level of quality that can be useful for detecting incomplete aspects of the model. For example, in Paulheim and Bizer [79] the authors estimated that DBpedia misses at least 2.7 million entity typing statements, by comparing it to YAGO, another model that is not fully accurate.

Apart from using standards, completeness can also be evaluated by employing reasoning or simple heuristics. For example, if you have an attribute or relation with a minimum cardinality restriction, then you can easily check how many of your entities violate this restriction. Or, if you have a class whose instances are expected to have an average number of values for a given attribute, then a large deviation from this average can indicate incompleteness (e.g., it is quite rare for a film to have only one or two actors).

It's also important to notice that completeness is often context-dependent because a semantic model may be seen as complete in one use-case scenario but not in another. For example, as exemplified in Bizer's *Quality-Driven Information Filtering in the Context of Web-Based Information Systems* [80], a list of German stocks is complete for an investor who is interested in German stocks, but it is not complete for an investor who is looking for an overview of the European stocks.

Beware of Inaccuracy and Incompleteness Due to Bias

A semantic model may be inaccurate and/or incomplete due to the biases of the people who contributed to its development, either by stating incorrect facts or leaving out important ones because they don't know or care about them. This can also happen if the gold standards you use to measure a model against have entrenched bias of some kind. In Chapter 8 we will discuss this issue in more detail.

Consistency

Consistency means that a semantic model is free of logical or semantic contradictions. For example, saying that "John's natural mother is Jane" and "John's natural mother is Kim" when Jane and Kim are not the same person, is inconsistent as a person can only have one natural mother. Similarly, if we have a constraint that two classes are *disjoint* (i.e., they share no common instances) and, despite that, we state that a particular entity is an instance of both these classes, then we also end up with an inconsistent model.

The main reason we get inconsistent models is the absence or nonenforcement of appropriate constraints that could trigger relevant warnings whenever they are violated. Thus, for example, if we can define that hasNaturalMother can relate an entity to at most one other entity, then we can prevent the inconsistency just discussed.

Sometimes we are just too lazy or too busy to create such constraints, but it can also be that the modeling framework we employ does not inherently support them. Neo4j, for example, a graph database implementing the property graph paradigm, supports various types of constraints [81] but not constraints regarding relation cardinality. This means that if our model is implemented in Neo4j, then we need a custom solution to implement these constraints ourselves.

There is also the case when the modeling framework does support the definition of constraints, but the latter's enforcement by some reasoner is computationally too complex. For example, for some variations of the OWL2 language, called profiles [82], consistency checking is known to be an undecidable or NP-Hard problem (i.e., not solvable in realistic time).

A Consistent Model Is Not Necessarily Accurate, Nor Is an Inaccurate Model Necessarily Inconsistent

Just because a model's logical constraints are not violated, it does not mean that the model is necessarily accurate. If two nonvague statements contradict each other, they definitely cannot both be true, but they can both be false. On the other hand, if the contradictory statements are vague, then it's pretty likely that they are not inconsistent but just refer to borderline cases.

Conciseness

Conciseness in a semantic model is the degree to which the model does not contain redundant elements. These are elements (or combinations of them) that already exist in the model in a different but semantically equivalent form, or that are no longer required to be in the model.

An example of semantic representation redundancy we find in DBpedia is where the relation between persons and their children is represented by two different relations that don't seem to have any real difference: `dbo:child` [83] and `dbp:children` [84]. Similarly, in the Organizational Ontology (*https://oreil.ly/6KigL*), the membership relation between an `Agent` and an `Organization` can be represented both via an `org:memberOf` binary relation [85] and a `Membership` class [86]. To be fair, the latter is explicitly stated that it is meant to be used for representing an n-ary relationship between an `Agent`, an `Organization`, and a `Role`, yet this does not prevent it from being used for binary, role-independent relations.

Now, there are several reasons why a model could be inconcise:

Uncoordinated modeling from multiple parties with inadequate governance
Different modelers may make different modeling decisions for the same modeling problem, so it's important that they coordinate when working on the same model. For example, in order to represent n-ary relations there are multiple modeling patterns available [87].

Optimizing for different applications at the same time
What is necessary for one application may be redundant for another. For example, a semantic model that is to be used for natural language processing and text analytics tasks is generally expected to contain a lot of lexicalization terms for its entities. Yet, if the same model is to be used for navigation or reasoning, then it does not really need all those terms. Similarly, for one application it may be better to model an entity's characteristic as an attribute, while for another, it may be better as a relation.

"Temporary" elements or hacks that haven't been removed
Sometimes we don't have the time to be concise because we are pressed to deliver. For example, let's say we have ten thousand new terms to add as new entities in our model, and many of them are synonyms of each other. Ideally, we should first detect the synonyms, group them together, and add them as entities in the model. This can take too much time, so, if our application allows it, we may choose to add all the terms as distinct entities and care for the synonyms later. The result of that will be that, for a period of time, we will have duplicate entities in our model.

Legacy elements not having been removed

>If a model is pretty old, it may contain elements that are no longer relevant for the domain, data, or task. For example, in the labor market domain, there are several professions or skills that are no longer mentioned either in vacancies or résumés, so having them in our model is not beneficial.

Inconciseness in a semantic model might not seem as problematic as inaccuracy or incompleteness, yet it carries its own risks.

First, if you are the creator and owner of an inconcise model, redundancies will increase its maintenance overhead, as well as the risk of introducing inconsistencies, especially if the same elements—though distinct in the model—are maintained by different parties. Second, if you use a model for some application and you are not aware that the information you need is distributed among duplicate elements (e.g., you want to get from DBpedia the children of certain persons and you don't know that there is both a relation and an attribute for that), you risk getting only part of it. Third, as we will see in "When Knowledge Can Hurt You" on page 171, if you use a model for some application and much of its information is irrelevant, there is a risk that the application will perform worse than if it didn't have this information.

A simple way to detect semantic representation redundancy is to consider the natural language questions that the model is supposed to answer and investigate if they can be transformed into formal queries in more than one equivalent way. For example, if the model is about geography and you can get the set of Asian countries either by asking for entities that are instances of the class `AsianCountry` or are related to `Asia` via the relation `isLocatedIn`, then you may have a redundancy problem.

Also, to detect duplicate elements, you can apply various similarity metrics, based on the elements' names, attribute values, incoming/outgoing relations, and anything else that may indicate duplicity.

Finally, to determine whether the model carries "dead weight," you can compare its content against a gold standard or other data that reflects the domain (e.g., a text corpus) and check if every element of it is also available there. For example, if the model is supposed to contain active startup companies, you can periodically scan the news to see if they are still relevant in the market.

You should be careful, though, as this technique will work only if a) the reference model or corpus is far more complete than the model, and b) the model under evaluation has rich lexicalization per element, as the inability to find an entity or relation in the corpus may as well be because it is not expressed within the corpus in the same way it is expressed in the model. For example, in an evaluation of ESCO that my team at Textkernel did in 2017, we looked for ESCO professions and skills in a large set of job vacancies and we found out that some entities were indeed not so useful or frequent in the data, but others were simply not discoverable because their lexicalization terms were too verbose.

Timeliness

Timeliness in a semantic model can be defined as the degree to which the model contains elements that reflect the current version of the world. For example, a model of world countries that still considers Yugoslavia as a single country and knows nothing about the countries that followed its dissolution (Serbia, Croatia, etc.) is not a timely model.

To keep a timely model, you need to detect and act upon changes that happen in your domain; i.e., add elements that appear valid and relevant and remove elements that are not valid or relevant anymore. Thus, for example, if like Yugoslavia, a country splits tomorrow into more countries, you would need to add these to the model and either remove the old country from the model (if you don't need it), or keep it, but in a way that reflects its change (e.g., make it an instance of a `FormerCountry` class).

Thus, a model's timeliness depends on the domain's dynamics (how often and to what extent it changes) and the efficiency of its maintainers to detect and incorporate these changes. For example, the day I first wrote these lines (March 23, 2019) Kazakhstan officially renamed its capital Astana as Nur-Sultan in honor of its former president Nazarbayev. Less than 24 hours later the Wikipedia article about Astana had been updated accordingly and, almost immediately, DBpedia Live (*https://oreil.ly/qXEiP*) (a version of DBpedia that is always in synchronization with Wikipedia) contained the new name.

Assessing a model's timeliness can be done by evaluating its accuracy and completeness with respect to contemporary knowledge. An indirect metric can also be the frequency and volume of updates combined with the volatility of the domain. You should be careful, though, that these updates will have to do with contemporary knowledge, not error fixes or completion of old knowledge.

Relevancy

A semantic model is relevant when its structure and content are useful and important for a given task or application. Conversely, a model has low relevancy if, no matter how accurate or complete it looks to be with respect to a domain, we still cannot easily or effectively use it for the particular task(s) we need it.

One case where this may happen is when the model contains relevant information about the domain but misses information that is critical for the task. For example, at Textkernel we use a knowledge graph to automatically extract skill and profession entities from résumés and job vacancies, utilizing the relevant entities and their synonyms. When we contemplated using ESCO for the same task, we realized that the number of available synonyms per entity was not adequate to give us a high enough recall.

Another case is when the model contains relevant information about the task but in a way that is not easily accessible. For example, again at Textkernel, we need a semantic model that will tell us what professions and skills are available in the labor market and how they are related to each other. When we considered DBpedia as a potential solution, we saw that it did contain many such entities, but not the relation between them. Moreover, these entities were not explicitly typed by means of a `Profession` or `Skill` class, thus making it really hard for us to directly retrieve them from the model.

In all cases, the main reason a model may not be so relevant for a task or application is that it has been developed without having considered the latter's requirements. This, as we will see in Chapter 10, may make the model not only irrelevant, but also harmful.

Understandability

Understandability or *comprehensibility* of a semantic model is the ease with which human consumers can understand and utilize the model's elements, without misunderstanding or doubting their meaning. From my experience, this is a quality dimension whose importance and difficulty semantic modelers most often underestimate, giving more emphasis to the computational properties of the model. This leads to models that are not only interpreted and used in a wrong way, but also score low in other quality dimensions like accuracy, relevancy, and trustworthiness.

Low understandability is mainly the result of bad or inadequate model descriptions. Of course, we could accuse the model's users for not trying hard enough to understand a model, yet it is usually ambiguous or inaccurate element names, obscure axioms, the lack of human-readable definitions, or undocumented biases and assumptions, that cause the problem. In Chapter 6, I describe in detail the most common mistakes we make when we describe our model's elements and provide tips and guidelines to effectively avoid them.

To assess a model's understandability, you can ask people directly about it and have them assess the clarity, specificity, and richness of its documentation. A more effective approach, though, is to observe how they actually use it and identify systematic errors. For example, as we will see in Chapter 7, many semantic relations like `rdfs:subclassOf` or `owl:sameAs` are very often applied incorrectly, indicating that their creators need to try harder in explaining how they are meant to be used.

Trustworthiness

Trustworthiness of a semantic model refers to the perception and confidence in the quality of the model by its users. This (inevitably subjective) perception is definitely related to other quality dimensions like correctness, completeness, or relevancy; yet you can have a model that is, in reality, less accurate than another and still regarded as more trustworthy. The reason is that trust is not merely a technical concept, but one with social and psychological dimensions that cannot be easily expressed by a mathematical formula.

One key factor that contributes to a model's trustworthiness (or the lack of it) is its reputation and the extent to which it has been endorsed or adopted by different communities and industries. For example, schema.org was founded by Google, Microsoft, Yahoo, and Yandex and, according to a 2015 study on 10 billion websites [88], around 31% of them use it.

A second important factor is the availability and content of formal evaluations and experience reports. Just like we can look for user reviews before we buy a product, we can also look for academic papers, technical reports, or other articles that describe the quality of a semantic model. DBpedia evaluations, for example, are reported in papers by Färber et al. [78], Zaveri et al. [89], and Acosta et al. [70], while Freire et al. [90] presents two case studies that analyzed Schema.org metadata from collections from cultural heritage institutions. The actual quality scores of these reports, their rigorousness and consistency, but also the sentiment they convey, can easily build or demolish trust.

A third trustworthiness factor is the model's provenance, namely the people, sources, methods, and processes that are involved in building, managing, and evolving the model. It is, for example, quite different having the model edited only by experts, in a centralized fashion, with rigorous and frequent quality checks, than having it developed by a loosely governed community of unregistered volunteers. Similarly, it is quite important whether the model is extracted automatically or manually from one or more data sources, as well as whether these sources are themselves structured, semi-structured, or unstructured, and, of course, reliable.

For example, Cyc (*https://www.cyc.com*), a massive semantic model of commonsense knowledge that started being developed in the 1980s, is being edited, expanded, and modified exclusively by a dedicated group of experts, while its free version OpenCyc (now discontinued [91]), used to be derived from Cyc, and only the data of a local mirror could be modified by the data consumers. Similarly, Wikidata (*https://oreil.ly/7virV*) is a collaboratively edited knowledge base that is curated and expanded manually by volunteers. Moreover, it allows the importation of data from external sources but only after they are approved by the community. Finally, the knowledge of both DBpedia and YAGO is extracted from Wikipedia, but DBpedia differs from YAGO with respect to the community involvement because any user can engage in the mappings of the Wikipedia infobox templates to the DBpedia ontology and in the development of the DBpedia extraction framework (*http://mappings.dbpedia.org*).

A model might also lose the trust of its users if the latter have reasons to believe that the model contains biases and reflects the own interests of its creators (no matter whether these are experts or not).

Finally, note that hyperbole and misrepresentation of the real quality of a semantic data model does surely not help build trust. A couple of years ago I came across a press release of a company that claimed to have built a Human Resources ontology that covered 1 billion words; a claim that is rather absurd. And, personally, I would trust a model that claims to have an accuracy of 60% and actually achieves that accuracy in my evaluation more than a model boasting 90% accuracy and achieving only 75%. In Chapter 8 I discuss the importance of scrutinizing third-party semantic models before using them in your applications.

Availability, Versatility, and Performance

Three additional semantic model dimensions that are usually mentioned in the relevant literature are *availability*, *versatility*, and *performance*.

Availability is the extent to which the model (or part of it) is present, obtainable, and ready for use, while versatility refers to the different ways and forms the model can be accessed. DBpedia, for example, can be queried directly online via the RDF query language SPARQL (*http://dbpedia.org/sparql*) [92] or downloaded as RDF files. Similarly, ESCO is is available both as a web service API (*https://oreil.ly/falF3*) and downloadable RDF files (*https://oreil.ly/UEukE*).

Performance, in turn, has to do with the efficiency and scalability with which we can access and use the model in an application (querying, reasoning, or other operations). As such, it's a dimension highly dependent on the characteristics of the modeling framework or language we decide to use (e.g., reasoning in some variations of OWL is known to be nonscalable), as well as the technology stack (e.g., storage techniques and tools, query languages, reasoners, etc.) that is available for this framework.

In the rest of the book I will not discuss these three dimensions so much; instead I will focus on pitfalls and dilemmas influencing the content and structure of semantic models.

Summary

You can't know if the semantic models you build or use are good unless you know what this "good" entails and how you can measure it. For that, in this chapter we saw the main quality dimensions that you need to consider every time you judge the quality of a model, as well as the main metrics and methods you can use for measuring these dimensions. Moreover, we saw some of the most common causes of bad model quality for each dimension; you can use these to investigate and discover the reasons behind your own models' quality problems.

In general, achieving high quality in a semantic model in all dimensions can be a very challenging task. In any case, we will revisit the problem of managing model quality, where you'll learn how to avoid some common pitfalls.

Important things to remember:

- In the presence of vagueness and subjectivity, agreement on the truth of a model's statement is not a given. Keep that in mind when measuring a vague model's accuracy.
- Completeness is hard to accurately measure because it's a moving target. You can try to use gold standards, but these are rarely available. In most cases you will need to work with partial standards and/or heuristics.
- Inference in a semantic model might multiply and propagate semantic inaccuracy; you can contain the latter either by limiting inference or by finding and fixing the inaccurate assertions.
- A consistent model is not necessarily accurate, nor an inaccurate model necessarily inconsistent.
- Always pay attention to a model's relevancy; it's crucial for the model's adoption and success.
- Don't underestimate the importance and difficulty of having a model with a high degree of human understandability.
- Trustworthiness of a semantic model is not simply a matter of accuracy or completeness; it's a concept that has social and psychological dimensions that cannot be easily expressed by a mathematical formula.

Now, let's move to the next chapter that discusses how semantic models can be developed.

CHAPTER 5

Semantic Model Development

"If you mine the data hard enough, you can also find messages from God." [Dogbert]
—Scott Adams, *Dilbert*

So far we've seen what a semantic model can consist of, what phenomena should concern us during its development and usage, and what quality dimensions we need to evaluate before we use it. In this chapter, we'll focus on the development process of a semantic model, looking at the challenges, steps, and activities it involves, and the methodological and technological support that is available for each of them.

If you are mainly a consumer of semantic models rather than a creator, this chapter will help you understand how challenging the development process can be, and how you can help model creators build you the models you actually need.

Development Activities

There are several methodologies and life cycles in the semantic modeling literature that attempt to define the steps and activities involved in the development of a semantic data model [93]. Some prescribe only a few high-level activities, while others contain more detailed and specific tasks. Some are specific to particular types of models and/or modeling frameworks, while others are more generic. Some are based on a more centralized philosophy, while others are based on a more collaborative one. And some enjoy comprehensive technology and tooling support, while others do not.

In my career as a semantic modeler I have had the chance to apply several of these methodologies in (nonacademic) projects, with mixed results. The three biggest lessons I learned were:

- You cannot force an off-the-shelf methodology onto a problem if it doesn't fit; it should always be the other way around, i.e., use the problem's context and realities to adapt the methodology. This might seem obvious but it is often forgotten.

- A semantic data modeling project is almost never a one-off engineering project; the models you build require a continuous effort to keep them relevant and useful.

- A semantic data modeling project is almost never purely technical; you have to take into account business, strategic, and organizational aspects.

That said, I now approach every semantic model development project as an iteration of six activities: *setting the stage*, *deciding what to build*, *building it*, *ensuring it's good*, *making it useful*, and *making it last*. Let's see what each of these entails.

Setting the Stage

Before you open your favorite semantic modeling editor or start drawing diagrams on a whiteboard, you need actually to define an appropriate strategy for your model's development and ensure you have everything you need to successfully execute it. This is essentially translated into asking (and getting as many clear and satisfactory answers as possible to) five key questions:

- What are we building?
- Why are we building it?
- How are we building it?
- Who is building it?
- Who cares?

The first question might seem trivial, but it's not. For example, let's say that a client asks you to build him a knowledge graph. Which of the following (quite different) definitions do you think they have in mind?

A knowledge graph acquires and integrates information into an ontology and applies a reasoner to derive new knowledge [94].

Knowledge graphs are database-like structures that facilitate the retrieval of related information [95].

A knowledge graph (i) mainly describes real-world entities and their interrelations, organized in a graph, (ii) defines possible classes and relations of entities in a schema, (iii) allows for potentially interrelating arbitrary entities with each other, and (iv) covers various topical domains [96].

Knowledge graphs could be envisaged as a network of all kind things which are relevant to a specific domain or to an organization. They are not limited to abstract concepts and relations but can also contain instances of things like documents and datasets [97].

We define a Knowledge Graph as an RDF graph. An RDF graph consists of a set of RDF triples where each RDF triple... [78].

Knowledge graphs are large networks of entities, their semantic types, properties, and relationships between entities [98].

In practice, you cannot expect that everyone in an organization or project knows or agrees on what an ontology, taxonomy, knowledge graph, or other kind of semantic data model is. Some will have no idea what you are talking about, others may have read about it or heard about it at some conference, and others will know it in a different way than you do, depending on their background. Semantic Web people will think of RDF and Linked Data, linguists and NLP people will think of WordNet, and data people of just another kind of database.

Your task (and challenge) is not to argue about which definition is correct (unless of course your model needs to semantically define the entity Knowledge Graph), but rather to understand what your client actually means, and then create one or more narratives that can effectively communicate this "what" to all the relevant stakeholders.

 You should always clarify whether the "what" involves merely the model or also the supporting technology and processes, especially if the organization has never had a semantic model developed before.

Now, the "what" is tightly coupled with the "why," namely the technical and business goals the model is trying to achieve. The latter is not so much needed to justify the model's development (unless you are still in the phase of making the business case), but mostly to give you a first rough idea of what the requirements and challenges will be.

For example, it might be that you simply want a taxonomy of product categories that the users of an ecommerce website can use to navigate within it. Then your main challenge is to define these categories in a way that is intuitive for all users and actually enhances the findability of products. But it might also be that you want a semantic model to provide some important domain knowledge to a chatbot and enhance the latter's natural language interaction capabilities. In such a case your model will have to deal with the nuances of ambiguity, vagueness, and other phenomena that we saw in Chapter 3, and enable the chatbot to interpret user requests and generate answers for them in a more effective way. In all cases, the more concrete and clear the model's goals are, the greater are its odds of success.

After the "what" and "why" comes the "how," though not as a detailed plan with concrete actions and methods, but rather as an overall philosophy, set of principles, or strategic directions on which the model's development will be based. For example, in my first months at Textkernel, while "setting the stage" for the company's knowledge graph, we defined three main principles that would guide its development [99]:

The scope, structure, and content of the graph would be driven by the actual data that our software products needed to analyze and process, as well as the way these products (could) use the graph to become more effective

> In other words, every entity, attribute, or relation defined in the ontology would need to not only be related to the domain(s) of the data, but also serve some concrete role in the products' functionality.

The graph's elements would be generated (and regularly updated) by mining a variety of structured and unstructured data sources

> Because the estimated size (several thousands of entities and statements) and volatility of the recruitment domain were pretty high, building the model in a top-down, expert-driven approach was infeasible in terms of cost and scalability. For that, we decided to invest in methods and tools for automatic mining of semantic elements, rather that doing it completely manually.

The automatic mining approach would be complemented with a human-in-the-loop approach to quality assurance and continuous improvement

> Even the best automatic semantics mining algorithms are prone to some level of inaccuracy which, depending on the concrete subtask, can be significant (see upcoming sections). That's why, to ensure the highest quality possible for Textkernel's knowledge graph, we would incorporate human judgments in the mining process, so as to deal with cases where the algorithms were not confident or reliable enough with respect to their own judgments.

These principles may not be applicable to the organization, domain, or problem you are trying to solve; you might not have a large amount of data to harvest, you might not care for very high accuracy, or you may be able to fully automate the model's development without the need for human involvement. That's fine, as long as your own principles are well articulated and communicated to all relevant stakeholders.

The "how" question is also an excellent way to align expectations and prevent fundamental misunderstandings. I still remember a client from 12 years ago who, when I told him that he would need to set up a dedicated team for his ontology's maintenance, asked me, "Why don't you simply automate this?" at a time when industry-strength automated ontology construction methods and tools were extremely hard to find (and actually still are).

In all cases, the answers you will get on the "how" will determine to a great extent the "who," namely the people who will be involved in the model's development. If, for example, your strategy involves a great degree of expert human input, then you will need to start recruiting domain experts. If your goal is to exploit large amounts of unstructured data from which to mine your semantics, then you will need experts in natural language processing and machine learning. And if you expect your model to be heavily axiomatized so as to enable automated reasoning, then you will need people who can work with formal logic. In Chapter 11 I discuss in more detail what pitfalls to avoid when assembling a semantic model development team.

Finally, the "who cares" question is nothing else than the famous "stakeholder analysis" that every project management framework teaches, namely the identification of all people (or teams) who the semantic model will involve or affect, and their grouping according to their levels of participation, interest, and influence in the project. This is particularly important when you operate in a complex environment and your semantic model is expected to affect (and get affected by) many different products, processes, and people.

Deciding What to Build

Once the stage has been set up, it's time to dive into the details of what exactly you want (and can) develop, by *specifying the model's requirements*. This typically includes the kind of data you want in your model, the kind of questions you want it to be able to answer, the domains you want to cover, the applications you want to support, or the dimensions and level of quality your users expect. For example:

- I want a model about cinema, history, and literature.
- I want a model that can tell me all the characters of a film and their equivalent characters in the book the film was based on.
- I want a model that covers the 20th century and the whole of Europe.
- I want a model that I can use to automatically identify and disambiguate the persons a news article talks about.
- I want a model that can be applied to data in English, French, and Italian.
- I want a model that can be used both by my data analytics platform and my content recommendation system.
- I want a model that has an accuracy of at least 90%.

Some requirements will be more vague and open-ended than others, and a good modeling process should ensure these are defined more tightly before development starts. For example, a request to build a model about cinema is not very informative; you probably want to know the time period, the geographic scope, or other parameters.

Along with such requirements, you might also get "nonfunctional" requirements such as the representation framework you have to use, the reasoning complexity and scalability you have to consider, or some third-party model that you must keep your model aligned and in sync with.

In all cases, you should be prepared for three things: First, the whole exercise will be less about "gathering" and more about "investigating" and "discovering" requirements that nobody would know or tell you. If you passively expect the requirements to come to you, it will be too late (more on this in Chapter 8).

Second, you will unavoidably get conflicting requirements that cannot be satisfied at the same time (e.g., wanting to support a particular reasoning task when the modeling language that *must* be used does not support it). Actually, the whole "Dilemmas" part of this book owes its existence to such conflicts. In any case, you need to resolve these conflicts as early as possible.

Third, more often than you think, you will get requirements that are either impossible or extremely difficult to satisfy, given the available technology and resources (e.g., wanting to fully automatically extract synonyms for your model with a 95% precision, when the best relevant algorithms perform much worse than that). To tackle such cases, but also for planning and project/product management purposes, you should always complement the list of requirements with some feasibility and priority analysis. You will find more details on pitfalls and dilemmas regarding model specification in Chapters 8 and 13.

Building It

Once you have concrete requirements for your model, you actually need to go on and build it. That means choosing, defining, and putting together the modeling elements that best satisfy these requirements, under the restrictions and constraints that your context imposes, and by following/implementing the principles, methodologies, and techniques you have decided are most appropriate and effective.

This is the activity where you will need to dive deep into the semantic representation requirements of your model and make decisions about the latter's structure and content. For example, given the requirement *I want a model that can tell me all the characters of a film and their equivalent characters in the book the film was based on*, you may decide that your model needs a class FilmCharacter, a class BookCharacter, and a relation isEquivalentTo between their instances. Or, considering the requirement *I want a model that can be applied to data in English, French, and Italian*, you may decide that all elements will need to have names and lexicalizations in these three languages.

This is also the activity where you have to design and implement (if they are not already in place) or change and adapt (if they are not the right ones) mechanisms and processes for *knowledge acquisition*, namely the generation of entities, relations, and other elements that will go into your model from appropriate sources (experts, data, users, etc.).

For example, a big part of the DBpedia project has been the development of DBpedia extractors, a set of software modules that are responsible for extracting specific pieces of data from Wikipedia articles [100]. Similarly, at Textkernel, along with the development and delivery of our knowledge graph, we developed a semiautomatic framework for discovering new profession and skill entities from job vacancies. And in the case of ESCO, there was much work on defining the required processes that allowed geographically distributed domain experts to collaboratively develop ESCO's content [101].

Finally, the building activity is the one that will make you revisit and revise your model's initial requirements, after discovering that many of these are either not feasible or conflicting with each other.

Ensuring It's Good

Whatever you build, and in whatever way, you always need to ensure it's of acceptable quality. So, this activity is about defining in detail the quality dimensions and metrics that matter most for your model (see Chapter 4), but also implementing the necessary mechanisms and processes to measure these metrics.

It's also an activity during which you will need to decide (and maybe revise your initial expectations and requirements) which dimensions and metrics are more important. For example, you may realize that you cannot achieve both a high degree of accuracy and also a completeness for some of your model's elements, and that you have to sacrifice one for the other. In Chapter 9 I discuss several such quality trade-offs.

Making It Useful

Let's say you have managed to build a high-quality semantic model that covers 100% of the requirements you were given. Unless the model is actually used by real users and systems, and brings apt benefits to them, it's practically useless.

In my career I have experienced several situations where a perfectly good model was never put into use or, when it was, did not really make a difference. The reasons for this varied per case, but all of them boiled down to one key reason: nobody made the (often significant) extra effort needed to incorporate the model into the applications that were to use it, and ensure they worked well together.

So, the "making it useful" activity is the one you focus on:

- *Understanding the annoying, yet very important, details of how the applications that are meant to use the model work.* Ideally you will have started doing that from the inception phase of your model, but in many cases you will be asked to apply an already developed model to some new application you have never heard about before.

- *Identifying points of incompatibility (technical, conceptual, or other) between your model and these applications, and developing ways to overcome them, both on the model's side and the application's.* For example, several years ago, I worked on a project where we had to incorporate a business ontology to a semantic tagging system in order to detect mentions of company entities in news articles. From the very first quality check it became obvious that the system could not handle the high level of the model's ambiguity and, for that, we actually had to develop a whole new disambiguation module for the system.

- *Tackling any conflicting requirements that different applications or users demand from the same model.* Different stakeholders will most likely give you different, single-sided requirements without realizing conflicts and trade-offs with other applications. It's your job to identify and reconcile these conflicts.

- *Measuring the end-to-end quality of the model-enhanced application and verifying its improvement.* This is typically done by comparing the application's effectiveness before and after the incorporation of the model; in all cases, it's imperative that you verify and demonstrate such an improvement.

Making It Last

Even when your model is successfully deployed in some production environment, and has already started bringing value to its users, your job is not done; you still need to ensure your model's longevity by establishing effective continuous improvement and change-management processes and mechanisms.

You will need such mechanisms for three reasons. The first is that it's highly unlikely that the first version of your model is perfect and that there are zero complaints by its users, meaning that you will need a systematic way to collect feedback and execute improvements. Most of the (public) models I mention in this book have known quality problems that they (hopefully) try to fix in every new version.

The second reason is the need to keep your model timely with respect to changes in the domain and data it represents (see the "Timeliness" quality dimension in Chapter 4). The more volatile and susceptible to semantic drift your domain is, the higher the risk is of it becoming irrelevant over time.

A third reason is potential changes in the model's requirements; you might be asked to expand it in a completely different domain, represent it in another modeling language, map it to some new standard, or make it usable by a new type of application.

In Chapter 14 I discuss dilemmas related to semantic model evolution, along with techniques for crafting an evolution strategy that best fits your model and its environment.

Vocabularies, Patterns, and Exemplary Models

Semantic modeling is about *shareability* and common understanding; so not reinventing the wheel, and reusing, where possible, existing semantic resources can potentially accelerate the development process and increase the chances of semantic interoperability. The circumstances under which this can happen are examined in Chapter 8, but before that, let's see what kind of resources we have at our disposal.

Upper Ontologies

Upper ontologies (also known as top-level or foundational ontologies) describe very general concepts and relations that are independent of any particular problem or domain and which are meant to be used as high-level, domain-neutral categories of more domain-specific modeling elements. The idea is that if multiple semantic models link to the same upper ontology, there can be better semantic interoperability between them.

In Figures 5-1 and 5-2, you can see the basic categories defined in two different foundational ontologies, namely DOLCE (Descriptive Ontology for Linguistic and Cognitive Engineering) [102] and BFO (Basic Formal Ontology) [103].

In general, upper ontologies are hard to develop as the concepts they define are more abstract and often epistemological in nature. Moreover, there is no such generally accepted, comprehensive, standardized ontology in use today. For these reasons, the effort needed to select a proper upper ontology for your model, and actually link the latter to it, can be considerable.

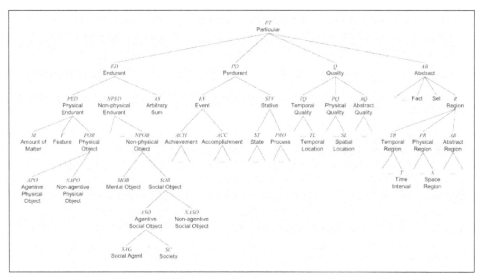

Figure 5-1. Taxonomy of basic categories in DOLCE

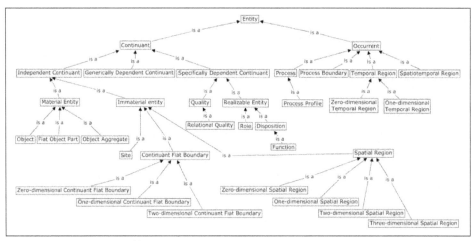

Figure 5-2. Taxonomy of basic categories in BFO

Design Patterns

In the context of semantic data modeling, *design patterns* are reusable, well-proven solutions to recurring modeling/design problems or scenarios. Their goal is to help modelers accelerate their work by providing them with ready-to-use templates that they can easily adapt/apply to their own context and situation.

For example, let's say you are developing an OWL ontology and you want to represent the fact that "John married Jane in California." This will be problematic because a known limitation of OWL is its inability to define ternary or higher-degree relations, and the relation married here relates three entities. To overcome this limitation, you can use a modeling pattern for n-ary relations that has been proposed by W3C [104], and which suggests representing the married relation as a class (e.g., Wedding) and the particular wedding between John and Jane as an instance of this class that can be then linked to California via a binary relation. Figure 5-3 illustrates this representation.

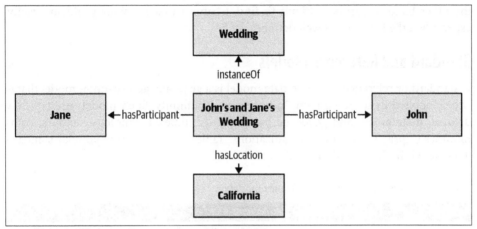

Figure 5-3. Example of the n-ary relation pattern

Semantic modeling patterns are characterized by:

The kinds of problems or situations they are designed for
> There are, for example, patterns designed to solve problems where the representation language does not directly support certain constructs (like the n-ary relation pattern we just saw). These are independent from a specific domain of interest but depend on the expressivity of the logical formalism that is used for representation. There are also "good practice" patterns whose goal is to obtain more robust, clean, and easy-to-maintain models. And there are patterns that provide solutions to concrete modeling problems in a variety of domains.

Their domain and applicability range
> There are, for example, patterns that are applicable in specific domains [105] [106], and universal patterns that span across industries and domains [107].

The modeling language they are expressed or applicable in
> For example, if you work mostly with E-R and relational database models, then the patterns described in Silverston's *The Data Model Resource Book* [105] or Hay's *Data Model Patterns* [108] can be useful. If, on the other hand, OWL is your cup of tea, then several patterns can be found in the W3C Semantic Web Best Practices and Deployment Working Group [109], the University of Manchester [110], and the OntologyDesignPatterns.org portal. However, nothing

prevents you from applying relational patterns in OWL models and vice versa, as long as they contain compatible elements.

In general, semantic design patterns provide a higher level of building blocks than the basic elements of a modeling language and can help modelers accelerate their work by not having to create everything from scratch. Moreover, carefully considered patterns are more likely to be correct and robust than an untested, custom solution. On the other hand, it can be difficult to find a pattern that fits your problem exactly, especially if the latter is not well defined.

Standard and Reference Models

A standard or reference semantic data model is a generally agreed-upon model that is widely applied in some domain, industry, or community. Such models are typically defined, maintained, and governed by standards bodies, technology vendors, communities of practice, or other organizations. Table 5-1 shows some popular standard data models in different domains.

Table 5-1. Sample standard and reference models

Model	Governing body	Description
SNOMED Clinical Terms	SNOMED International	A systematically organized collection of medical terms providing codes, terms, synonyms, and definitions used in clinical documentation and reporting
Schema.org	Schema.org Community Group	A common set of metadata schemas for structured data markup on web pages
International Standard Classification of Occupations (ISCO)	International Labour Organization	An International Labour Organization classification structure for organizing information on labor and jobs
Financial Industry Business Ontology (FIBO)	EDM Council	A formal model of the legal structures, rights, and obligations contained in the contracts and agreements that form the foundation of the financial industry
HL7 Reference Information Model (RIM)	Health Level Seven International (HL7)	Expresses the data content needed in a specific clinical or administrative context and provides an explicit representation of the semantic and lexical connections that exist between the information carried in the fields of HL7 messages

Public Models and Datasets

Last but not least, we have models that are publicly available on the web, without necessarily claiming the status of a standard or pattern. A characteristic example is Linked Open Data [111], a large set of interlinked semantic models and datasets that are expressed in RDF and OWL, and which are released under an open license that allows their free reuse. In Table 5-2 you can find some characteristic linked open datasets, while in Figure 5-4 you can see an overview of this set in 2011.

Table 5-2. Datasets available as Linked Open Data

Dataset	Description
DBpedia	A dataset containing extracted data from Wikipedia
GeoNames	Information about over seven million places and geographic features worldwide
Diseasome	A dataset of 4,300 disorders and disease genes linked by known disorder-gene associations
CrunchBase	A dataset describing people, companies, and products
Eurostat Countries and Regions	Statistical information about European countries and regions
MusicBrainz	Data about artists and their albums

A similar, though smaller in scale, set of public semantic models is Linked Open Vocabularies [112] [113]. The models within this set contain mostly classes rather than individual entities, and are meant to help modelers more with the structure of their model rather than its content. Thus, for example, you can use the classes, relations, and attributes of the Music Ontology [114] to semantically describe your own songs, but you won't find in it entities regarding concrete songs and artists.

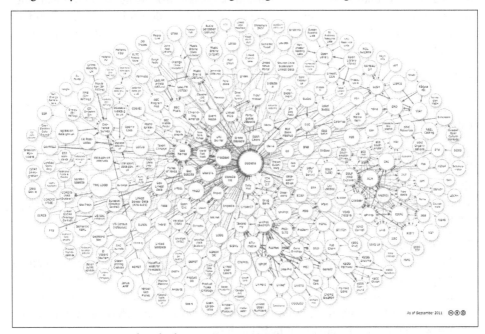

Figure 5-4. Overview of Linked Open Data in 2011

Semantic Model Mining

When the semantic model we want to develop (and maintain) is potentially very large, a human-only development approach can be too expensive and time-consuming. As an example, consider Cyc. In 2017, its inventor, Douglas Lenat, estimated that the accumulated development cost for Cyc (comprising at that time 21 million statements) had reached $120 million [115]. On the other hand, English DBpedia managed to reach 400 million statements in less time and for lower cost, mainly thanks to the fact that these statements are automatically extracted from Wikipedia [115]. This difference is, of course, not indicative of the comparative quality of the two models; however, it is of the positive effect of semantic model mining in scaling the development process and making it more efficient.

Semantic model mining can be defined as the task of acquiring and incorporating terms, entities, relations, and other elements from data in a model, with limited human effort. It's a task typically performed through methods and techniques from the areas of information extraction, natural language processing, machine learning, and information retrieval, and can take many forms, depending on the kind of semantic elements we want to mine, the data we have at our disposal, and the available state-of-the-art methods, algorithms, and tools.

In this section we'll see the basic tasks that semantic model mining involves, their key dimensions, and the main methods and tools that can be used to tackle them. You will find more in-depth discussion of how these methods can be effectively applied in real-world settings in Chapter 8.

Mining Tasks

Given the modeling elements we saw in Chapter 2, there are four main information extraction tasks that can help us automate aspects of the semantic model development process:

Terminology extraction
> This is the task of automatically extracting from a given data source (usually a corpus) terms that are relevant and important for the model's domain(s), and which can potentially signify entities, relations, or other elements. It's a task we typically perform when we build a model in a bottom-up fashion and don't really know what kinds of elements it needs to have.

Entity extraction
> This is the task of automatically extracting, from a given data source, terms that denote entities of some particular entity type, such as persons, organizations, locations, or other. It's a task also known as *entity recognition* and it differs from terminology extraction in that the extracted term is assigned to some known entity type. As such, we perform it when we already know the entity types we

need in the model and we are looking to instantiate them. At Textkernel, for example, we regularly mine job vacancies to discover (previously unknown) entities that denote professional skills.

Relation extraction

This is the task of automatically extracting, from a given data source, relations that hold between different entities and/or other elements, such as synonymy, meaning inclusion, semantic relatedness, or any other relation that we want in our model.

Rule and axiom extraction

This is the task of automatically extracting, from a given data source, complex axioms and rules that can be used for reasoning purposes.

As an example, let's say we are developing a semantic model to describe historical events and we have the following text from Wikipedia [116]:

> The Battle of Waterloo was fought on Sunday June 18, 1815 near Waterloo in Belgium, part of the United Kingdom of the Netherlands at the time. A French army under the command of Napoleon Bonaparte was defeated by two of the armies of the Seventh Coalition: a British-led allied army under the command of the Duke of Wellington, and a Prussian army under the command of Field Marshal Blücher.

If we apply a terminology extraction tool on this text, we will most likely get back terms like `Field Marshal Blücher`, `Prussian Army`, `Seventh Coalition`, `Napoleon Bonaparte`, `fought`, or `command`, all of which are good potential entities and relations to enter our model. If, in addition, we have at our disposal a competent Entity Extraction system, we will also get the information that `Napoleon Bonaparte` is an entity of type `Person`, `Waterloo` of `Location`, and `Seventh Coalition` of `Organization`. And if we apply some algorithm to discover potential relations between these entities, we might be able to extract the fact that "Waterloo is located in Belgium" or that "Field Marshal Blücher was the commander of the Prussian Army."

Mention-Level Versus Global-Level Extraction

The term information extraction (IE) is often used in the literature to refer to either *global-level IE* or *mention-level IE*. A global-level IE system is expected to take some input data and produce a list of distinct entities, relations, or other elements, without caring where exactly these were found. A mention-level IE system, on the other hand, will return not only the semantic elements, but also the exact data (e.g., a sentence) where they have been found. For the purposes of semantic model mining, we typically need global-level IE systems. This does not mean that we cannot use mention-level systems for this purpose, but we need to adapt them for our task.

Something to keep in mind is that there is no standard order by which these tasks should be performed; in the preceding example, we could have just as well applied the relation discovery system first, gotten the relation statements, and then determined what kind of entities the subjects and objects of these statements were. Whether that would be more effective is another story, though, and this is exactly the challenge of developing semantic mining pipelines from individual information extraction algorithms and tools, namely coming up with the configuration and orchestration that works best for your model.

Also, how effective these tasks will be depends on several factors, including:

The complexity of the target information
For example, it is generally easier to find salient terms in a text than identifying their entity types. Similarly, it is easier to extract a binary relation than a more complex one (e.g., an event).

The specificity of the target information
For example, it is generally easier to identify semantically similar entities than identifying ones that are synonyms. Similarly, establishing that a person is somehow related to a location is typically easier than finding the exact nature of this relation.

The appropriateness of the available input data
For example, looking for synonyms or hyponyms of an entity is easier in an encyclopedic text than in a news article. Similarly, determining which skills are in most demand for a particular profession is easier in a job vacancies corpus than a news one.

The structure degree of the available input data
For example, if instead of the text about the Battle of Waterloo we had used the respective infobox that its Wikipedia page provides (see Figure 5-5), we could have much more easily extracted `Napoleon Bonaparte` as one of the participating commanders.

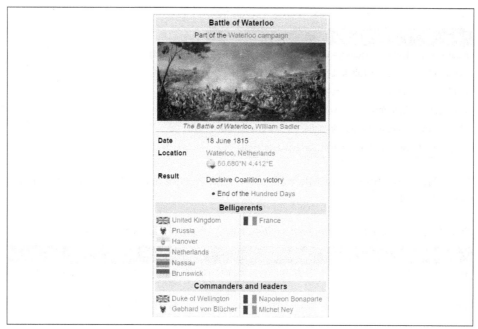

Figure 5-5. Wikipedia infobox for the Battle of Waterloo

Let's see the different approaches and techniques that most information extraction systems use to tackle the aforementioned tasks.

Mining Methods and Techniques

The common component of all information extraction systems is some set of extraction patterns (or extraction rules) that can be used to extract the desired information from the input data. Where these systems usually differ is in the different ways they acquire these patterns.

Hand-built patterns and rules

Even though they might not admit it (because everybody does machine learning these days), many information extraction systems still rely on manually crafted extraction rules and patterns that linguists, domain experts, or other professionals meticulously create.

A well-known example is Hearst patterns, a set of lexico-syntactic patterns that can be used to recognize instances of the generic-specific relation in texts (see Table 5-3).

Table 5-3. Hearst patterns for extracting is-a relations

Pattern	Occurrence example
X and other Y	Temples, treasuries, and other important buildings
X or other Y	Bruises, wounds, broken bones, or other injuries
Y such as X	The social sciences, such as archeology or psychology
Such Y as X	Such authors as Roth or Bellow
Y including X	Common-law countries, including Canada and England
Y, especially X	European countries, especially France and Spain

A similar set of patterns for other common relations are defined in Araúz et al. [117] (see Table 5-4).

Table 5-4. Patterns for extracting part-whole, cause-effect, and location relations

Part-Whole	Cause-Effect	Location
WHOLE is comprised/composed/ constituted (in part) of/by PART	CAUSE (is) responsible for EFFECT	ENTITY (is) connected/delimited to/by PLACE
WHOLE comprises PART	CAUSE causes/produces/... EFFECT	ENTITY (is) found/built/... in/on/... PLACE
PART composes WHOLE	CAUSE leads/contributes/gives (rise) to EFFECT	ENTITY (is) formed/forms in/on/... PLACE
PART is/constitutes (a/the/...) part/ component/... of WHOLE	CAUSE-driven/-induced/-caused EFFECT	ENTITY (is) extended/extends (out) into/ parallel/... (of/to) PLACE

The main reasons why such patterns are popular are their simplicity; the speed at which they can be created, tested, and customized; and their high accuracy when the domain is well defined and the text's structure easily predictable. On the other hand, they are not easily transferable to other domains or types of texts, their coverage of all possible cases is typically low, and they can require too much manual labor.

Supervised machine learning methods

As writing useful extraction patterns can be a difficult, time-consuming task, several approaches focus on automatically learning the extraction rules, using supervised machine learning and human-labeled training data. Considering again the Waterloo example, if you wanted to follow a supervised approach you would need to take several texts like that and have human annotators mark the entities and relations found in them. Then you would use this data to train a supervised machine learning model that you could use to automatically detect entities and relations in unseen texts.

For example, the Stanford Named Entity Recognizer system [118] provides a machine learning model that recognizes seven entity types (Location, Person, Organization, Money, Percent, Date, and Time), and has been trained on a set of annotated newswire articles, known as the Message Understanding Conference (MUC) datasets [119]. Similar approaches in other domains include extraction of biomedical entities (such as proteins, DNAs, RNAs, cells, etc.) [120], and labor market entities (such as job titles, skills, companies, etc.) [121].

The main advantage of supervised systems is that they can learn complex extraction patterns that a human can either not see or express. Also, they can be easily adapted to a different domain as long as there is adequate training data available. On the other hand, this training data can be expensive to produce. And if the training has been done for a very specific domain or type of texts, then these systems may incorporate biases that prevent them from being equally effective in different domains.

Semi-supervised methods

Semi-supervised (or weakly supervised) methods work as follows: First they use a small number of labeled seed data to extract an initial set of patterns from a large corpus. Then they use these patterns to automatically generate more labeled data, and those again to extract new patterns in an iterative way.

A characteristic example of this approach is a system called NELL (Never-Ending Language Learner), developed at Carnegie Mellon University as part of a research project [122]. NELL started its operation in January 2010, with an initial ontology of approximately 800 classes (e.g., Person, SportsTeam, Fruit, Emotion) and relations (e.g., playsOnTeam, playsInstrument), and with 10 to 20 instances per class and relation. Every day, NELL extracts new instances from unstructured web pages by finding noun phrases that represent new examples of the input entity types (e.g., George Washington is a person and politician), and pairs of noun phrases that correspond to instances of the input relations (e.g., the pair Jason Giambi and Yankees is an instance of the playsOnTeam relation). These new instances are added to the growing knowledge base [123] and are used to retrain NELL's extractors. NELL is still in operation and, at the time of writing these lines, has accumulated 2.8 million asserted instances of 1,100 different classes and relations.

The major motivation behind these techniques is to reduce the manual efforts required to create labeled data, and to exploit the large amount of unlabeled data that is generally easily available without investing much effort. An important risk, however, is *error propagation*, as extraction mistakes at the initial stages will result in choosing incorrect seeds for the later stages, thus generating more mistakes and decreasing the accuracy of the overall extraction process. In the case of NELL, the system ran for six months without human supervision, achieving a very high precision for 75% of the model's classes and relations, but a very low one for the remaining 25%. Therefore, the selection of initial seeds is very important; if they do not accurately reflect the knowledge contained in the corpus, the quality of extractions might remain low.

Distant supervision

The idea behind distant supervision is to exploit existing semantic models to automatically generate labeled data, and use these as training data for traditional supervised learning algorithms.

For example, in Mintz et al. [124] the authors exported from Freebase (a large collaborative knowledge base with data harvested mainly from user contributions [125]) three hundred relations between nine million named entities and, for each pair of related entities, they identified all sentences that contained them in a large unlabeled corpus. Then they used these sentences to train a relation classifier. Their intuition (and assumption) was that any sentence that contained a pair of entities that participate in a known Freebase relation was likely to express that relation in some way.

The obvious benefit of such methods is that they do not require any manual effort to label data and can be applied to large corpora. Also, since they extract relations already defined in some existing semantic model, they are less likely to produce uninformative or incoherent relations.

On the other hand, there are certain drawbacks. For example, if we consider the relation extraction system of Mintz et al. [124], then it might be that:

- The same two entities can be related in multiple different ways in the same corpus, adding incorrect examples to the training data
- Several entities are ambiguous, meaning that if the algorithm that tags the sentences with the entity pairs makes many ambiguity-related mistakes, these will be propagated to the training data and the machine learning model
- Several of the entity relations in the used semantic model are actually wrong, also resulting in training data that is wrong

Also, since distant supervision is limited to a fixed set of relations in a given knowledge base, it can be very hard to adapt it to new domains.

Unsupervised methods

Unsupervised information extraction methods require no labeled data to be trained with, nor carefully handcrafted rules. Instead, they rely on large amounts of unlabeled data and algorithms/techniques from the areas of statistical semantics and unsupervised machine learning, to discover meaningful patterns. As such, these methods are usually employed when the target elements to be extracted cannot be specified in advance, or getting an adequate amount of labeled data or handcrafted rules is just too difficult.

An example of this philosophy is found in Hasegawa et al. [126], where the authors discover relations between pairs of (already known) named entities within a corpus of newspaper articles in the following way: First, they tag the corpus with the entities. Then, for each pair of entities that co-occur in one or more sentences they find their accumulated context, i.e., the set of all distinct words that appear between the entities in all their co-occurrences. Then, they cluster together these entity pairs by calculating the cosine similarity [127] between their accumulated contexts. The (desired) result is that the obtained clusters contain pairs of entities linked by the same relation.

Another, more famous example is *Word2Vec* [128], a neural network–based system that takes as input a large text corpus and maps each term of it to a vector of real numbers. The calculation of these vectors (which are also known as *word embeddings*) is done in such a way that terms that share common contexts in the corpus have closer vectors. The intuition behind this is that if two terms have very similar neighbors, then they are probably quite similar in meaning, or are at least related. Thus, using Word2Vec, one can identify semantically related terms by, for example, calculating the cosine similarity of their vectors. Table 5-5 illustrates examples of semantically similar terms generated by a Word2Vec model trained on a Google News corpus [129].

Table 5-5. Examples of semantically similar terms using Word2Vec

Term	Top-10 nearest terms
Plato	Socrates, Aristotle, Hegel, Nietzsche, ancients, Karl Marx, philosopher, Marx, Goethe, ancient Greek
ontology	Semantic, taxonomy, schema, Semantic Web, meta, contextual, computational, associative, bioinformatics, semantics
biology	Biochemistry, molecular biology, biological sciences, Biology, physiology, science, developmental biology, molecular genetics, evolutionary biology, microbiology
fiction	Nonfiction, novels, Fiction, novelist, fictions, science fiction, novelists, literary, graphic novels, romance novels
car	Vehicle, cars, SUV, minivan, truck, car, Ford Focus, Honda Civic, Jeep, pickup truck
good	Great, bad, terrific, decent, nice, excellent, fantastic, better, solid, lousy

The obvious advantage of unsupervised approaches is that they do not need any annotated data for training, and can be easily applied to very large amounts of data without much effort. On the other hand, the information they extract can be incoherent, uninformative, and hard to map and disambiguate to specific entities, relations, or other elements. For example, the group of terms related to the entity Biology in Table 5-5 includes synonyms ("biological sciences"), broader entities ("science"), and narrower entities ("microbiology"); Word2Vec has no way of distinguishing between them.

> ## Open Information Extraction
>
> Open Information Extraction (OIE) is not so much a different technique but rather a different philosophy on how information extraction should be approached. Whereas traditional approaches focus on a small set of well-defined target elements and operate on relatively small domain-specific homogeneous corpora, OIE approaches aim at extracting all types of elements that can be found in large heterogeneous corpora [130] [131].
>
> Because of this, most OIE systems like TextRunner [132], StatSnowball [133], or Reverb [134], are unsupervised, though semi-supervised techniques can also be designed to work on a large scale (e.g., the NELL system I mentioned earlier).

Summary

In this chapter we concluded the "Basics" part of the book by taking an overview of the semantic model development process, and showing you how you can organize and support it. You have seen what activities you need to include, from *setting the stage* to *making it last*, as well as what kind of existing semantic resources and information extraction methods you can use to accelerate the process.

Important things to remember:

- A semantic data modeling project is almost never a one-off engineering project; the models we build require a continuous effort to keep them relevant and useful.

- A semantic data modeling project is almost never purely technical; you have to take into account business, strategic, and organizational aspects.

- Use the model's context and realities to adapt your development strategy and methodology, not the other way around.

- Push for concrete answers to the "what", "why," and "how" questions to prevent misunderstandings and manage expectations.

- Try not to reinvent the wheel and see if you can reuse, where possible, existing semantic resources. Don't rely exclusively on them, though, nor take them at face value.

- Try to exploit machine learning and information extraction methods to mine your model from data; they can be a great help for automating and scaling the development process.

Now it's time to move to the "Pitfalls" part of the book, where you will learn how to identify and avoid common mistakes and bad practices that usually result in bad semantic models.

PART II

The Pitfalls

CHAPTER 6

Bad Descriptions

The limits of my language means the limits of my world.
—Ludwig Wittgenstein

When we develop a semantic model, we define aspects of it that contribute to human-interpretability (element names, textual definitions, usage guidelines, and other documentation), as well as aspects that aim for machine-interpretability (relations with other elements, logical axioms, inference rules, etc.). As creators of semantic models, we place a lot of emphasis on the machine-interpretability aspects, and rightly so, but we often underestimate the importance and difficulty of creating semantic models that are clearly understood by humans. Conversely, as semantic model users we often underestimate the probability that we have actually misunderstood what a semantic model is really about, and we end up using it in incorrect ways. This is perhaps the biggest reason the semantic gap between data suppliers and consumers exists.

This chapter describes some common mistakes we make when we describe a semantic model's elements via names, textual definitions, and other types of human-readable information, and provides tips and guidelines to improve the quality of these descriptions.

Giving Bad Names

My favorite quiz when I give lectures on semantic modeling or when I interview people for hiring is the following: Assume you want to model the customers of a company, and that these clients can either be physical persons or other companies. Which of the two semantic models in Figure 6-1 is correct, the left or the right one?

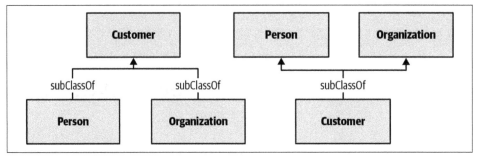

Figure 6-1. A modeling dilemma

The left model suggests that there is a class Customer and two subclasses of it called Person and Organization. The right model, on the other hand, suggests that the class Customer should be a subclass of the class Person but also of the class Organization. Most people are tempted to answer that the left model is the correct one, but they smell a trap and remain hesitant. And, indeed, there is a trap, namely that both models are wrong. Let's see why.

The model on the right, if you try to express it in natural language, says that "all customers are persons and organizations *at the same time*." However, this is impossible because an individual person cannot be an organization (a one-person company is still a company, not a person). The model on the left, on the other hand, says that "all persons and organizations are also customers"; this is also problematic as it implies that there are no persons or organizations in the domain or the data that are not customers. This latter example of bad modeling is just one case of *bad naming*.

A modeling element's name is bad when it doesn't help human users understand what the element is about or, even worse, when it leads them to wrong interpretations. In the left model of Figure 6-1, the class Person is badly named because, in reality, the modeler wanted to represent the class of customers that are physical persons, not all persons. The same applies for the class Organization. Therefore, a more accurate name for each of these two classes would be PrivateCustomer and Corporate Customer, respectively, and a much better model would be that of Figure 6-2. And that should be the case even if in your domain you are only interested in those persons and organizations that are customers.

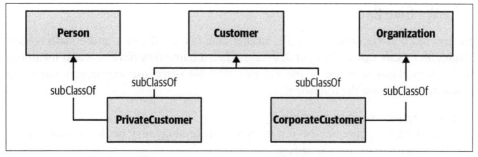

Figure 6-2. A solution to the modeling dilemma of Figure 6-1

Setting a Bad Example

Bad naming happens more often than you may think, even in models designed by experts in semantic modeling. For example, the relation that the SKOS framework defines for modeling meaning inclusion is named skos:broader. This is an obviously ambiguous name that does not provide any information about the intended direction of the relation, i.e., if "A skos:broader B" then is A broader than B or vice versa. Now, in the SKOS specification, this is clarified via a note stating that the word *broader* should be read as "has broader concept," meaning that one should say "cheese skos:broader dairy" rather than the inverse. Still, the naming of the relation should have been more accurate.

Similar cases of bad naming are found in popular public semantic models and datasets like Schema.org and DBpedia. For example, the class Agent [135] in DBpedia has an attribute called cost that is defined as "cost of building an ArchitecturalStructure, Ship, etc." Given this definition, a better name for the attribute would be hasConstructionCost, or something similar, as the term *cost* is way more generic than what the definition implies.

Another telling example is the class ExerciseAction [136] from Schema.org and its two relations sportsEvent and sportsTeam. The first is defined as "A sub property of location. The sports event where this action occurred" while the second as "A sub property of participant. The sports team that participated on this action." The problem with both relations' names is that they don't reflect their parent relations and their exact meaning. It is more accurate to say that "Action A isLocatedAt SportsEvent B" rather than "Action A SportsEvent B" as now the location aspect is clearly communicated. Similarly, hasParticipatingSportsTeam conveys more accurately the intended meaning of the sportsTeam relation.

Why We Give Bad Names

In general, bad element names are ambiguous, inaccurate, or unnecessarily vague. Ambiguity, as we saw in Chapter 3, occurs when a name may have different meanings and interpretations. Some of the reasons why we often use ambiguous names in semantic models are the following:

Not knowing any other interpretations
> For example, someone who doesn't follow technology may not know that Python is also a programming language.

Assuming other interpretations are irrelevant to the domain or application of the model, and that users will know what is meant
> For example, if the model contains only entities related to computer science, then nobody is expected to think that Python refers to the snake species

Assuming that the element's meaning will be inferred by its context
> For example, if there is an entity with the name `Barcelona` related to an entity with the name `Santiago Bernabeu` via the relation `visited`, then we can infer from the context that `Barcelona` refers to the soccer team and `Santiago Bernabeu` to the stadium

Inaccuracy, on the other hand, occurs when the element's name represents something similar but essentially different than what the modeler intends to express. Very often the name is more generic or more specific than it should be, and sometimes it is totally irrelevant, but in most cases it refers to something closely related but not exactly the same. The main reason behind this phenomenon is how, as humans, we are used to expressing ourselves in natural language and managing to understand each other, despite obvious inaccuracies.

For example, if someone asks you "What car do you drive?" you most likely won't answer "I drive the car with license plate ABC," but rather something like "I drive an Audi A4." The reason you would do that is that, even though you know that *Audi A4* is not actually the specific car you drive but rather the model of it, you guessed that when the questioner used the word "car," they really meant "car model." In most cases you would be right, but even if you were wrong, the questioner would clarify the question and then you would give the right answer. In a semantic model, however, you don't always have the luxury of context or interaction with the user, so if you want to create a class whose instances are car models, you would be safer and more accurate if you named it `CarModel` rather than `Car`.

Another example is the table of contents of this book when viewed as a taxonomy. There is a part called "The Dilemmas" and a chapter called "Expressiveness Dilemmas." When naming the chapters, I could have easily named the chapter "Expressiveness," expecting that when you see it under the "Dilemmas" part, you will understand what is it about. But I didn't, precisely because if someone opened the book directly to that chapter, it would be unclear to them what "Expressiveness" was all about.

In general, an element name is inaccurate when it is totally wrong, when it is more generic or more specific than it should be, or when it refers to something closely related but not exactly the same. Table 6-1 shows naming-related bad and better modeling decisions.

Table 6-1. Bad and better names for semantic model elements

Natural language expression	Bad modeling	Better modeling
"United States of America is a democracy"	Creating a class `Democracy` and making the entity `United States of America` an instance of it	Creating a class `Democratic Country` and making the entity `United States of America` an instance of it
"Jane scored high in deep learning"	Creating an entity `Deep Learning` and relating it to the entity `Jane` via a relation `scoredHighIn`	Creating an entity `Deep Learning Course` and relating it to the entity `Jane` via a relation `scoredHighInCourse`
"Barcelona visited Santiago Bernabeu"	Creating an entity `Barcelona` and relating it to the entity `Santiago Bernabeu` via a relation `visited`	Creating an entity `Barcelona FC` and relating it to the entity `Santiago Bernabeu stadium` via a relation `visited`

Pushing for Clarity

In my first months at Textkernel, I came across a semantic model that was used by the company's semantic search software for *query parsing and expansion*. Query expansion is a technique in search systems where the user's query (e.g., "Java") is expanded with semantically similar terms so that relevant documents that don't contain the user's input term can still be retrieved (e.g., expand "Java" with "C#"). To achieve that, the model already contained a large amount of good-quality semantically related terms, defined by experts and mined from user data. There was a small problem though: practically all people involved in developing, maintaining, and using that model referred to these terms as "synonyms," something that obviously was not the case (`Java` and `C#` have similarities but are different entities). Even worse, the actual name of the relation within the model was `belongsTo`, a rather abstract and uninformative name that often led to confusion.

To improve the situation, my team and I did two things. The first, and relatively easy task, was to change the name of the relation within the model's representation and documentation from `belongs` to `expandsInSearchQuery`. The second, and harder task, was to change the name in people's heads, so as to stop considering the expansion relation as synonymy. In the end, we achieved that as well by, gradually but steadily, promoting the new name in all communications, formal and informal.

To avoid having bad names in your semantic models, you need to learn to continuously scrutinize them for clarity and accuracy, and (gently but firmly) push for clarity, starting with yourself. Some techniques to do that include the following:

- *Always contemplate an element's name in isolation, i.e., without its related elements or other definition, and try to think of all the possible and legitimate ways this can be interpreted by a human.* Include multiple people in this. Alternatively, you could search the name within one or more corpora (or even Google it), and see how many different meanings arise.

- *If a name has more than one interpretation, make it more specific, even if the other interpretations are not within the domain or not very likely to occur.* Please note that this does not mean that the model should not contain ambiguous element lexicalizations, just that the main names of the entities should be unambiguous. For example, if your entity is Barcelona FC, then it's OK to use the term "Barcelona" as a label of it but not as a name, even if the meaning looks clear because of the entity's related entities.

- *If a definition is available for the element, compare the name with it.* If the definition expresses something more general or more specific than the name, then you need to change the latter.

- *Study how the element is used in practice by your modelers, annotators, developers, and users.* For example, if most of the human-made assertions for a given relation are wrong, then the relation's problematic name may have been the cause.

- *Ask for edge cases.* For example, if you have an attribute called cost, ask whether this name includes all the different types of costs you can think of.

- *When naming relations, use verb phrases and make their direction clear.* For example, as we saw in SKOS, hasBroader is a better name than broader.

Omitting Definitions or Giving Bad Ones

Imagine that it's a warm summer night and you are having drinks in a bar with a friend. At some point you tell them that yesterday you had to work overtime because your colleagues found a bug in your system and you had to deal with it. What is your friend's reaction?

1. They think that you caught some disease and ask you if you have already gone to the doctor.

2. Knowing you work as a software engineer, they guess that *bug* is some jargon term for something related to your work but have no idea what.

3. They're also a software engineer, so they know that *bug* in a software context "is an error, flaw, failure, or fault in a computer program or system that causes it to produce an incorrect or unexpected result, or to behave in unintended ways."

If your friend reacts in the first way, then it means that they do not have enough context to disambiguate the term *bug*, and that you should have been more specific, for example, by using the term *software bug*. In other words, you should have used a *better entity name*. If, however, they react in the second way, then the problem is not the ambiguity of the term, but the fact that they lack the domain knowledge needed to understand the term's meaning in this context. In other words, your friend is *missing a good definition*.

When You Need Definitions

Several years ago, I was working on a project that involved the merging of two taxonomies. For that purpose, we had developed a couple of semantic matching algorithms that identified synonymous entities from the two taxonomies that should be merged. As the algorithms were not 100% precise, the identified synonyms were ranked according to some confidence measure, and were given to a group of annotators to verify or reject their correctness. The feedback we got from the annotators focused on one important issue: they were spending a lot of time searching Google or other search engines for the meaning of the entities they had to annotate, because they could not always understand what they were by their names alone. That was to be expected because our annotators were more generalists than specialists in any particular domain.

Textual definitions of elements are necessary in a semantic model when you can't reasonably expect that all model stakeholders (creators, maintainers, and users) have the same background or domain knowledge. This is particularly true in highly specialized domains and communities where there are many special terms and concepts that are difficult for anyone outside of them to understand. These include:

Highly specialized terms that are used in the given domain and are not likely to be common knowledge
For example, "Agonal" is a term found in the medical domain, signifying a major, negative change in a patient's condition.

Acronyms
For example, "AWOL" in the military domain stands for "absent without leave" and indicates that someone is absent from where one should be but without intent to desert.

General terms, or terms from other domains, that get a specialized meaning in the given domain

For example, the term "Ability to pay" in the financial domain denotes "an economic principle that states that the amount of tax an individual pays should be dependent on the level of burden the tax will create relative to the wealth of the individual" [137].

In cases like these, giving a better name, e.g., including a domain qualifier, can help but is not always enough. You can say bug (`software`) instead of merely bug, but the entity's meaning will still be elusive to most nonsoftware experts.

Why We Omit Definitions

If you inspect many public semantic models you will notice that the use of definitions is inconsistent, both in terms of coverage and quality. For example, Eurovoc (*https://oreil.ly/THTTs*) provides no definitions or descriptions for the terms it contains, while ESCO does. DBpedia, on the other hand, contains definitions for most of the instance-level entities it contains (via the `rdfs:comment` attribute), but not for the majority of its schema elements, namely classes, relations, and attributes. Thus, for example, we get to know that the class `Broadcaster` is "an organisation responsible for the production of radio or television programs and/or their transmission" [138] but we get no information about what a `Naruto Character` [139] is.

Now, there are several reasons why a semantic model may lack definitions:

"Everybody knows this" assumption

When we build a semantic model for a domain we know very well, we tend to assume that everyone has the same background knowledge as us and, thus, is able to understand everything we include in the model. Bad names are one consequence of that assumption, while missing (or sloppy) definitions are another.

Difficulty and cost

If the elements to be defined are many, and there's no available automatic mechanism for getting definitions about them, it may be too costly to try to manually define them. Moreover, if the elements to be defined are rather abstract and vague, it may be hard to come up with accurate and consensual definitions.

Optionality

In many semantic modeling frameworks, definitions are optional elements that are not considered core to a semantic model.

"Not contributing to inference" attitude

For most logicians and knowledge representation experts, textual descriptions of entities are pretty much useless because they do not contribute to inference and reasoning like relations and axioms or rules do. This is a valid argument only if a) your model is to be used primarily for automated reasoning, and b) you are highly confident that any humans who will interact with it (for consumption but also for maintenance) will be able to understand it without much effort.

Good and Bad Definitions

Equally if not more problematic than no definitions are bad definitions, i.e., definitions that, just like with names, are inaccurate, ambiguous, or (unnecessarily) vague. For example, consider the concept `Fishing Industry` from the International Press Telecommunications Council (IPTC) Subject Code Taxonomy (*https://oreil.ly/nlxSO*) that is defined as "raising or gathering of fish" [140]. This is a partially accurate definition because it covers only the *fishing* part of the concept's name and leaves the *industry* one out.

Similarly, the concept `statistic` [141] in the same taxonomy is defined as "numerical facts about the weather such as temperature, barometric pressure, river levels, humidity, high and low tides and the like." This is also an inaccurate definition because the concept's name does not imply weather specificity. Table 6-2 shows additional examples of good and bad definitions from the IPTC taxonomy.

Table 6-2. Good and bad IPTC term definitions

Good definitions	Bad definitions
Dance: The expression of emotion or message through movement	*Cinema*: Cinema as art and entertainment
Newspapers: Daily or weekly publications that present the day to day history of the world, as well as features, comics, etc.	*Forecast*: Prediction of the course of the weather in the future either near term or long term
Homicide: Killing of one person by another	*Alternative energy*: Alternative energy business
Pollution: Emissions of unwanted materials in areas where it can be harmful	*Jewelry*: Accessories to clothing.
Farms: Agricultural areas for the production of foodstuffs, including dairy products, fruits, and livestock, such as cattle and fish	*Traffic*: Traffic reports and/or warnings

A common problem with definitions is circularity, namely defining a term solely using etymologically or morphologically related terms. For example, again in IPTC, `Poetry` [142] is defined as "the art, structure, forms of poetic expression," shifting the focus from the noun *poetry* to the adjective *poetic*. While it is possible to define concepts this way, definitions should ideally stand on their own. Thus, a much better definition would be that of DBpedia, according to which "Poetry is a form of literature that uses aesthetic and rhythmic qualities of language—such as phonaesthetics, sound symbolism, and metre—to evoke meanings in addition to, or in place of, the prosaic ostensible meaning" [143].

To check for circularity, you need to check the primary words in the definition to see whether any of them points right back at the term being defined. If two entries are defined solely or primarily as each other, then there will be no basis for a reader to understand either definition.

Defining Classes in a "Nonclass" Way

A common definition-related mistake is when we define a class in a way that does not make clear what instances it should have. For example, if we want to use in our model the entity Democracy as a class whose instances are democratic countries, then defining it as "a political system in which the supreme power lies in a body of citizens who can elect people to represent them" [144] hides the important information that the instances should be countries. A more accurate definition would thus be "a country governed by a political system in which...."

How to Get Definitions

There are four ways to produce definitions for your semantic model. The first is to hire a team of experts to provide them for you. This, for example, is what the European Commission did when building ESCO, both for occupations and skill concepts. This is obviously quite an expensive and nonscalable approach that makes sense to adopt either when you operate in a very specialized domain for which it's hard to find existing definitions, or when you need your definitions to be endorsed by "experts."

The second way is to get the definitions you need *as is* from some already available dictionary, glossary, or other source. For example, if your domain is software, then you can find quite good definitions for many relevant technologies in Stackoverflow Tags (*https://stackoverflow.com/tags*). Or, if you care mostly about the oil and gas domain, then Schlumberger's Oilfield Glossary (*https://www.glossary.oilfield.slb.com*) can be pretty useful. You need to be aware of three things when you reuse such sources, though:

The resource's copyright
 You may not be allowed to use the resource for your own purposes.

The resource's quality and trustworthiness
 As we saw with IPTC, not all public definitions are good.

The resource's domain specificity
 Domain glossaries may be defining ambiguous or generic terms in very specific ways that you don't necessarily expect or want. For example, the term Elasticity, according to Investopedia, "refers to the degree to which individuals, consumers or producers change their demand or the amount supplied in response to price or income changes" [145], meaning that if you want a definition of the term in the physics domain, you should not use this glossary.

The third way to get definitions is to extract them from text using relevant specialized algorithms and techniques [146] [147] [148] [149]. The majority of these approaches use symbolic methods that depend on lexico-syntactic patterns or features, which are manually crafted or semiautomatically learned [150] [151] [152]. Patterns may be simple sequences of words like "refers to," "is defined as," "is a," or more complex sequences of words, parts of speech, and chunks.

These systems work best on texts with strong structuring (stylistic or otherwise), such as technical or medical texts. For instance, in most mathematical textbooks, definitions are explicitly marked in the text, and usually follow a regular form. In less-structured texts such as programming tutorials, identifying which sentences are definitions can be much more challenging, since they are typically expressed more informally.

A fourth and seemingly counterintuitive way to generate definitions for your model's elements is to synthesize them from your own or other available semantic models. For example, assume that your model contains the relations "JavaDeveloper subclassOf SoftwareDeveloper" and "Java Developer specializesIn Java Programming Language." Then, by using methods like the one described in Androutsopoulos et al. [153], you can combine and verbalize these two relations into a definition like "A Java developer is a kind of software developer who specializes in the Java programming language."

In this way you can generate extensional definitions (by listing all instances of an element you know is complete), ostensive ones (by listing a subset of the element's instances) and intensional ones (by verbalizing subsumption, synonymy, instantiation, or other relations). The main challenge in the latter two cases is to determine which instances or relations contribute more to the element's meaning. For example, saying that "A Java developer is a kind of software developer" is more useful in a definitional context than "A Java developer has an average salary of $50,000."

Ignoring Vagueness

As we saw in Chapter 3, vagueness is a phenomenon that makes it difficult to precisely determine the extensions of classes, relations, and other elements. When building semantic models, engineers and domain experts often use predicates that are vague, and this is evident from several publicly available ontologies that contain elements with vague definitions.

For example, the relation hasFilmGenre that is found in DBpedia, and which relates films with the genres they belong to, is vague. The reason is that most genres have no clear applicability criteria and, therefore, there will be films for which it is difficult to decide whether or not they belong to a given genre. Other examples of vague classes include `Famous Person` and `Big Building` in Cyc, and `Competitor`, found in the Business Role Ontology [154].

The important thing to notice in these examples is the lack of any further definitions that may clarify the intended meaning of the vague entities. For example, the definition of the concept `Famous Person` does not include the dimensions of fame according to which someone is judged as famous or not. This may lead to problematic situations.

More specifically, the presence of vague elements in a semantic model can cause disagreements among the people who develop, maintain, or use it. Such a situation arose in an actual project where my team of domain experts faced significant difficulties in defining concepts like `Critical System Process` or `Strategic Market Participant` while trying to develop an electricity market ontology. When I asked our domain experts to provide exemplary instances of critical processes, there was dispute among them about whether certain processes qualified. Not only did different domain experts have different criteria of process criticality, but neither could anyone really decide which of those criteria were sufficient for the classification. In other words, the problem was the vagueness of the predicate *critical*.

While disagreements may be overcome by enforcing consensus or some voting mechanism, they are inevitable as more users alter, extend, or use semantic models. For example, imagine that you are developing an enterprise ontology and you need to instantiate the concept `Strategic Client`. For that you ask the company's executives, who provide instances by using as criterion the amount of revenue a given client generates for the company. Then a new R&D director joins the company and, in order to craft an R&D strategy, they consult the instances of this concept in the company's knowledge management system. If their own applicability criteria for the term "Strategic" does not coincide with the ones used by the other executives, then using the returned list of strategic clients might lead to poor decisions.

Generalizing these examples, some typical use-case scenarios where vagueness may cause problems include:

Instantiating vague classes and relations
> When domain experts are asked to define instances of vague classes and relations, then disagreements may occur on whether particular entities constitute instances of them.

Using vague facts in applications
> When systems reason with vague facts, their output might not be optimal for those users who disagree with these facts. For example, if a recommendation system knows that "John likes comedy films" and that "film A is a comedy," then it can infer that "John will like film A." Yet, John may disagree that film A is indeed a comedy because this is can be a quite vague and subjective statement.

Integrating vaguely described data

When you need to merge data from several different sources, then the merging of particular vague elements can lead to data that will not be considered correct by all users (imagine, for example, two different sets of instances of the `Strategic Market Participant` class that I mentioned before).

Reusing vaguely described semantic models

When data practitioners need to decide whether a particular semantic data model is suitable for their needs, the existence of vague elements can make this decision harder, because it can be quite difficult for them to assess a priori whether the meaning of these elements is compatible with their application context.

Training a Machine Learning Model with Vague Features and Data

Imagine having to develop a film rating prediction system by training a machine learning model, and the features you want to use are vague or have vague values in the training data. For example, instead of having the exact year or decade the film was released, you only have the characterization old or new. Or, instead of knowing the exact actors that starred in the film, you only have the Boolean attribute `includesFamousActors`. In such a case, your prediction model will learn the interpretations of "new," "old," and "famous actor" that are reflected in the training data, but not necessarily in other data where you will want to apply the trained system.

Vagueness Is a Feature, Not a Bug

It can be quite tempting to think that you can avoid the negative impact of vagueness in your model by making an extra effort to define everything in a crisp way. This is indeed possible, but can you be certain that your users will do the same? Let's see three scenarios where this doesn't happen.

In the first scenario, a user wants to find a restaurant in Madrid with "moderate prices" and "exotic cuisine." For the restaurants stored in the database, we keep their cuisine (French, Chinese, Spanish, etc.) and their price range. In order for a system to answer the user's query it needs to know two things, namely what cuisine qualifies as *exotic* and what prices are considered *moderate*.

Apart from the obvious context dependency of this knowledge (e.g., for a Chinese person, Chinese cuisine is not exotic), the more general problem that the semantic modeler needs to address is where to draw the line between *cheap* and *moderate* restaurants or between *exotic* and *nonexotic* cuisines. The reason is that both the predicates *moderate* and *exotic* are vague. In fact, the predicate *moderate* has degree-vagueness along the dimension of the price, while *exotic* has combinatory vagueness (as the necessary criteria for classifying a cuisine as exotic cannot be determinately defined).

In traditional systems and models, what usually happens is that either a strict border is imposed (e.g., a price over €20 is moderate, while below it is cheap), or some borderline cases are classified as both true and false (e.g., a certain cuisine is classified as both exotic and nonexotic). With the second solution, the problem is not really solved as someone needs still to decide which restaurants are borderline cases and which are not. On the other hand, the problem with the first solution is that the system might not retrieve results that are potentially relevant for the user (e.g., it won't get any restaurants with a price of €19.90).

The second scenario involves a business manager who receives a *request for proposal* (RFP) about a potential project and wants to decide whether it's worth devoting time and work in preparing a competitive proposal. For this decision, the manager wants to evaluate the probability that the proposal will be successful, and for that they need to know a number of things about their own company, such as whether the business and technical areas required in the RFP fall within the company's core competence areas, whether the budget of the potential project is high enough, or whether the competition for the project is expected to be strong or weak.

Ideally, the manager would like these questions answered by some intelligent system that would keep in mind the company's knowledge about its expertise, its projects, its people, and its competitors. To do that, however, the system would need to have definitions about what constitutes a core competence area, a strong or weak competitor, and a high or low budget. Yet, all these predicates (core competence, strong competitor, high budget) are vague so the same problems as in the restaurant example arise.

Finally, imagine a job seeker who uses a job search engine to find vacancies that best match to his professional profile, and one of his profile characteristics is that he has two years of experience in Java development. If there is a job vacancy in the system's database that asks for a moderately experienced Java developer (without specifying an exact number of years), then the system will need to know to what degree two years of experience satisfies the requirement "moderately experienced." The latter, of course, is a vague term, so again the same problems arises. The only difference here is that vagueness is not contained within the query but in the content (job vacancy).

Detecting and Describing Vagueness

The only legitimate reason to avoid talking about vagueness in your model should be the fact that you don't have it, i.e., all the model's elements have a crisp definition that does not leave room for borderline cases. If that's not possible (or desirable), then the least you can do is to warn your model's users about the existence of vagueness. For that you need to do four things:

1. Identify which of your model's elements have a vague meaning (via its name and/or definition). This you can do manually or, if your model is too big, use an automated vagueness detection method that I describe in the following section.

2. Investigate whether these elements are indeed vague, or whether it just happened that they were defined in a vague way even though they had a completely crisp meaning (see "Giving Bad Names" on page 87).

3. Investigate and make the vague meaning of the element as specific as possible by specifying the type of vagueness, potential dimensions, and applicability contexts.

4. Make sure that everyone is aware of the specifications you added in step 3 by explicitly mentioning this in the description and documentation of the element.

A simple vagueness detector

In 2014, a colleague and I developed a method for automatically identifying vague semantic model elements by training a classifier that may distinguish between vague and nonvague term senses [155]. For example, the definition of the ontology class StrategicClient as "a client that has a high value for the company" is (and should be) characterized as vague, while the definition of AmericanCompany as "a company that has legal status in the Unites States" is not. The classifier was trained in a supervised way, using vague and nonvague sense examples, carefully constructed from WordNet.

In particular we created a dataset of two thousand adjective senses, such that one thousand of them had a vague definition and the rest a nonvague definition. A sample of these senses is shown in Table 3-1 in Chapter 3. As the task of classifying a text as vague or not can be quite subjective, we constructed this dataset by asking three human judges to annotate a subset of the dataset's definitions (one hundred), and we measured inter-annotator agreement. We found mean pairwise Joint Probability of Agreement (JPA) equal to 0.81 and Cohen's Kappa [156] equal to 0.64, both of which indicate a reasonable agreement.

Having this dataset, we used the first 80% of it (i.e., eight hundred vague and eight hundred nonvague instances) to train a binary classifier, using the bag of words assumption to represent each instance. We used the remaining 20% of the data (i.e., two hundred vague and two hundred nonvague instances) as a test set. We found accuracy to be 84%, which is considerably high.

To evaluate the effectiveness and potential of our classifier for detecting vague ontological definitions, we applied it to CiTO. In order to compare the experts' vague/nonvague classification with the output of our system, we worked as follows. We selected 44 relations from CiTO (making sure to avoid duplications, for example, by avoiding having both a relation and its inverse) and we had three human judges manually classify again them as vague or not. In the end we got 27 vague relations and 17 nonvague, a sample of which is shown in Table 3-2 in Chapter 3.

Then we applied the trained vagueness classifier of the previous section on the textual definitions of the relations. The results of this were highly encouraging: 36 out of 44 relations were correctly classified as vague/nonvague (82%), with 74% accuracy for vague relations and 94% for nonvague ones.

Investigating the Relation Between Vagueness and Subjectiveness

While vagueness is related to subjectiveness and sentiment polarity (as polarized words are often vague, and vague words are typically subjective), subjective statements do not always involve vagueness and, thus, require specialized treatment.

To verify this intuition, we used the subjective sense classifier of [157] to classify our vague and nonvague terms as subjective or objective, assuming that vague senses are subjective while nonvague ones are objective. The particular classifier is part of the OpinionFinder system (*https://oreil.ly/gbvRK*) and the results of its application in the 2,000 adjective senses of our dataset were as follows. From the 1,000 vague senses, only 167 were classified as subjective while 993 were from the 1,000 nonvague ones. Similar results we found when we applied OpinionFinder on the CiTO relations: 18 out of 44 overall correctly classified relations (40%), with 94% accuracy for nonvague relations but only 7% for vague ones.

Of course, these numbers do not reflect the quality of OpinionFinder as a subjectivity detection system, but they illustrate the fact that treating vagueness in the same way as subjectiveness is not really effective.

Describing vagueness

The first thing a description of vagueness should explicitly state is whether the entity is actually vague or not. This is important, because it can often be the case that a seemingly vague element can have a nonvague definition (e.g., TallPerson when defined as "a person whose height is at least 180cm"). Then this element is not vague in the given ontology and that is something that needs to be explicitly stated.

The second important vagueness characteristic to be explicitly represented is its type. As we saw in Chapter 3, vagueness can be described according to at least two complementary types: quantitative (or degree) vagueness and qualitative (or combinatory) vagueness. Based on this typology, it's very useful that for a given vague element we explicitly document the following:

The type of the element's vagueness
    Knowing whether an element has quantitative or qualitative vagueness is important because elements with an intended (but not explicitly stated) quantitative

vagueness can be considered by others as having qualitative vagueness, and vice versa. Assume, for example, that a company's CEO does not make explicit that for a client to be classified as strategic, the amount of its R&D budget should be the only factor to be considered. Then, even though according to the CEO the vague class StrategicClient has quantitative vagueness in the dimension of the R&D budget amount, it will be hard for other company members to share the same view as this term has typically qualitative vagueness.

The dimensions of the element's quantitative vagueness

When the element has quantitative vagueness it is important to state explicitly its intended dimensions. For example, if a CEO does not make explicit that for a client to be classified as strategic, its R&D budget should be the only pertinent factor, it will be rare for other company members to share the same view as the vagueness of the term *strategic* is multidimensional.

Furthermore, vagueness is subjective and context-dependent. The first has to do with the same vague entity being interpreted differently by different users. For example, two company executives might have different criteria for the entity StrategicClient: one the amount of revenue this client has generated, and the other the market in which it operates. Similarly, context dependence has to do with the same vague entity being interpreted or applied differently in different contexts even by the same user; hiring a researcher in industry is different from hiring one in academia when it comes to judging their expertise and experience.

Therefore, you should also explicitly describe, if possible, the provenance of a vague element as well as the applicability context for which it is defined or in which it is used in a vague way. In particular, context-dependent can be i) the description of vagueness of an element (i.e., the same element can be vague in one context and non-vague in another) and ii) the dimensions related to a description of vagueness having quantitative type (i.e., the same element can be vague in dimension A in one context and in dimension B in another). Table 6-3 shows sample descriptions of vague relations.

Table 6-3. Sample descriptions for vague relations

Element	Vagueness nature
isNearTo	Degree-vagueness along the dimension of distance
isFunctionalPartOf	Degree-vagueness along the dimension of the part's contribution to the functionality of the whole
isCompetitorOf	Degree-vagueness along the dimension of the competitor's business areas and the dimension of the competitor's target markets
belongsToCategory	Combinatory vagueness due to the lack of sharp discrimination between those conditions that are necessary for something to belong to a given category
isExpertAt	Degree-vagueness along the dimension of the level of knowledge on a subject

Keep in mind that the goal of these descriptions is not to eliminate vagueness, nor to create models that work for all people and contexts. The goal is to make vagueness and its characteristics explicit so that it is clearer to the model's users when and how they can use the model safely, without surprises. On the other hand, there are techniques, like fuzzification and contextualization, that can help us reduce the impact of vagueness. We will see these in Chapters 12 and 13.

Case study: Detecting vagueness in business process ontologies

In business process management, the term *process knowledge* refers to the information describing the control flow of a process as well as its content, namely all artifacts that its definition may refer to. These artifacts are typically derived from and express the business environment and the organizational context of the process. Vague pieces of information and knowledge may appear in all three dimensions of process knowledge, namely structure, domain, and organizational context.

To illustrate this point, we had conducted a study in the past where we considered and analyzed two different cases of business process knowledge [158]. The first case involved a set of generic business process–related ontologies, developed in project SUPER, which were meant to serve as reusable knowledge schemas in practical semantic business process modeling scenarios [154]. The analysis of these ontologies, which included among others the Business Process Modeling Ontology (BPMO), the Business Goals Ontology (BGO), the Business Roles Ontology (BROnt), and the Business Motivation Ontology (BMO), involved the identification within them of elements that can be interpreted as vague, according to the definitions of the previous paragraph. Our criterion for classifying an element as vague or not was merely the potential existence of borderline cases, not the number of them. That meant that even if an element could potentially have only one borderline case, we considered it to be vague.

The outcome of this analysis is summarized in Table 6-4, where a sample of the elements we managed to identify as vague, along with a brief explanation of their vagueness, is presented. As you can easily see, the elements identified as vague are quite central to their respective ontologies (e.g., the hasBusinessGoal relation) and as such they are expected to be found in many relevant application scenarios. Furthermore, the use of vague terms like *desired* in the definition of elements (e.g., Desired Result) indicates that in practice there could be an almost infinite number of vague ontological elements in these ontologies that would be the result of the combination of such terms with nonvague elements (e.g., Loyal Customer, Expert Analyst, etc.).

Table 6-4. *Vague elements from business process ontologies*

Element	Ontology	Vagueness description
Managerial Role	BROnt	Combinatory vagueness due to the lack of sharp discrimination between those conditions that are necessary for someone to be considered as having a managerial role
CompetitorRole	BROnt	Degree-vagueness along the dimensions of the number of an organization's shared business areas and target markets that make it a competitor
hasBusinessDomain	BPMO	Combinatory vagueness due to the lack of sharp discrimination between those conditions that are necessary for something to belong to a given domain
Strategic Goal	BGO	Combinatory vagueness due to the lack of sharp discrimination between those conditions that are necessary for a goal to be strategic
Desired Result	BMO	Combinatory vagueness when criteria for desirability have not been set or are vague, degree-vagueness when these criteria are arithmetic

The second case involved a business process for tender call evaluation that we had to model as part of a decision support system. A tender call is an open request made by some organization for a written offer concerning the procurement of goods or services at a specified cost or rate. The evaluation of a tender call by a company refers to the process of deciding whether it should devote resources for preparing a competitive tender in order to be awarded the bid. A diagram describing this business process is depicted in Figure 6-3.

Our analysis of this process involved identifying which aspects of it (structure, domain knowledge, etc.) had vague characteristics. Our findings can be summarized as follows: First, some of the process's various decision conditions, according to which a specific action is decided, are vague. For example, in order to make the decision about pursuing the call, two criteria that need to be satisfied are i) the budget of the project to be "high" and ii) the company's experience to be "adequate." In both cases there could be borderline cases as it is indeterminate where the exact threshold is over which the budget is considered high (degree-vagueness), or exactly how many years and how many projects are required for the company to be considered experienced in a given area (degree-vagueness in two dimensions).

Second, many of the underlying organizational and domain pieces of knowledge that are needed for performing various steps of the overall process are also vague. For example, the assessment of the potential competition for the call requires knowledge about the company's competitors. Yet, the existence of other companies that are borderline competitors is possible, mainly due to the lack of clear criteria about what constitutes a competitor and what does not (combinatory vagueness). A similar argument can be made for the knowledge about the company's areas of expertise.

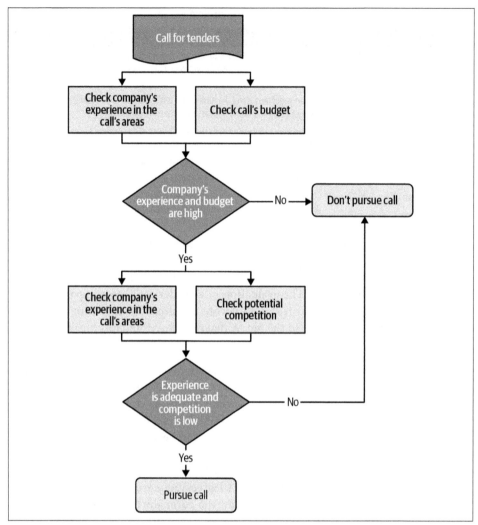

Figure 6-3. A tender call evaluation process

This second case illustrates, apart from the existence of vagueness in a common business process, the potential problems that may be caused during the latter's execution when this vagueness is not properly considered. Different people who will perform the same process will most likely produce different results, exactly because they will interpret various pieces of knowledge in a different manner (e.g., what budget is considered "high" or which companies are competitors). And it should be noted that this is not merely a problem of inadequate measurement or lack of concrete business rules, but an inherent problem caused by the vagueness of human thinking. For example, even if there is a business rule suggesting that competitors are those who have clients in the same industries and services in the same areas, the question remains: what is the minimum number of similar clients or services that a given company needs to have in order to be considered a competitor?

Not Documenting Biases and Assumptions

A couple of years ago, I was examining a client's taxonomy and I noticed that the term `tester` was a label of the entity `Software Tester` but not of other similar entities like `Car Tester` or `Drug Tester`. When I asked the taxonomy creators about this, they told me that because the application that used the taxonomy could not handle ambiguity, they had decided to assign each term to a single entity. And because they had measured in their data that the term `tester` referred to `Software Tester` 90% of the time, they had picked that to be the term's default meaning.

This annoyed me, but not because of the choice the model creators made; it annoyed me because this choice was not documented anywhere, and that made me anxious about what other similar choices, assumptions, and (perhaps) biases were incorporated into the model without all relevant stakeholders being aware of them.

Keeping Your Enemies Close

In real-world semantic modeling, we often need to make decisions and choices based on restrictions imposed by our environment and which are often beyond our control. This is reasonable and perfectly acceptable as long as a) we do it conscientiously and b) we inform all relevant parties about it. In the case of `tester`, the problem is not that the application that uses the taxonomy will interpret the term incorrectly 10% of the time, if that's an acceptable quality level. The problem will be when someone new to the modeling team who is unaware of the nonambiguity guideline will add `tester` as a lexicalization of other entities as well.

Generalizing this, here are some common pieces of information often not documented in a semantic model:

Constraints and restrictions
> For example, multiple parenthood (or, when a concept is linked to more than one broader concept) is not allowed in the taxonomy, an entity's labels should be case-sensitive and no longer than four words, etc.

Context dependence
> For example, a concept or relation is applicable only for application X, user Y, or location Z

Provenance
> For example, the model has been populated by using data source X, knowledge extraction tool Y, and Z number of domain experts

Quality

For example, the precision of the statements of relation X is 85%, or the coverage of the oil and gas domain for the French language is only 25%

Applicability

For example, model X is optimized for semantic search, but not for navigation

Design decisions and potential biases

For example, the particular model about domain X is optimized for accuracy rather than completeness, and has a bias toward entities related to the subdomain Y

Not having such information as part of your model makes it less usable, more prone to mistakes, and harder to maintain and evolve.

Summary

This chapter was all about how we humans end up creating semantic data models that few other humans understand and can correctly use. Giving wrong or misleading names to elements, omitting crucial definitions, assuming truth is binary, or not documenting biases and assumptions are all practices that you need to be aware of when using a semantic model, and that you need to avoid when building one.

Important things to remember:

- Don't overestimate human ability to understand ambiguous or inaccurate names based on context; be as specific and clear as possible when naming semantic model elements
- Don't look down on textual definitions; use them for uncommon knowledge
- Don't ignore vagueness, nor treat it as a flaw; detect it and if you cannot avoid it, document it
- Be conscientious about biases, assumptions, and design decisions in models, and inform all relevant stakeholders about them

In the next chapter we move from humans to machines and we look at how the latter end up drawing wrong inferences when human modelers fail to correctly use the semantic modeling languages and frameworks they have at their disposal.

CHAPTER 7

Bad Semantics

Words are wonderfully elastic. They can be mispronounced, misspelled, misused or mistranslated. Even the most precise technical term can be stretched into a verb or adjective, slang or idiom, stretched all the way around until it finds itself facing itself, a mirror image, the exact opposite of itself. Mark my words, it can.
—Ron Brackin

In Chapter 2, we saw how many semantic modeling languages and frameworks provide certain predefined modeling elements with a specific meaning and behavior in mind (e.g., `rdfs:subClassOf` for class subsumption or `skos:exactMatch` for entity interlinking). Nevertheless, it is not always the case that modelers follow this meaning when using the language. Defining hyponyms as synonyms, instances as classes, or nontransitive relations as transitive ones, are all examples of common semantic mistakes that lead to problematic models.

This chapter brings together the most common of these mistakes that you should anticipate when building or using a semantic model, and provides guidelines and heuristics for avoiding them.

Bad Identity

Identity in semantic modeling refers to the problem of determining whether two elements have the same meaning. Depending on the domain and kinds of elements, this can be a pretty difficult task that, if we don't carefully address it, can lead to inaccurate semantic models that might produce erroneous inferences. Let's see why this is the case and how we can avoid some common pitfalls.

Bad Synonymy

As we saw in Chapter 2, lexicalization relations relate the elements of a semantic model (entity, relation, attribute, etc.) to one or more terms that can be used to express them in natural language. As a consequence, these terms are interpreted as synonyms to each other.

Problems start when people (and therefore models) define as synonyms terms that do not really have the same meaning. As an example, consider in Table 7-1 the labels of the entities Economist and Arsenal FC as found in ESCO and Babelnet (*https://babel net.org*) (a large multilingual encyclopedic dictionary and semantic network integrating Wikipedia, WordNet, and other resources), respectively. According to these, an Interest Analyst is synonymous with a Labor Economist and Arsenal FC is the same team as Manchester United.

So, if you are a job seeker and you use an ESCO-powered semantic search engine to find vacancies for Interest Analyst, you will also get vacancies for economic scholars (and vice versa). Or, if you are a Manchester United fan and you want your Babelnet-based intelligent assistant to book tickets for you for the next match, you may well end up in London instead of Manchester. In other words, because synonymy means (almost) interchangeability of meaning, if you don't get it right then terms with different meanings may be wrongly considered as fully equivalent.

Table 7-1. Examples of synonyms found in different public semantic models

Model	Entity	Synonyms
ESCO	Economist	Economics science researcher, macro analyst, economics analyst, economics research scientist, labor economist, social economist, interest analyst, econometrician, economics researcher, econophysicist, economics scientist, economics scholar, economics research analyst
ESCO	Chief Executive Officer	Senior executive officer, chairman, CEO, managing director, president
WordNet	Chief Executive Officer	CEO, chief operating officer
Babelnet	Arsenal FC	Red Devils, Arsenal FC, Diablos Rojos, Manchester United
ESCO	Coach clients	Manage clients, prepare clients, supervise clients
KBpedia	Accountant	Professional accountant, Accountancy qualifications and regulation, Public Accounting, Bean counter

Now, automatic synonym detection is a quite challenging and still inaccurate task, so models like Babelnet that have no manual curation of their content are expected to contain bad synonyms. There are several reasons why a semantic model may end up with bad synonyms, though, even after human checking:

We need the term but we don't want to create a new entity

In an ideal semantic model all distinct meanings of a term would be modeled as different entities, each fully defined and related to other entities. Yet, for several reasons, we may not want to have too many entities in our model. One such reason is development and maintenance overhead; adding a term as a label of an existing entity is much less work than creating a new entity. In ESCO, for example, if `Interest Analyst` were to become a distinct entity, it would need its own textual definition, labels in 27 languages, and a set of related essential and optional skills. Another reason is application constraints. In a taxonomy project I worked for, I got the explicit requirement that the taxonomy should not contain more than five to six thousand entities because it would become too cumbersome for the users to navigate it in the application's user interface.

We mix synonymy with search expansion similarity

Those of you who have worked with taxonomies will be aware of *synonym rings*, namely groups of terms that are treated as equivalent for search purposes. This means that, when a user enters, for instance, the term "J2EE," this term will be sent through the synonym ring to see if there are any equivalent terms. For "J2EE" we would find "Java 2 Enterprise Edition" as a synonym. The search engine would then retrieve all documents with either "J2EE" or "Java 2 Enterprise Edition" in their metadata, and the searcher would get the complete set of relevant documents as though they had searched both terms. Now, since synonym rings are optimized for search applications, it is pretty tempting to start adding terms to them that are not synonyms but merely similar. For example, if I am a recruiter and I am looking for a candidate with knowledge of Java but I cannot find one, I would also be satisfied with someone who knows C++ because these programming languages are very similar in terms of philosophy and principles. To consider them as synonymous, however, would be totally wrong.

We are unaware of "false friends"

False friends are terms in two or more different languages that look or sound similar, but differ significantly in meaning. An example is the English *embarrassed* and the Spanish *embarazada* (which means "pregnant"), or the word *sensible*, which means "reasonable" in English, but "sensitive" in French and Spanish. Such terms can appear in (multilingual) semantic models as synonyms, usually due to human error, but also because of automatic synonym detection methods that are heavily based on string similarity metrics. Table 7-2 shows several such examples.

We forget or ignore context dependence

Some terms may indeed be synonyms in some contexts but not in others. For example, *big* and *large* can be used interchangeably when referring to sizes and numbers, but not when referring to importance. Also, in American English *vacations* are different from *holidays* in the sense that the latter refers to days celebrated by a lot of people, including national and religious holidays. In British English, though, they are often used interchangeably (e.g., "I am going on holiday next week").

We are unaware of subtle but important differences in meaning for our domain or context

For example, for most people, a violin and a fiddle are the same thing. If your model, however, is to be used by classical music players, most of them will not want to use the term *fiddle* as they associate it with folk music [159]. Similarly, for someone not familiar with the corporate world, the difference between a *Chief Executive Officer* and a *Chief Operating Officer* (which are synonyms according to WordNet) may not be immediately apparent.

Table 7-2. Examples of "false friends" between English and other languages

English term	False friend
Ambulance	*Ambulanz* (German): Emergency room
Rat	*Rat* (German): Advice/Council
Stadium	*Stadion* (German): Stage
Excited	*Excité* (French): Aroused
Pain	*Pain* (French): Bread
Library	*Librairie* (French): Book shop
Travel	*Travail* (French): Job/Work
Compromise	*Compromiso* (Spanish): Commitment/Obligation
Preoccupied	*Preocupado* (Spanish): Concerned/Worried
Lecture	*Lectura* (Spanish): Reading

To avoid having problematic synonyms in your model, there are a number of things you can do:

1. You need to communicate to anyone responsible for generating, validating, and maintaining synonyms for your model that you are not just looking for any kind of semantic similarity but for meaning equivalence in as many different contexts as possible. In other words, make sure that your people understand that the meaning similarity threshold for synonymy should be very high and, when in doubt, they should look for more evidence and corroboration.

2. Try to get your synonyms validated by more than one human judge, and use inter-agreement metrics to detect borderline cases. Remember that synonymy is a vague relation and, as such, prone to disagreements.

3. Make sure your judges understand the differences between synonymy, hyponymy, and mere relatedness, and provide them with several nonsynonym examples to use for reference.

4. Try to evaluate your synonyms as a set, not just pairwise. This will help you avoid inconsistencies and understand the context better. For example, imagine that you have three pairs of candidate synonym terms—A with B, B with C, and C with A—but these are presented to your judges in isolation. Then it is pretty possible that even the same judge decides that two of the three pairs are indeed synonyms but the third isn't. If, instead, the judge gets to review all candidates together, then it's easier to detect the outliers.

5. You should always document the criteria, assumptions, and biases for synonymy that you decide to apply to your model. For example, it may be that in your domain or application you don't care about distinguishing between different distributions of Linux (Fedora, Ubuntu, etc.) and you decide to represent all of them as lexicalizations of the entity rather than as distinct entities. That's fine, as long as all people involved (modelers and users) are aware of this. And, moreover, make sure that any such guideline is applied consistently across your model.

6. If you can't be sure that your synonyms are indeed synonyms, then don't call them synonyms. In the Textkernel Knowledge Graph, we named the relation that lexicalizes entities `hasAttractor` instead of `rdfs:Label`, exactly because we knowingly don't populate it only with 100% synonyms.

Finally, as Table 7-1 illustrates, if you are reusing data in your model from one or more external semantic models, then be extra careful with the latter's assumptions about synonymy.

Bad Mapping and Interlinking

As discussed in Chapter 2, mapping relations are used to link elements that belong to different semantic models. A popular mapping relation is `owl:sameAs` (from the OWL ontology modeling language), that we use to denote that two or more entities actually refer to the same thing. This is useful (and necessary) if we want to interlink models and datasets that have been developed independently by different people, organizations, and communities, as we cannot reasonably expect that all of them have used the same names for their entities.

And indeed, `owl:sameAs` has been extensively used in the Linked Data world for interlinking purposes. For example, the entity that represents the city of Paris in English DBpedia [160] is stated as being the same with 26 other entities from other models, including LinkedGeodata [161], and the *New York Times* Linked Open Data. Nevertheless, as mentioned in Halpin et al. [162], "there is a lurking suspicion within the Linked Data community that this use of `owl:sameAs` may be somehow incorrect, in particular with regards to its interactions with inference."

More specifically, the authors in Halpin et al. [162] identify two cases of `owl:sameAs` misuse that are more or less the bad synonymy problem we analyzed in the previous section: The linked entities are very similar but not identical to each other, or refer to the same thing but only in a specific context. They also, however, identify a third case of misuse that happens when the linked entities refer to the same thing but the attributes and relations they have in one model are not necessarily acceptable by the other model. This phenomenon is known as *referential opacity*.

The problem of referential opacity is best illustrated via an email that David Baxter, a modeler at Cycorp, sent to the Public Linked Open Data mailing list in 2009, regarding the use of owl:sameAs [163]. In that email, Baxter was mentioning that he wanted to link OpenCyc concepts to WordNet synsets but the latter contained assertions that did not make sense for OpenCyc. As an example, he gave the OpenCyc concept of India that he wanted to link with the corresponding WordNet synset, yet the latter contained assertions like "...is an instance of NounSynset or "...contains WordSense 'Republic of India 1,'" which did not make sense to OpenCyc.

Interlinking Traps for OWL and SKOS Fans

If you use OWL as a modeling language, you should be aware that relating two classes via owl:sameAs is a very different thing than relating them via owl:equivalentClass. The former says that the two classes are in fact the same, while the latter is merely an assertion that the extension of the classes is equivalent. Moreover, using owl:sameAs requires treating classes as individuals, meaning that class equality can only be expressed in OWL Full, a variation of OWL with problematic reasoning performance.

Also, owl:sameAs might at first glance appear to be the same as skos:exactMatch, but it's not. When two resources are linked with owl:sameAs they are considered to be the same resource, and all statements involving these resources are merged. This is not the intended usage of skos:exactMatch as it does not require nor imply any statement merging.

To avoid your model being "contaminated" by undesired elements and inferences, there are a number of things you can do:

Think twice before you decide to link to another mode

In many cases, modelers add mappings to external models (especially public ones) just because it's considered good practice and promotes the vision of Linked Data and Semantic Web. This is noble, but it does not always support a business case. If the benefits of interlinking your model to an external model don't outweigh the potential risks and maintenance costs, then it may not be worth doing it. For example, at Textkernel we have strategically decided to map our knowledge graph to ESCO, as the latter is set to become a shared standard among public employment agencies in Europe. On the other hand, we have no interlinking with DBpedia or other community-based model. In Chapter 13 I discuss this dilemma in more detail.

Check the semantics of the external model carefully
Before we mapped our Textkernel Knowledge Graph to ESCO, we analyzed the latter in detail to ensure that its semantics were compatible with our graph. This may not always be easy (the external model may be opaque or not well documented), but it is necessary. In Chapter 8 I provide a framework for scrutinizing semantic models for reuse and interlinking purposes.

Be selective about what you import from the external model
Just because you map to an external model, it doesn't mean that you are obliged to accept all its statements as true or valid for your model. For example, as we saw in the previous section, ESCO's labels for profession concepts are not really synonyms for each other. Therefore, in the Textkernel Knowledge Graph we do map our profession concepts to the ones of ESCO but we don't automatically import their labels.

Avoid the `skos:closeMatch` *temptation*
Since `owl:sameAs` or `skos:exactMatch` have quite strict semantics, it can be tempting to try to relax them by using vague variations like `skos:closeMatch`. What will most likely happen, though, is that this vagueness will cause even more misuses, disagreements, and wrong inferences. So, unless you are certain you can handle vagueness in an effective and efficient way, you should refrain from introducing it.

Bad Subclasses

In Chapter 2 we saw that an important element in semantic models is the class subsumption relation, which has the logical implication that if a class A is a subclass of class B, then all entities that instantiate A are also instances of B. Unfortunately, pretty often, this relation is used incorrectly, leading to problematic reasoning behavior. Let's see the different ways this misuse might happen and how to avoid it.

Instantiation as Subclassing

A pretty common problem we find in class hierarchies is having entities linked to their respective entity types via the subclass relation instead of the instantiation one.

For example, in KBpedia, we find the city of Calgary in Canada being a subclass of `City` and the temple of Parthenon of Athens in Greece being a subclass of `Landmark` [164]. This is profoundly wrong as both Calgary and Parthenon cannot be classes since they represent individual entities.

In SNOMED (*https://oreil.ly/t3R7c*), we find that several occupations like `Factory Worker` or `Secretary` are represented as subclasses of the class `Occupation`. This means that, if we apply a reasoner, we can infer that all instances of these occupations, which are individual persons, are also occupations.

Now, there are quite a few reasons why we make this mistake:

The ambiguity of the "is a" expression
Both the instantiation and the subclass relations can be expressed via the "is a" pattern (e.g., "John is a Football Player" and "A Football Player is an Athlete"), and that can be confusing for both relation extraction systems and human modelers.

Second-order classes not allowed
A second-order class is a class whose instances are other classes (e.g., `Human` is an instance of `Species`). In some modeling languages, like OWL-DL, defining such classes is not allowed due to reasoning complexity. This often makes modelers think that the only way to include both first- and second-order classes is to make one a subclass of the other.

Defining two senses in one entity
The term *democracy* may refer to "a system of government by the whole population or all the eligible members of a state" or to "a state governed under a system of democracy." These two senses, though similar, are not exactly the same; the first primarily describes a governance system (or variations of it) while the second primarily describes states.

Assuming subclass hierarchies are the same as narrower/broader hierarchies
As we saw in Chapter 2, instantiation and meaning inclusion relations are both hierarchical relations, without the explicit need to distinguish between them in a taxonomy, and without any kind of formal reasoning accompanying them. A subclass hierarchy, on the other hand, has more formal semantics and logical implications that we might not immediately realize when we are used to working with taxonomies.

Misleading modeling guidelines
In many papers, tutorials, and books we find semantic modeling guidelines that are not 100% correct. For example, in Description Logics and OWL, the term *concept* is used interchangeably with the term *class*, giving the illusion that a concept should always be modeled as a class and never as an instance. Similarly, in one of the most popular and cited ontology development tutorials, we are told that "individual instances are the most specific concepts represented in a knowledge base" and that "if concepts form a natural hierarchy, then we should represent them as classes." Both these statements are wrong [165].

The simplest way to detect instantiation relations disguised as subclassing ones, is to check whether the instances of your subclasses are also instances of their superclasses. If you cannot find any instances for your subclass, then most likely you shouldn't have modeled it as a class in the first place (like "Parthenon" in the KBpedia example). If, on the other hand, you can find instances of the subclass but these are not also instances of its superclass, then the relation is not a subclass one.

Another technique is to try to express the subclass relation with the "is a kind of" pattern instead of "is a" and see if it makes sense. If it doesn't, then most likely the relation is an instantiation. For example, you cannot say that "a Human is a kind of Species," nor that "Parthenon is a kind of Monument."

You can also use the notion of identity that we first saw in Chapter 3 as part of the OntoClean methodology, and check if the two classes share identity criteria. Remember that identity refers to the problem of determining whether or not two entities are the same, so if two classes provide different identity criteria for their instances then one cannot subsume the other. For example, Occupation has different identity criteria than Person as two persons are different even if they have the same occupation.

Finally, you can apply the guidelines of Chapter 6 to naming and defining your classes in a more accurate and clear way so as to prevent misunderstandings. For example, if you want a class for countries that have democracy as their governance system, then it's more effective (and accurate) to name it DemocraticCountry rather than Democracy. The reason is that the latter can be also interpreted as a Governance System, leading to the second-order class trap I described earlier.

Parts as Subclasses

Another pretty common misuse of the subclass relation is to use it to represent part-whole relations. That is, instead of saying, for example, that an Engine is part of a Car, we say that it is a subclass of it. This is obviously wrong, but we do it for a couple of reasons:

- A subclass is analogous to subset, and a subset of a set is a part of it. We can overcome this confusion if we realize the difference between the parts of a set and the parts of the set's members.

- Part-whole relations typically form hierarchies and, as in the case of instantiation, when we implement them in languages like OWL we get the illusion that we can only model them by means of classes and subclasses.

So, how can we effectively model part-whole relations in a class-based modeling language? Well, it depends on whether we really need to represent our parts as classes, or whether we can model them as individuals. If it's the latter then we can simply define a part-of relation and use it to directly link these individuals. If, on the other hand, we want to link classes we need to use some more complex representation patterns as the ones proposed by W3C [166] or others [167] [168]. The reason for this complexity is that saying, for example, that "An Engine is part of a Car" is equivalent to saying that "All instances of a Car (need to) have an instance of Engine as a part," and this statement cannot be simply expressed via a binary relation.

Rigid Classes as Subclasses of Nonrigid Classes

In Chapter 6 I demonstrated the problem of bad naming of semantic modeling elements via an example where the class Customer has as subclasses the classes Person and Organization (see the left model in Figure 6-1). Apart from bad naming, though, this example also demonstrates a semantic error: representing classes that are rigid as subclasses of classes that are nonrigid.

In particular, the class Customer is nonrigid because an entity can stop being an instance of it without ceasing to exist (see "Rigidity, Identity, Unity, and Dependence" on page 41). On the other hand, Person entities are essentially instances of this class, and the same applies for Organization. Thus, having Customer as a superclass of Person would imply that any instance of the latter is essentially an instance of the former—something that is obviously wrong.

The same argument can be made for the classes Bacterium and InfectiveAgent. The latter is nonrigid because an *agent* here refers to entities that play a causal part in some event and, as such, can stop playing this part without ceasing to exist. So, being a superclass of Bacterium implies that all bacteria are essentially infective agents, which is not correct because this happens only under certain circumstances. In short, a rigid class cannot be a subclass of a nonrigid class because it would have to inherit its nonrigidity. Table 7-3 juxtaposes rigid and nonrigid classes.

Table 7-3. Rigid versus nonrigid classes

Rigid	Nonrigid
Person	Teacher
Organization	Customer
Fruit	Food
Country	Contestant
Engine	CarPart

The main reason we often make this mistake is because we try to use subclassing to represent alternative possible classes that can fulfill a role (like Customer and InfectiveAgent). Yet a subclass-superclass relation is not about entities of the subclass that are *possibly* instances of the superclass, but about entities that are *definitely* instances of it.

Common Superclasses with Incompatible Identity Criteria

Let's now revisit the right model of Figure 6-1 which suggests that the class Customer should be a subclass of Person and Organization. The implication of this representation is that any instance of Customer is at the same time an instance of Person and of Organization. This is obviously wrong and the reason is that the two superclasses are disjoint, i.e., they provide incompatible identity criteria to their instances.

This means that if you have a class in your model that has more than one superclass, then you should always check if these have compatible identity. If this not the case, then one way to fix the problem is to refactor your model as depicted in Figure 6-2; i.e., split the class (in this case Customer) into as many classes as the different identities it inherits (in this case PrivateCustomer and CorporateCustomer).

Bad Axioms and Rules

In addition to identity relations and subclasses, problematic modeling is also observed in certain types of axioms and reasoning rules. Let's see some characteristic cases.

Defining Hierarchical Relations as Transitive

When we define hierarchies, we tend to consider them as transitive, i.e., if A is narrower than B and B is narrower than C, then A is also narrower than C. For example:

- A Mammal is an Animal and a Cat is a Mammal, hence a Cat is an Animal.
- Albert Einstein is a Physicist and a Physicist is a Scientist, hence Albert Einstein is a Scientist.
- Amsterdam is part of The Netherlands, and The Netherlands is part of Europe, hence Amsterdam is part of Europe.

Nevertheless, transitivity in a hierarchy should not always be taken for granted as there are several cases in which this kind of reasoning leads to nonsensical assertions:

- Albert Einstein is a Physicist and Physicist is a Profession, yet Albert Einstein is not a Profession.
- Vehicles is broader than Cars and Cars is broader than Wheels, yet Vehicles is not broader than Wheels.
- Amsterdam is part of The Netherlands and Brazil is part of the United Nations, yet Amsterdam is not part of the United Nations.

One reason these inferences don't make sense is that we are combining different types of relations that are not necessarily combinable from a reasoning perspective. The fact that A is part of B does not mean that it's necessarily part of all things that are more general than B, as the vehicle-wheels example illustrates. But even if the hierarchy consists of only one relation, transitivity is not guaranteed. For example, in the case of `Einstein` being a `Profession`, the two combined relations are both instantiation ones.

Of particular interest is the part-of relation, which we often consider to be transitive by default, yet it has a lot of problematic cases. Amsterdam being part of the United Nations is one of those, but also consider the following examples:

- The heart is part of the musician and the musician is part of the orchestra. Is the heart part of the orchestra?
- Hydrogen is part of water, and water is part of the cooling system. Is hydrogen part of the cooling system?
- The house has a door and the door has a handle. Does the house have a handle?
- The endocarp is part of the apple, and the fruit is part of the cooking recipe. Is the endocarp part of the cooking recipe?

Again, one reason these inferences don't make sense is that they are the result of mixing together different types of part-whole relations that we saw in Chapter 2, namely Component-Integral, Member-Collection, Portion-Mass, Stuff-Object, Feature-Activity, and Place-Area. For example, the invalidity of the musician's heart example is due to the fact that it combines a Component-Integral relation with a Member-Collection one. Another reason is that some of these types, even in isolation, are not always transitive. Member-Collection, for example, is never transitive, while the example of the house and the handle illustrates that Component-Integral can sometimes be nontransitive.

SKOS and Transitivity

The SKOS modeling framework very nicely anticipates the transitivity problems that we saw in this section, and does not define `skos:broader` and `skos:narrower` as default transitive relations. Instead, it supports transitivity reasoning via two other relations called `skos:broaderTransitive` and `skos:narrowerTransitive`. However, these relations are defined as transitive super-relations of `skos:broader` and `skos:narrower`, and that may actually lead to problematic inferences.

For example, if we state that "Amsterdam `skos:broader` TheNetherlands" and "TheNetherlands `skos:broader` UnitedNations," a reasoner will infer that "Amsterdam `skos:broaderTransitive` TheNetherlands" and "TheNetherlands `skos:broader` UnitedNations," since any two entities related via a relation A are also related via its super-relation B. The transitivity of `skos:broaderTransitive`, however, will lead the reasoner to also infer that "Amsterdam `skos:broaderTransitive` UnitedNations."

This essentially means that you shouldn't assume that `skos:broaderTransitive` assertions will be always transitive, just because the relation's name suggests so. Instead use this relation in your applications only when you are sure that your broader/narrower relations are indeed transitive!

Defining Vague Relations as Transitive

Transitivity is not only problematic with hierarchical relations but also with vague ones. Take for example the relation `isNearTo`; Italy can be considered near to Greece and Greece near to Turkey, yet Italy might not be considered near to Turkey. Or, a client A of a company can be similar to a client B because they generate the same revenue, and client B can be similar to a client C because they are in the same industry, yet client A will differ from C in both revenue and industry, so they may not be considered so similar.

In other words, vagueness destroys transitivity, and that's because the dimensions and applicability criteria of a vague relation are unclear and, thus, potentially different between different pairs of related entities. It is exactly for this reason that SKOS explicitly warns its users that `skos:related` is not a transitive relation and that doing so "may have unwanted consequences" [169].

Complementary Vague Classes

In OWL we are able to define a class as the complement of another class via the `owl:complementOf` relation. For example, we can define the class `ChildlessPerson` as the set of entities that are instances of `Person` and instances of the complement of `Parent`. In other words, the complement of a class corresponds to logical negation as it consists of exactly those entities that are not members of the class itself. When, however, a class is vague, its logical negation is not necessarily equal to its complement.

As an example, consider the class `HappyPerson`. One way to express the negated version of it would be to define the class `UnhappyPerson` as a complement of it. Another way, seemingly equivalent, would be to name the complementary class `NotHappyPerson`. Based on this, two questions arise:

- Are the instance sets of `HappyPerson` and `NotHappyPerson` really mutually exclusive?

- Are the instance sets of `NotHappyPerson` and `UnhappyPerson` really the same?

The answer to both questions is "not necessarily." Regarding the first question, the vagueness of the predicate *happy* means that there are borderline situations where it's not clear whether a person is happy or not. So, inferring that someone is not happy just because they are not explicitly stated as happy is not always correct.

Regarding the second question, in a recent study described in [170], the authors observed two interesting behaviors of vague gradable predicates. First, that morphological antonyms (like "unhappy") do not behave the same as genuine antonyms (like "sad") or as explicit negations (like "not happy"), especially when these are uttered by the same speaker in close proximity. Similarly, the negation of morphological antonyms (like "not unhappy") is not always equivalent to the original predicate (like "happy"). In other words, the way you decide to name your complementary classes can make a big difference when vagueness is involved (see Chapter 6).

Mistaking Inference Rules for Constraints

When we build semantic models in RDF(S) or OWL, we can define for a given relation its domain and range, namely the classes that the potential subjects and objects of this relation may belong to. Thus, for example, for the relation wasBornIn, we can define Person as its domain and Location as its range. If you are familiar with E-R modeling, then you will definitely recognize this pattern. However, there is a big difference: in RDF(S), domain and range axioms do not behave as constraints but as inference rules.

More specifically, if a relation R has as domain the class C1 and as range the class C2, then if you relate via R two entities that are not instances of either C1 or C2, your reasoner will not complain. Instead it will infer that the subject entity is an instance of C1 and the object entity an instance of C2. In other words, if you nonsensically state that "Amsterdam wasBornIn Ajax," then Amsterdam will be inferred as an instance of Person, and Ajax as a instance of Location.

This happens because Semantic Web languages are designed with the open-world assumption in mind, meaning that inferences and deductions can be done only based on statements that are explicitly true or false in the model (see Chapter 3). This assumption can generally have unexpected and potentially harmful effects in your models and the applications they are applied to, so you should always read the "fine print" of your chosen modeling language very carefully.

SHACL to the Rescue?

Exactly because Semantic Web languages are designed for open-world inference rather than data validation, W3C introduced the Shapes Constraint Language (SHACL) in 2017 [171]. SHACL enables the definition of constraints that can be validated against RDF models (e.g., constraining the number of values an attribute may have), as well as of inference rules that OWL doesn't support.

Summary

In this chapter we covered several situations where as modelers we fail to understand and correctly use the elements that our semantic modeling language or framework provides, the result being inaccurate models. We saw some typical reasons for these failures, and practices you can follow in order to anticipate and prevent them.

Important things to remember:

- Always make sure you understand the characteristics and peculiarities of your modeling framework, and how each of its available elements is meant to be used and behave

- Semantic inference is not the same as logical inference; if the input to a logical rule is wrong, it's output will also be wrong

- Be careful with synonyms and equivalence relations; they are not as straightforward as they might seem

- Don't abuse subclassing; you don't have to model all your concepts as classes, nor all hierarchical relations as subclasses

- Hierarchies are not always transitive

- Beware of inferences disguised as constraints

The next chapter continues with pitfalls that lead to models with wrong structure and content—not because we don't use the modeling framework correctly, but because we fail to get the right requirements or implement the appropriate knowledge acquisition mechanisms.

CHAPTER 8

Bad Model Specification and Knowledge Acquisition

> *"Mulla, you lost your ring in the room, why are you looking for it in the yard?"*
> *Mulla stroked his beard and said: "The room is too dark and I can't see very well. I came out to the courtyard to look for my ring because there is much more light out here."*
>
> —Classic Tales of Mulla Nasreddin

As we saw in Chapter 5, before we start building a semantic model we need to decide what exactly we want to develop by specifying the model's requirements. Moreover, while we are building the model, we need to design, implement, and apply appropriate knowledge acquisition mechanisms that will provide us with all the entities, relations, and other model elements that will satisfy these requirements.

Unfortunately, very often, we perform both these activities in a suboptimal way that results in expensive models that provide little value to their users. This chapter illustrates several problematic practices with respect to these activities, and provides useful insights on how to improve them. Many of these practices and insights (e.g., data specification and selection) are applicable to any kind of data science project, not merely semantic model development.

Building the Wrong Thing

When I joined Textkernel in early 2016, I was all too eager to start building the knowledge graph I had been hired for. Within my first month at the company I had already gathered the main requirements for the graph and specified the elements it should contain. Then I spent another six months giving substance to the graph by mining and incorporating these elements in a semiautomatic way from a variety of sources. The result of that work was a rich knowledge graph with thousands of entities and with an acceptable accuracy.

My next task was to have this graph integrated into Textkernel's CV and vacancy parsing and search products, and actually help them improve their performance. Suffice to say that both the integration and the performance improvement proved to be extremely difficult and took much more time than initially estimated. Why? Because I had failed to specify the graph correctly and ended up building something that nobody could use. If that has happened to you too, keep reading.

Why We Get Bad Specifications

The main mistakes I made during that first period of my work at Textkernel can be summarized as follows:

I specified features for my model that did not cover the requirements exactly
> For example, I implemented in my model a very strict synonymy relation between terms while the semantic search system that would use the model actually required a looser interpretation of synonymy that would optimize the system's recall rather than its precision.

I did not specify features that were crucial for the usage of the model
> For example, I implemented in my model a hierarchy of profession entities (using the hierarchical relation narrowerThan) with a depth that was far greater than what the CV parsing system that would use the model could handle.

I specified features that were actually harmful to the model's usage
> For example, I added way more lexicalization to the model's entities than the parsing system could effectively disambiguate, reducing the latter's precision more than increasing its recall.

I specified features that nobody (yet) needed or was able to use
> For example, I added and populated a relation to the model representing the typical skills a particular profession requires in the job market, yet none of our products at that moment could actually make productive use of this relation.

In retrospect, I can think of several reasons why these things happened.

For starters, I did not push for clarity and specificity during the requirements gathering stage, especially with respect to semantic elements and phenomena. People would tell me that their application needed synonyms, but what they really meant and wanted were semantically related terms for search expansion purposes. People would tell me that they wanted the knowledge graph's entities to be hierarchically related, but they would forget to mention that this hierarchy needed to have a maximum depth. And people would say that they would like to have a particular element in the graph without knowing exactly how they would use it.

This is not a blame game but a reality; all of us operate in our daily work with implicit assumptions, biases, and interpretations of things, so it's only natural to get such misalignments (see Table 8-1 for additional examples). In the early chapters of this book we saw how ambiguous, versatile, and vague the terminology we all use in the field of data modeling can be. At the same time, we need to learn to anticipate these misalignments and work toward fixing them.

Table 8-1. Expressed versus desired features for a semantic data model

What people say	What they most likely mean
We want the model to contain entities from the legal domain.	We want the model to contain entities from the legal domain, but only for the US legal system.
We want the model to be lexicalized in Spanish.	We want the model to be lexicalized in all the languages spoken in Spain.
We want the model to relate films with their actors.	We want the model to relate films with their star actors.
We want the model to be used for inference.	We want the model to be used for inductive inference.
We want to be able to use the model for semantic search.	We want to be able to use the model in the particular search system we have just bought.
Our biggest problem is the ambiguity of our business terms.	Our biggest problem is the vagueness of our business terms.

A second source of problems was that I did not specify the knowledge graph in tandem with its intended applications; instead, I focused solely on the domains and data the graph had to cover, leaving the application aspects as an afterthought. By doing that I missed crucial requirements and constraints that eventually canceled key design decisions I had initially made.

A third sin was that I didn't anticipate conflicting requirements. People and teams would give me biased and single-sided requirements, often not realizing conflicts and trade-offs with other applications. And as I was not considering all applications at the same time, I would often specify and implement a feature in the knowledge graph that made sense for one application but later proved problematic for another. The fault, of course, was all mine as I failed to recognize and involve all relevant stakeholders in the specification process from the very beginning.

Equally problematic was the fact that I pretty much ignored legacy and history. Upon my arrival at the company, I inspected the current semantic models that were in use and found that they suffered from certain design flaws. But instead of trying to understand how these flaws came to be, I just dismissed these models and went on to define new ones from scratch. Nevertheless, as I later discovered, many of these flaws were actually deliberate design decisions that had been taken in light of certain application constraints that were, unfortunately, still applicable.

Finally, a major reason for bad specifications was my misunderstanding of the pain points that the knowledge graph was meant to treat. Biased from semantic modeling projects I had worked in the recent past, I (incorrectly) assumed that the problems and challenges I had faced there were equally applicable and important in my new project. This assumption resulted in specified features of the knowledge graph that were either redundant or badly prioritized.

How to Get the Right Specifications

Getting the right specifications for your semantic model is almost never an easy and smooth process; it requires patience, humbleness, inquisitiveness, and proactiveness. Moreover, it's a process that will inevitably be iterative as you will rarely get all requirements from the beginning.

In any case, it's best to work in three phases: first understand in detail the model's context and environment, then specify its required features and characteristics and, finally, assess the importance and feasibility of each requirement.

Investigating the model's context

Before you even start writing down and documenting the required features and characteristics, you need first to understand the environment where the model will be developed and applied. To do that, you need to ask the following questions:

- What systems or applications, if any, are expected to use the semantic data model, and who develops and maintains them?
- What semantic models, if any, do these systems currently use and who develops and maintains them?
- What are the pain points of each system with respect to data and its semantics?
- Have these pain points been addressed in the past and, if so, how and with what results?

The first question is about identifying your model's most important stakeholders, namely the applications that will use it. In most cases, your model's success will be directly tied to the success of these applications, so it's vital that you understand in adequate detail how they work and what they need. Thus, the people who develop and maintain them are your best source for your model's requirements.

Ideally you would like your model to have to support a single application so that you don't have too many conflicting requirements. If this is not the case, and you have more than one application, you might be tempted to just focus on one and leave the others for later (especially if you don't have relative experience in them). Well, don't; even if you are able to prioritize the different applications and start with only one of them, you should put in your radar anything that may sooner or later affect your model so as to avoid future surprises.

Moreover, knowing beforehand all the applications your model will be used in, will help you to better structure the specification process. For example, whenever I build a semantic model for entity recognition and disambiguation in texts, I already know a set of general characteristics it needs to have, but also how some of these characteristics are in conflict with other applications like, for example, navigation or semantic search. Thus, the specification discussions focus around these characteristics and how feasible they are.

The second question is about understanding the status quo with respect to what semantic data models are in use and in what ways, before trying to replace or improve them. Completely discarding these models is rarely a good idea; instead, you want to understand from their creators, maintainers, and users their development history, their design principles, decisions, and compromises, and their strengths and weaknesses. These will give you valuable insights on how you can realistically design your model to overcome the weaknesses and maintain the strengths.

The third question is about focus. A semantic model may be able to improve an application's effectiveness in multiple ways, yet only some of them may be important or desirable. For example, as I discuss in Chapter 10, an entity recognition and disambiguation system can exploit a semantic model both for the task of detecting potential entity mentions in the text (recognition) and the task of deciding the correct entity for each mention (disambiguation). Yet, it may be that the main problem of a particular such system that your company uses suffers more from low coverage of terms and entities in a particular domain rather than from low disambiguation effectiveness. Of course, you will almost always hear different and conflicting opinions about whether and to what extent something is a pain point.

Finally, the fourth question is about knowing history so that you don't repeat it. It may be that a semantics-related pain point hasn't yet been addressed due to lack of resources, know-how, or priority. It may, however, also be that there have been attempts to address it but they failed due to technological, organizational, or other hurdles. Well, you want to know these hurdles so that you adapt your model's specification and design accordingly.

Observe and Decipher the Terminology People Use

Throughout the semantic model life cycle, but especially during the specification phase, you should pay attention to the terminology your model's stakeholders use when discussing data models and semantics. Because different people use different terms for the same things and same terms for different things (see Chapter 2), you need to ensure that you all speak the same language.

Specifying features and characteristics

After getting an accurate and complete understanding of your model's context, it's time to dive into the concrete features and characteristics it needs to have in order to alleviate the identified pain points. For that, there are many formal and semi-formal frameworks and techniques in the literature (e.g., brainstorming, document analysis, focus groups, interviews, etc.) that you can definitely use. For me, however, the starting point of any semantic model specification process should be the identification of its *core entity types*.

By "core" I mean those entity types that you would use in a one- or two-sentence description of your model. The creators of ESCO, for example, describe the model as "the European multilingual classification of Skills, Competences, Qualifications and Occupations." This is an excellent description as it not only explicitly states the main entity types that ESCO contains, but also its geographical scope.

The important thing in identifying core entity types is to do it in the right level of generality, not too high nor too low. For example, if you want to model specific types of persons, such as athletes or actors, then your core entity types should be `Athlete` and `Actor`, not `Person` (even if you eventually define a class `Person` in your model), or more specific types of athletes or actors. If you start too generic then you risk having requirements you don't need. If you start too specific then you risk having a lot of repetitive requirements.

The next step is to specify the information you want your model to have for these core entity types. This is best done by means of *competency questions*, namely questions expressed in natural language that the model should be able to provide answers to. By working together with your stakeholders to form such questions you are enabling them to tell you what elements they want/need the model to have (relations, attributes, axioms, other entity types, etc.) without them being experts in semantic modeling.

As an example, consider Table 8-2, which contains sample competency questions for pizzas and professions. If you consider the question "What is the average salary of a data scientist in the US?" you can immediately understand that your model needs to contain salary information for each individual profession, but also that this information needs to be country specific. Similarly, the question "What are the ingredients of a pizza napolitana?" indicates that your model needs to define specific pizza types (napolitana, margherita, etc.) as well as the different ingredients per type.

Table 8-2. Competency questions for pizzas and professions

Questions about pizzas	Questions about professions
Which pizzas do not contain nuts?	What is the average salary of a data scientist in the US?
How much does a pizza margherita weigh?	Which professions are specializations of an economist?
Which pizzas share three or more ingredients?	What skill set does a quantitative analyst need?
What is the third least popular pizza topping?	Which professions were in demand in Europe in the 1980s?
What are the ingredients of a pizza napolitana?	How many professions require studying for more than four years?
Which pizzas have a single meat ingredient?	Which professions have faced the biggest decline in the number of people exercising them in the last 20 years?

Premature Modeling

As you define the competency questions you will very likely start thinking about the exact elements your model needs to have in order to answer them (e.g., contemplating whether to represent the salary information of professions as an attribute or a distinct entity). This is normal and potentially useful because quite often there are elements of exploration in the initial stages that can help you identify conflicting requirements and explore alternative solutions. You should be careful, though, that you don't lose focus from your goal of gathering all possible requirements, and that you don't alienate your stakeholders by dragging them into overly technical discussions that they cannot follow or just don't care about.

Keep in mind that, since the competency questions will be expressed in natural language and by humans, their initial form will inevitably be incomplete, vague, or ambiguous. It's your job to make them as clear as possible, generalize them where appropriate, and fill in the missing pieces.

For example, when I see the question "Which professions were most in demand in Europe in the 1980s?" I can immediately think of three things to ask the person who wrote it:

1. What is their exact definition of the vague predicate *in demand*, and how would they decide whether it's true or false for a given profession?

2. By *Europe* do they mean the continent, or maybe just the European Union?

3. At what geographical granularity would they like this competency question answered: continents (as the use of *Europe* in the question implies), countries, states, or other?

In practice, your probing questions should aim to discover constraints, limitations, and special requirements about the model that its stakeholders may otherwise not tell you, either because they never thought of them as relevant, or because they have been taking them for granted. Especially when your model is to be used by specific applications and systems, learning the details of how this usage is going to happen will help you discover many hidden requirements.

Assessing feasibility and importance

From all the requirements you will get for your semantic model, not all will be equally feasible or important. For example, you may be asked to lexicalize your model's entities in a language for which acquisition sources (data and people) are not available or are too expensive. Similarly, you may be asked that your entities be lexicalized in five languages, yet only two of them will be really important and of high priority. What you want is to assess feasibility, inform the stakeholders about it, and let them decide the importance.

In general, there are two main sets of factors that affect the feasibility of a semantic model's requirements:

The features and constraints of the modeling language and framework you have at your disposal
> These factors typically affect requirements related to the structure and reasoning behavior of the model. Some of these will be directly supported by the framework, some will require minor adjustments, and some will require a complete customization. For example, in 2007 I worked on a project involving the development of a semantic search system for Greek history documents. There I got the requirement to include in the system's underlying semantic model several different entity relations like, for example, which people participated in which events. Yet the modeling framework I had to use could only support one "is related to" relation.

The availability, quality, and cost of knowledge acquisition resources and tools/processes
> These factors typically affect requirements related to the content and expressiveness of the model. For some of the content, you will have at your disposal ample resources and highly effective methods and processes, but for others you will not. For example, in the Greek history project I just mentioned, I did not have an entity recognition system available that I could apply to the Greek history texts and automatically mine them for mentions of relevant persons, locations, and events. Instead, I had to rely on a small team of history graduates who defined these events and persons in a manual fashion. That, of course, affected the size and coverage of the model.

Beware of the Hype

Many semantic and data technology vendors (and sometimes academics) will tell you that it's pretty easy to build a semantic model using their methods and tools. This is true but in a misleading way; you can indeed build "a" model relatively easily but that won't necessarily be the one you want.

Compared to feasibility, the importance of a model's requirements is less dependent on the available resources and technology and more on strategic and business factors; some domains, markets, or applications will inevitably be more important than others. Therefore, this is information that only your stakeholders can give you, and you really need to push for it if you want to build something useful and impactful.

Of course, you should anticipate contradictory opinions on what is important and how much (besides, *important* is a vague predicate). As I am writing these lines, we still have debates at Textkernel as to whether including soft skills in the knowledge graph is of any use.

Requirements' Importance Drives Quality Strategy

Knowing the relative importance of your model's requirements will also help you determine the quality strategy you will need to follow. Optimizing the quality of a low-importance requirement at the expense of other more important ones is a sure way to failure.

In any case, the combination of feasibility and importance will help set priorities because not having clear prioritization usually leads to a waste of time and resources. One thing to be aware of, though, is what I call the tyranny of "low hanging fruits." In theory, the feasibility of requirements is independent of their importance as the latter typically depends on business strategy and priorities. In practice, though, easy requirements often get highest priority and difficult ones get pushed back. This is OK as long as the continuously postponed requirements do not cause significant technical debt to the model. For example, I don't really care if I never get to expand my model in a challenging but unimportant domain for which I would have limited resources anyway. I do care if I have a model that is currently maintained in a way that causes quality problems, though, and instead of taking the time to improve its maintenance process, I merely keep adding content to it.

Bad Knowledge Acquisition

Even when the requirements of a semantic model are properly specified, its development may still suffer from not using (or developing) the right knowledge acquisition mechanisms. For example, we may have made clear in the model's specification that we want to have in it a synonymy relation between terms, yet we end up getting terms that are merely related to each other. Or, we may want to get textual definitions for our model's entities, yet we cannot find any in the data we have chosen to extract them from. This happens when we use the wrong knowledge sources and acquisition methods.

Wrong Knowledge Sources

When developing a semantic model, we mainly use two types of element sources: data and people. Data can be used in four ways:

As sources of semantic model elements that we can add to the model as-is
This is the case for existing databases, ontologies, taxonomies, and other semantic data models from which we can reuse some or all of their entities, relations, or other elements, with very little additional processing.

As sources of data from which we can extract semantic model elements
This is the case for text corpora, conversational logs, wikis, and any other data from which we can derive elements for our model by applying some semantic model mining method.

As training examples for (semi-)supervised semantics model mining methods
This is the case for data that has been annotated with the semantic elements it contains and, as such, can be used to train supervised or semi-supervised methods for semantic model mining.

As sources of elements for distantly supervised model mining methods
This is the case for existing semantic data models that can be used for distant supervision; i.e., for automatically generating training data for supervised model mining methods.

People, on the other hand, are mainly used as:

Providers, curators, and maintainers of semantic model elements
This is the case when we ask people, directly or indirectly, to provide us with terms, entities, relations, and other elements that we can incorporate into the model with little processing. This includes asking them to validate the output of automatic semantic model mining methods. They may not be semantic modelers per se, but their input is vital.

Annotators of training data
This is the case when we ask people to identify and annotate mentions of semantic elements within texts or other data in order to use the latter as training examples for (semi-)supervised methods.

Now, in the world of journalism there is a saying that journalists are only as good as their sources. Well, the same applies to the world of semantic modeling, namely that a model will be as good as the data and people we build it with. If these do not have the elements we need, or provide them in a misleading, confusing, and error-prone way, then both the quality of our model and the efficiency of its development will be sub-par. Let's see when and how this may happen.

When data is wrong

There are three potential problems with data as a source of semantic information. First, the information it contains may be semantically inaccurate. As we have already seen in Chapters 5 and 7, several publicly available data sources, like Wikipedia, DBpedia, SNOMED, and others, contain factual and semantic errors. By using these sources without proper care, we risk transferring the same errors into our model.

Second, the information it contains may be accurate, but not what we need or have specified. For example, we might want to mine for our model natural language defini-tions of technology concepts, but the data we have available is about CVs and job vacancies which typically don't contain such definitions. Or, we may want to find which skills are most in demand for a given profession, but the data we have available is only about CVs, which reflect the supply side of skills in the labor market, rather than the demand side. By using such inappropriate sources, we risk not only wasting time and resources trying to find something that does not exist (like definitions in CVs), but also adding inaccurate assertions to our model (for example, by populating the demand relation between professions and skills with supply instances).

Third, it may be that the information the data sources contain is accurate and in line with our specifications, but provided in a way that makes it hard to extract it in an accurate and efficient fashion. This is mainly the case for data sources with such a low degree of structure and such a high degree of ambiguity and linguistic variance and complexity that the application of mining methods proves to be quite ineffective. Again, the risk here is wasting time and resources that could be saved if we used "eas-ier" data, as well as increasing the chances that the extracted elements are inaccurate.

Now, there are several reasons why we end up using problematic data sources:

We blindly trust data that is not so trustworthy after all
> We don't take the time to do our own scrutinization of the data sources in ade-quate depth and breadth. We base our evaluation of their quality or suitability mainly on the credentials of their creators and the documentation they provide. This documentation, however, is often high-level, inaccurate, vague, and incom-plete, especially when it comes to aspects like quality, or biases and design choices. ESCO, for example, has extensive documentation about the model's structure, content, and the methodologies followed for its development and

quality control, yet any concrete figures about its accuracy and coverage are nowhere to be found.

We don't specify and describe the semantics of our model accurately enough
Even if we are willing to scrutinize a data source for accuracy and suitability, we will still do a bad job if we have an inaccurate, ambiguous, or too vague idea of what elements our model is supposed to have. If, for example, we are looking for data to instantiate the vague class `Strategic Client` and we haven't explicitly defined the vagueness dimensions and instantiation criteria that the users of the class have in their minds (see Chapter 6 for how to do that), we might select data that is incompatible with these dimensions and criteria.

We fall into the "because there is much more light out here" trap
We believe that just because we have a lot of data at our disposal that is related to our model's domain or application context, we must definitely use it even if it doesn't fit our task. This happens both when this data has been obtained in a very easy way (and therefore we should start with it), or a very difficult and expensive one (and therefore we should make the best out of it).

So, what can you do to avoid using the wrong data in your model? Well, for starters, make it a habit to pick the data to use after you have clearly specified the semantics of your target elements, not the other way around. Avoid the temptation of diving directly into the data you already have, no matter how relevant it seems to be to your model's domain. It might indeed be useful, but you won't really be in a position to know this if you don't know exactly what you are looking for.

You should also make a habit of scrutinizing the data you are thinking of using for correctness, semantic compatibility, and easiness to extract semantics from, no matter how compatible and trustworthy it seems to be. Looks can be deceiving, and the devil is usually in the details, so you need to critically read the data's documentation (when available), do your own investigation, and carefully and selectively use that which best satisfies your needs.

Look for Systematic Problems

When scrutinizing a data resource, you should be looking for systematic errors rather than isolated and anecdotal ones. For example, when I was contemplating DBpedia as a data source for a project on computer science concepts, I found that it considered the entity Machine Learning to be an instance of the class Disease [36]. Now, that could have been a single mistake, but as I continued checking additional entities, I noticed that most of them were assigned to the wrong class (see Table 8-3 for more examples). Triggered by that, I went to check the classes of DBpedia and I realized that very few of them could serve as types of abstract entities. So now I know that I cannot really use DBpedia for getting classes for my abstract entities.

Table 8-3. Wrong classes of abstract entities in DBpedia

Entity	Class
http://dbpedia.org/resource/Supervised_learning	http://dbpedia.org/ontology/Software
http://dbpedia.org/resource/Macroeconomics	http://dbpedia.org/ontology/Organisation
http://dbpedia.org/resource/Accounting	http://dbpedia.org/ontology/Company
http://dbpedia.org/resource/Drama	http://dbpedia.org/ontology/single
http://dbpedia.org/resource/First-order_logic	http://dbpedia.org/ontology/Book

When people are wrong

Just like data, people can also be an inaccurate or inappropriate source of semantic information, even if they are experts in the model's domain. As an example, consider again ESCO, a model whose content was derived solely by experts from the labor market and education and training sectors. One piece of information these experts had to provide was the knowledge, skills, and competences that are required when working in a particular occupation. We already saw some examples of such "essential" knowledge for some data-related occupations in Table 1-1. What do you think of their quality?

Personally, I find some of this information pretty inaccurate. For example, according to ESCO, an essential skill for a data scientist is the Resource Description Framework Query Language, and for a knowledge engineer Web programming. As I am writing these lines, a search in LinkedIn of the first term (and its spelling variation "RDF Query Language") returns 64 people's profiles (out of around 300,000 data scientists on the platform) and no vacancies (out of around 50,000 data scientist job vacancies). Similarly, a search for knowledge engineering jobs mentioning "web programming" as a requirement returns no results. These are pretty low numbers for essential skills.

Another case of expert inaccuracy is described in Aroyo and Welty [172], where both medical experts and nonexperts were asked to detect causality relations in sentences. Surprisingly enough, the authors found that experts were far more likely than nonexperts to see such relations where none were expressed in a sentence, most likely because they knew them to be true. For example, in the sentence "He was the first physician to identify the relationship between Hemophilia and Hemophilic arthropathy," medical experts annotated a cause relation between the two diseases, even though the sentence doesn't explicitly say that.

Now, there are three main reasons why experts (and people in general) would be a bad source of semantic information:

They don't really have the knowledge and expertise we need, but we fail to recognize it
This may happen when, like with data selection, we don't specify and describe our model accurately enough, but also when we erroneously believe that expertise is a single skill. For example, if our model is about historical events in Medieval Europe, it doesn't mean that any history expert can be equally helpful. People may be highly expert in some part of a domain and a complete novice in others.

They don't really have the knowledge and expertise we need, but they fail to recognize it
Ideally we would expect that people, and especially experts, would know the limits of their expertise, but unfortunately this is not always the case. Several psychological studies have identified overconfidence as one of the most common (and potentially severe) problems in human judgment; low-competence individuals often incorrectly rate themselves as highly knowledgeable in a subject because they are too ignorant to know otherwise (a phenomenon known as the Dunning–Kruger effect), and high-competence individuals become so entrenched in a particular way of viewing the world that they believe this view is globally applicable.

They are susceptible to cognitive and behavioral biases
One such bias is the so-called availability bias, according to which, people often put too much confidence in the result of small samples and have a tendency to estimate the frequency of an event according to the ease with which instances of the event can be recalled. The problematic occupation-skill pairs that we saw in Table 1-1 are most likely a result of this bias. Table 8-4 shows additional biases that may affect human judgments in semantic modeling.

Table 8-4. Cognitive and behavioral biases that affect human judgments in semantic modeling

Bias	Description
Groupthink	The tendency as members of a group to try to minimize conflict and reach a consensus without critically evaluating all alternative viewpoints.
Self-contradiction	The tendency to give different answers when we are asked to evaluate the same information twice. This is usually observed when the information has a high degree of vagueness and context dependence.
Desirability bias	The tendency to assign higher probabilities to desirable outcomes and lower probabilities to undesired outcomes.
Confirmation bias	The tendency to search for information, interpret it, and remember it in a way that confirms our preconceptions.
Distinction bias	The tendency to view two options as more dissimilar when evaluating them simultaneously than when evaluating them separately.
Framing effect	The tendency to draw different conclusions from the same information, depending on how that information is presented.
Pygmalion effect	The tendency to let other people's expectations influence our judgments.
Naïve realism	The tendency to believe that we see the world around us objectively, and that people who disagree with us are either uninformed, lazy, irrational, or biased.
Shared information bias	The tendency for group members to spend more time and energy discussing information that all members are already familiar with, and less discussing information that only some members are aware of.
False causality bias	The tendency to cite sequential events as evidence that the first caused the second.
Action bias	The tendency to act despite the presence of high ambiguity or vagueness, especially when time is limited.
Ambiguity bias	The tendency to favor options where the outcome is more knowable.
Anchoring bias	The tendency to be influenced by information that is already known or that is first shown.

So, how can you ensure that you have the right people for your model? Well, just like with data sources, pick them only after you have clearly specified the semantics of your target model and identified the exact expertise you need. Aim to have as many different and independent viewpoints as you can get, as a diversity of inputs nearly always results in a more robust outcome. It's not just about the biases of people you consult, it's also the about the biases you are introducing by not asking the right people in the first place.

More importantly, scrutinize your experts; i.e., don't give them a free pass based merely on their credentials or role, but run test knowledge acquisition sessions with them and watch out for systematic errors and symptoms of biases. It's highly unlikely that you will find completely unbiased people, but that is not your goal. Your goal is to make yourself aware of these biases and their intensity and adjust your knowledge acquisition methods accordingly. To see how to do this, keep reading.

Wrong Acquisition Methods and Tools

Even when the quality of the data and people we have at our disposal for our semantic model is high, the latter's development may still suffer if we apply the wrong acquisition methods and tools to them. Let's see how this may happen and how we can avoid it.

Misunderstanding model mining tools and frameworks

Some years ago I was interviewing candidates for a knowledge mining position on my team at Textkernel, and one of the pertaining questions I would ask them was how would they approach the problem of synonym extraction. To my disappointment, most people would reply with something along the lines of "Easy, just use Word2Vec."

As we saw in Chapter 5, Word2Vec is a neural network–based system that takes as input a large text corpus and maps terms in it to vectors of real numbers that can then be used to identify semantically related terms. It is a quite important and useful tool that has helped researchers and practitioners improve the effectiveness of several natural language processing and information extraction tasks. It is not an out-of-the-box solution for synonym extraction, though, and there are good reasons for that:

It does not give you only synonyms
>   Word2Vec tends to indicate similar words, but the similarity it learns includes not only pure synonymy but also antonymy, hyponymy, and other kinds of similarity (see Table 5-5 for examples). Thus, if we want only synonymy, we need a way to filter out the others.

It does not distinguish between term senses
>   Word2Vec has no standard way of distinguishing between different meanings of the same term. Even if the text corpus on which you train it contains two or more senses of the same term (e.g., "Apple" both as the fruit and the company), you will still get only one vector for this term that will probably encode multiple meanings. Thus, if our terms and corpus are ambiguous, we need to complement Word2Vec with disambiguation techniques.

Please note that my problem with the answer "Just use Word2Vec" was not that the particular tool could not completely solve the requested task. My problem was that the people who gave this answer had obviously misunderstood its capabilities. This is a general pitfall that we all often fall into and makes us use suboptimal model mining methods and tools that, in the worst case, produce inaccurate models or, in the best case, waste much of our time and resources.

Now, one reason for this misunderstanding is that we don't dedicate enough time and effort to understanding what a method or tool can do, and how well it can do it. We tend to over-rely on familiar tools that seem to have some relevance to our problem without critically scrutinizing this relevance. This is a common cognitive bias, also known as *Maslow's hammer*, which is usually phrased as follows: "If all you have is a hammer, everything looks like a nail."

There is a second reason why we misunderstand methods and tools, and that's the inaccurate and incomplete description and documentation by their creators, both in terms of capabilities and effectiveness. As an example, consider the entity recognition system described in a paper by Shalaby et al. [121], which I tried to use in 2017 at Textkernel to automatically discover skill entities for the knowledge graph I was building. The particular system took as input a single term and decided whether it denoted a Profession, a Skill, a Company, or a School. If the system did not have enough confidence that the term belonged to one of these four entity types, it returned Unknown.

According to the experiments reported by its creators, the system achieved an average precision of 94% and an average recall of 96%. These numbers were pretty impressive and indicated that the system could be used in a fully automatic way, without a need for humans to validate its output. Unfortunately, this was not the case. When I applied the system on my own set of input terms that could be either skills or something else, the precision I measured was between 60% and 75% (depending on the minimum confidence I wanted the system to have before returning an answer), and the recall between 85% and 15%.

The reason for that difference was, as I later discovered, a methodological flaw in the system's evaluation because the test dataset its creators used did not contain any terms that belonged to the Unknown category. That flaw resulted in an inaccurately reported effectiveness that I only identified through my own evaluation.

In general, judging the suitability of a semantic information extraction framework or tool for your model merely by the effectiveness scores its creators report from a couple of (usually not generic enough) experiments is not a good idea. This is not because these scores are falsified, but because they can be pretty sensitive to changes in the characteristics of the task, such as the type of target elements or input data.

For example, in a paper by Hoffart et al. [173] the effectiveness of the AIDA named entity resolution system is found to be 83% on the AIDA-YAGO2 dataset and 62% on Reuters-21578. Similarly, in Mendez et al. [174], the effectiveness of DBpedia Spotlight (another named entity resolution system) is found to be 81% when applied on a set of 155,000 wikilink samples and 56% on a set of 35 paragraphs from *New York Times* documents. In another paper [175], Spotlight achieves an F1 score of 34% on the AIDA/CO-NLL-TestB dataset (created in [173]). Finally, the AGDISTIS system [175] scores 76% on the AQUAINT (Corpus of English News Text) dataset (created in [176]), 60% on the AIDA/CO-NLL-TestB dataset, and 31% on the IITB dataset (created in [177]).

In other words, a semantics extraction tool's satisfactory performance in a given scenario does not constitute a trustworthy predictor of its performance in a different one. Or, to put it differently, it's always likely that the system will perform poorly when the scenario's characteristics change. Therefore, you should always test the tool with your own data and under your own conditions that reflect the realities of your model.

Moreover, the tool's effectiveness score should not be the only criterion you apply when deciding whether or not to use it. Instead, you should look for the framework that can provide you with comprehensive and convincing answers to the following questions:

- *What extraction tasks and semantics does the tool support exactly?* The goal of this question is to determine whether and to what extent the tool can support the exact tasks you want to perform. Generic taglines and descriptions like "knowledge extraction from textual resources" or "machine reading for the Semantic Web" are not enough, especially given the overloading of the relevant terminology. Instead, it is important that both the input/output and the extracted semantics the tool supports are clearly and completely defined.

- *Does the tool deliver the semantics it promises?* If the tool promises to give you synonyms but it gives you hyponyms, it's no good. If it promises to give you classes but it gives you individuals, it's also no good. In general, if the tool falls into semantic representation pitfalls like the ones in Chapter 7, you should be careful about it.

- *Does the tool succeed in avoiding biases?* If the tool extracts biased semantic information (maybe because it has been trained on biased data), using it will carry this bias into your semantic model. Word2Vec, for example, is often cited as an example of how gender-based stereotypes make their way from data to machine learning models [178].

- *What effectiveness range can you expect from the tool, and under what conditions?* With this question you are looking to learn something more than the precision/recall scores (or other evaluation metrics) that the tool has achieved in a couple of experiments. What you need is a clearly expressed and educated generalization of the tool's performance, including known strengths and weaknesses and conditions under which it will perform best and worst. For example, you need to be aware if the tool works very well with some types of input data (e.g., opinionated or definitional texts) but very bad with others.

- *What are the ingredients and recipe(s) you need in order to use the tool?* This question is not so much about the technical details of how to install or run the tool, nor about its licensing or pricing options. What you should be looking for are methodological guidelines and best practices on how (not) to use the tool so as to get the best possible results. This is especially important for middleware tools that are highly versatile and configurable and require specific procedures and expertise to adapt them for a given use case.

- *How can you troubleshoot/optimize the tool's performance?* This is another very important question about how you can troubleshoot and improve the tool's performance if the latter proves not to be satisfying for your case or data. Some tools may be black boxes, only specifying input and output, but others often have user-exposed parameters that can be configured to affect performance. In both cases, tool creators often don't realize that engineers who have not studied the tool's knowledge extraction topic and underlying theory will find it hard to diagnose a problematic performance and figure out how to improve it without explicit guidance.

- *How do you operationalize and maintain the tool?* With this question you seek to understand what it would take to put the particular tool in a production environment, either on its own or as part of a larger pipeline, as well as how easy its maintenance would be. For example, if the tool is provided as a service, you need to know how much you can trust it to be available and up to date. Or, if the tool uses particular data or semantic models, it's important to know how often and in what ways these should be updated so that the tool's performance does not decay.

These questions will help you decide what available knowledge extraction tools are worth considering and how to use them (e.g., by doing your own experiments, contacting the creators and setting up a pilot project, or immediately buying/licensing and using them).

Scrutinizing FRED

A couple of years ago, I spent some time evaluating FRED (*https://oreil.ly/7UcCd*), a tool that automatically generates RDF/OWL ontologies from multilingual natural language text [179]. My evaluation was qualitative rather than quantitative, and focused on detecting any systematic errors and biases of the tool. Here are some of my findings:

Different output for very similar input
> For example, when I asked the system to analyze the sentence "Alex has studied Greek history," it identified Greek History as an individual entity, but when I did the same for the sentence "Alex has studied Greek literature," it identified Greek Literature as a class.

Different modeling of verb/noun variations of the same entity
> For example, in the sentence "Maria is expert in managing projects," FRED modeled the term managing projects as an event entity, whereas in the sentence "Maria is expert in project management," it modeled the term Project Management as a class.

Modeling of the "is-a" pattern almost always as an instance-class relation
   For example, in the sentence "A web developer is a professional who builds websites," the term `Web Developer` was modeled as an individual entity that belonged to the class `Professional`. Similarly, in the sentence "A macroeconomist is an economist who looks at the big picture," `Macroeconomist` was modeled as an individual entity and instance of the class `Economist`.

Creation of artificial entities for wrongly identified classes
   For example, in the sentence "Paul is a semantic modeler who knows good machine learning," FRED suggests that there is an entity `learning_1` that is an instance of the class `Machine Learning`. There's no such instance, and `Machine Learning` is actually an individual entity, not a class.

No recognition of events that are not expressed via verbs
   For example, in the sentence "We implemented the project in four months," FRED correctly identifies the mentioned event but it fails to do so in the sentences "Implementing the project took us four months" and "The implementation of the project took us four months."

Bias toward (wrongly) modeling entities as classes rather than individual entities
   In almost all the examples I used for my evaluation, FRED tended to model entities that could not have any instances, such as `Project Management` and `Machine Learning`, as classes.

Unnecessary complexity
   For example, given the sentence "John is expert in project management," a human modeler would most likely create an entity `John` and an entity `Project Management` and would relate them through the relation `isExpertIn`. FRED, on the other hand, produced the model shown in Figure 8-1, which suggests that there is some situation involving the entity `John` who is an instance of the class `Expert`, and this situation is associated with something that is an instance of `Project Management`.

Based on these findings—which, by the way, are not mentioned anywhere in the tool's relevant papers or documentation—I decided not to use FRED in my projects.

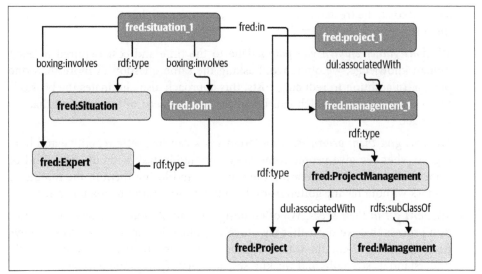

Figure 8-1. How FRED semantically models the sentence "John is expert in project management"

Failing your humans-in-the-loop

In the same way that we use the wrong tools and frameworks to extract semantic information from data, we follow bad practices when acquiring knowledge from people. Here are some of the mistakes we often make:

- *We ask people ambiguous or inaccurate questions.* For example, assume you have two entities, A and B, and you want to know if A is a subclass of B. If you ask "Is A a B?" then you will get a positive answer even if A is an instance of B. A better question would be "Is A a kind of B?" but the best question is actually "Are all A's instances also instances of B?" as it also checks whether A and B are indeed classes. In any case, be very careful with the wording of your questions.

- *We don't give them adequate guidelines and supporting information, especially in the presence of vagueness.* Assume, for example, that you ask history experts how important a particular event has been for a particular historical period, but you don't give them the importance criteria and dimensions you have in mind. They will probably spend either too much or too little time thinking of an answer which will most likely be incompatible with your criteria.

- *We push them for consensus.* Rather than accepting that disagreement is a natural property of semantic interpretation, we often consider it as an indication of poor quality, either because the task is poorly defined or because the human judges lack sufficient training or expertise. Of course, this may be case, but it can also be that the information we seek to elicit from people is ambiguous or vague and, as such, needs to be treated in a special way in our model. In other words, disagreement is not noise, but a signal.

- *We don't gather enough viewpoints.* Due to the time and cost required to elicit human knowledge, we often avoid asking the same question of more than one person. In addition to reducing costs, this approach also eliminates the possibility of disagreements, which can be an important piece of information that we never get.

- *We don't give them priorities.* Annotation work can be pretty repetitive and boring, so when we give people some large annotation task without some kind of prioritization, we risk increasing their anxiety and losing them in the middle of the task without having gotten from them the information that matters most.

- *We don't get in their shoes.* We often design an annotation or knowledge elicitation process that we don't first try ourselves, but it is important to do so. Why? Because only by doing the work our process is meant to make easy can we really understand its strengths and weaknesses, and identify ways to improve it.

A Specification and Knowledge Acquisition Story

In 2015, I worked on a project that involved developing a semantic model that could support the task of *aspect-based sentiment analysis* (ABSA). ABSA is an opinion mining process where texts are analyzed to extract the sentiments that their authors express toward certain features and characteristics of particular entities, such as products or persons. The accurate and complete identification of the aspects of the entities discussed within the text, as well as the evaluation expressions that accompany these aspects, plays a key role in the effectiveness of this process. Nevertheless, what entities may be considered as aspects and what evaluation expressions may characterize them, depends largely on the domain at hand. For that, we needed a semantic model that would provide domain-specific aspect-evaluation-polarity relations and which could be (re-)used toward more effective ABSA in concrete domains and scenarios.

Model Specification and Design

The model's specification consisted of the following competency questions:

- *Given a domain, what are the entities that may have the role of an aspect, i.e., entities for which a sentiment may be expressed?* For a given domain (e.g., films) not all entity characteristics are necessarily subject to opinions (e.g., it is rather rare for one to express a positive or negative opinion about a film's genre). For that, knowing a priori what entities are potential aspects can increase ABSA's precision as non-aspect entities would be filtered out.

- *What are the evaluation expressions that may be used to express a sentiment for a given aspect?* For example, the aspect Food for a restaurant can be characterized as `tasteless`, while the aspect `Price` can be characterized as `expensive`. Knowing what expressions go with what aspects can lead to better aspect identification by simply using these expressions as evidence of the implied aspect.

- *What is the typical polarity an evaluation expression has for a given aspect?* For example, saying that "prices are high" for a restaurant is typically negative, while saying that "standards are high" is positive. This means that i) the evaluation expression's polarity cannot be isolated from the aspect it characterizes, and ii) knowing this domain-specific polarity can help identify more accurately the aspect's sentiment within the text.

Using these questions, we went on and defined the model in Figure 8-2, using the SKOS modeling framework to represent aspect-evaluation-polarity relations.

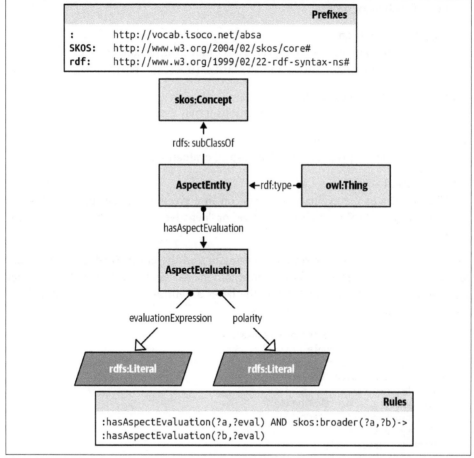

Figure 8-2. Aspect-evaluation-polarity ontology

The main elements of the model are:

Class `AspectEntity`

Consists of the characteristics for which an opinion or sentiment can be expressed in a given domain. If the domain is already represented as a semantic model, then these characteristics may be classes (e.g., `Restaurant`, `Location`, `Food`, `Author`, `Actor`, etc.), individuals (e.g., `Steak`, `Windows 8`, etc.), relations (e.g. `hasSubject`, `hasLocation`, `servesFood`, `hasOperatingSystem`, etc.), or even attributes (e.g., `price`, `capacity`, `size`, etc.). To capture this generality, we modeled the `Aspect` class as a subclass of `skos:Concept`. Another reason for this modeling choice was that aspects may form taxonomies in which a child node is a more specific aspect of its parent (e.g., `Linux` is more specific than `Operating System`). SKOS's broader and narrower relations effectively enable the representation of such taxonomies.

Class `AspectEvaluation`

Describes an evaluation that a given aspect may assume, and consists of an evaluation expression (e.g., "tasty") and a polarity score (e.g., "positive").

Relation `hasAspectEvaluation`

Links an aspect to one or more evaluations it may assume.

Attribute `hasEvaluationExpression`

The evaluation expression of a given aspect evaluation.

Attribute `hasPolarity`

The polarity of the evaluation expression in a given aspect evaluation. This can be a categorical value, such as "positive" or "negative," or a number in some sentiment scale.

As an example, consider the restaurant domain and the entity `Food`. In a restaurant review, one may characterize food, among others, as "tasty" or "decent," the former expressing a positive sentiment, while the latter a neutral one. Using the model, we can represent this information as follows:

```
@prefix : <http://vocab.isoco.net/absa/> .
@prefix ex:<http://example.org/> .
ex:DecentFood a :AspectEvaluation ;
:evaluationExpression "decent":
:polarity "neutral".
ex:TastyFood a :AspectEvaluation
:evaluationExpression "tasty":
:polarity "positive".
ex:Food a :AspectEntity ;
:hasAspectEvaluation ex:DecentFood ;
:hasAspectEvaluation ex:TastyFood ;
```

Moreover, in an aspect taxonomy, the children aspects typically inherit the evaluations their parents can assume. For example, the term *tasty* can apply to the entity Food, but also to specific foods such as soup or chicken. Therefore, it makes sense to assign these common evaluations only to the most generic aspect they are applicable to and have its children aspect inherit them by means of reasoning. To facilitate that in our model, we defined a rule suggesting that if an aspect A has an evaluation E, then all the narrower aspects of A have also this evaluation.

Model Population

To populate the model with concrete entities and relations, we designed and implemented a semiautomatic process that is depicted in Figure 8-3 and was designed to serve two goals:

1. The discovery of evaluation expressions (and their polarity) for already known/ identified aspects in a given domain.

2. The discovery of aspect-evaluation-polarity triples involving aspects that were previously unknown.

For both goals, we selected as input data a corpus of opinionated sentences about our target domain (e.g., restaurant reviews). A second input, required for the first goal, was a set of known domain aspect entities. Given these, the population process worked as follows. First, the corpus sentences were processed by a subjectivity detection system in order to filter out sentences that do not express an opinion. Then, we applied a named entity resolution system in order to identify which of these opinionated sentences mention a known aspect entity.

Subsequently, we applied a relation extraction system to all sentences in order to extract pairs of aspects and evaluation expressions. As a parameter for ranking the extracted pairs and fine-tuning the precision/recall of the process, we used the tf-idf score of the extracted pairs within the corpus. This score is a numerical statistic that is intended to reflect how important a word is to a document in a collection or corpus [180], and higher values of it provide more confidence that the extracted pair is accurate.

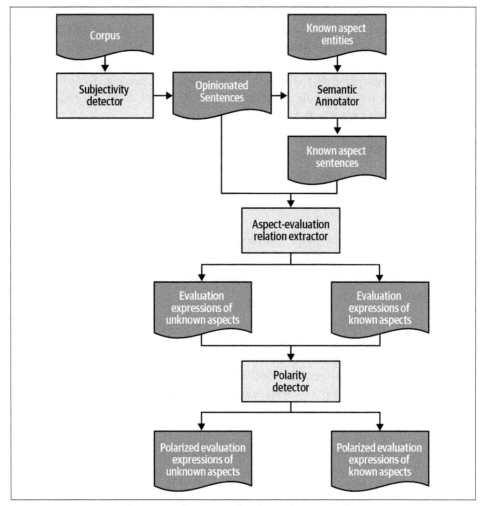

Figure 8-3. Aspect-evaluation-polarity ontology population pipeline

The final step of the process involved determining the polarity of each extracted pair. To do that we made the hypothesis that positive aspect evaluations appeared mostly in positive contexts and vice versa. Given this, we calculated pair polarity as follows:

1. For each unique pair, we gathered (from the sentence collection) the textual contexts it was detected in (one context per sentence)

2. To each context we performed sentiment analysis (via some existing tool) in order to derive a polarity score for it

3. We assigned to the pair the average of these scores

We then went on to incorporate the polarized aspect-evaluation pairs into the model. For a given extracted pair related to an already known aspect, we created an instance of the `AspectEvaluation` class and assigned to it the extracted evaluation expression. If an evaluation expression was shared by two or more aspects, then it was assigned only to the most generic ones.

Moreover, we manually checked for generality expressions that were shared between aspects at the same level of the taxonomy, i.e., whether they may refer to more generic aspects. For example, the expression `tasty` should be linked to the aspect Food even if in the corpus only specific foods were characterized as such. If that was the case, then the expression was moved to the more generic aspect. For extracted pairs that contained previously unknown aspects, we worked in a similar fashion, although first we needed to manually validate the newly discovered aspects.

Population process evaluation

In order to assess the feasibility and effectiveness of our model population process, we applied it in the restaurant domain, using a relevant domain ontology that we developed and whose aspect entities we manually identified. We also used a corpus of two thousand restaurant review sentences and a concrete implementation of the pipeline shown in Figure 8-3.

In the implemented pipeline, subjectivity detection was facilitated by OpinionFinder, while semantic annotation was performed via a named entity resolution tool that we developed in-house. For the aspect-evaluation extraction part, we utilized a pattern-based framework [181] that used dependency grammars to learn relation occurrence patterns, which was then applied to extract new relations from text. The framework required sentences that were already annotated with pairs of the target relations as training input; for that we (manually) annotated the sentences of the restaurant reviews corpus with pairs of aspects and evaluation expressions. Finally, for the polarity detection part, we used the Stanford Sentiment Analysis Tool (*https://oreil.ly/ p1dGH*).

Our first evaluation task was to measure the precision and recall of the aspect-evaluation pair extraction process, both for previously known aspects (i.e., aspects that we had identified in our domain ontology) and for unknown ones. We measured precision as the ratio of the correctly extracted pairs to the total extracted pairs, while we measured recall as the ratio of the correctly extracted pairs to the total actual pairs in the corpus. To perform this measurement we used 75% of the 2,000 sentences as training data for the relation extraction component and 25% for testing.

As a result of this process we obtained (via ten-fold cross-validation) the precision-recall curves in Figure 8-4, one for the extraction of aspect-evaluation pairs involving known aspects, and one for pairs involving unknown aspects. Each point on a curve corresponds to a different combination of precision and recall, obtained by using a different threshold for the tf-idf score of the extracted pairs.

As you can see, the system achieved a precision as high as 80% for known aspects and 72% for unknown ones, though, in the latter case, recall was relatively small. This was mainly a consequence of the corpus we used and the learning difficulty of the aspect-evaluation patterns it contained. To verify this, we used another pattern-based relation extraction tool, called LEILA (*https://oreil.ly/p7x7z*), and we got very similar results.

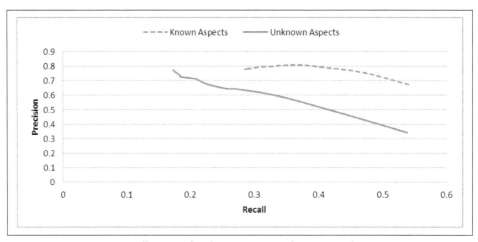

Figure 8-4. Precision-recall curves for the extraction of aspect-evaluation pairs

In any case, we found that higher thresholds result in higher levels of precision, and that meant we could use that particular parameter to control the size and quality of the system's output. If a small number of correct results were returned, then we could lower the threshold in order to increase their number, whereas if many incorrect results were returned, we could increase the threshold to increase their precision.

To evaluate the accuracy of the pair polarity detection, we considered 56 (distinct) aspect-evaluation pairs from our dataset along with the sentences they were found in. The number of sentences per pair was between 3 and 10. We then determined the polarity of these pairs both manually (using two human judges) and automatically (using the context polarity calculation approach we described in the previous section). The comparison between the manual and automatic assignments indicated an 80% accuracy of the automatic approach.

Summary

In this chapter we covered several pitfalls related to how we specify a semantic model and acquire knowledge about it. We saw how we might risk building the wrong model by failing to understand its context and by not being clear, thorough, and persistent enough in our interaction with its stakeholders. We saw also how, even with the right specifications, we may still end up with a bad model by selecting and using the wrong knowledge acquisition sources and methods.

Important things to remember:

- Push for clarity and specificity during requirements gathering
- Don't focus solely on the domains and data; give a central role to all the model's intended applications
- Anticipate biased and conflicting requirements
- Don't ignore legacy and history
- Always assess feasibility and importance
- Beware of the hype; building a good and useful semantic model is usually hard
- Pick the knowledge sources and acquisition methods for your model's elements after you have clearly specified their desired semantics, not the other way around
- Scrutinize knowledge sources and methods; look beyond their credentials
- Be aware of biases and take measures to neutralize them or make them transparent

In the next chapter we shift our focus to another crucial aspect of semantic model development, namely the management of its quality, and we describe a number of misunderstandings and pitfalls that prevent us from building models that have the quality we need.

CHAPTER 9

Bad Quality Management

If you give a manager a numerical target, he'll make it, even if he has to destroy the company in the process.
—W. Edwards Deming

The quality of a semantic data model (and any product, for that matter) is not only affected by mistakes made during its specification and development, but also by bad practices followed when measuring and managing that quality. The dimensions we choose to measure, the metrics we use for these measurements, and the ways we interpret the values of these metrics can make a big difference between a successful and a not-so-successful model. This chapter describes some common problematic quality-related practices and suggests ways to prevent them.

Not Treating Quality as a Set of Trade-Offs

We all want semantic models to be 100% accurate, complete, timely, and relevant, yet, more often than not, this is not possible or realistic. A key reason for that (apart from the fact that semantic modeling is a human activity, by and for humans) is that there are several trade-offs between the quality dimensions we saw in Chapter 4 (accuracy, completeness, consistency, etc.) that make it difficult to maximize a model's quality in all of them at the same time.

The problem with these trade-offs is not that they exist, but rather that we sometimes ignore or forget their existence and we don't take the time to create a concrete strategy to manage them. Let's see the most common quality trade-offs we are up against.

Semantic Accuracy Versus Completeness

As we saw in Chapter 4, semantic accuracy is the extent to which the semantic assertions of a model are accepted to be true, while completeness is the extent to which all required assertions are present in the model. How fast we can make our model complete depends on how fast we can add new (accurate) knowledge to it, especially when the domain is large and evolves at a fast pace.

Now, based on their definitions, completeness and accuracy do not really depend on each other, nor does one care so much if the other is high or not. Assume, for example, a model that contains the class `EuropeanUnionMemberState` and defines the latter's instances as not only the 27 countries that are actually members of the European Union, but also another 100 countries that are not. Thus this model's accuracy is really low (approximately 21%), but its completeness is 100%. Conversely, assume that the same model defines just two instances of the class, all correct. Its accuracy then would be 100% but its completeness only 7%.

This lack of positive correlation between the two dimensions gives us model developers a tempting but risky option, namely to accelerate the completion rate of our model by loosening the accuracy controls we have in place and allowing more knowledge to enter the model unchecked. Accuracy might suffer, but completeness will definitely be increased.

This trade-off becomes less relevant when the automatic knowledge acquisition mechanisms we have at our disposal are highly accurate and our model's domain is relatively small and static. In all other cases, a strategic decision has to be made as to whether or not completeness is more important than accuracy, and to what extent.

Conciseness Versus Completeness

Being in a hurry to make a semantic model complete also affects conciseness in a negative way, the reason being the lack of time needed to detect and avoid or remove redundant elements.

Imagine, for example, that we have a model with 10,000 entities and we want to add to it an additional 10,000 terms. The most concise way to do that would include the following steps:

1. Take each term, identify the existing entities (if any) of which it is a lexicalization (via synonym detection), and add it to the model as such

2. Take the remaining terms, group them into synonyms, and add each group as a distinct entity in the model

Depending on the technological support we have available for this task (e.g., a highly effective synonym detector), these two steps can take a considerable amount of time and effort. If, instead, we chose to skip the synonym detection and grouping steps and simply added all terms as distinct entities, our model would still be accurate, definitely more complete, but, in all probability, less concise.

Another reason why conciseness may be at odds with completeness is because the latter can be subjective and context-dependent, thus making it hard to decide whether or not certain elements are redundant. For example, the product owner of the Textkernel knowledge graph did not want the graph to contain any entities with a frequency in labor market data below a certain threshold, as he considered them an unnecessary burden to the model, without adding any value. Yet, an outsider could correctly argue that without these entities, the graph was incomplete.

As a result, the only way to make the conciseness–completeness dilemma less relevant to your models is to develop effective redundancy detection mechanisms and agree on relevant criteria and thresholds.

Conciseness Versus Understandability

Focusing too much on the conciseness of a semantic model without having clear and agreed redundancy criteria is also pretty likely to harm the ease with which human users can understand and utilize the model's elements.

For example, in an ontology development project I participated in several years ago, the client explicitly forbade us from adding any textual definitions to entities that were not classes. They also thought that names and lexicalizations of entities that were longer than three words were too verbose and should be avoided. The latter meant that for many entities that represented acronyms, we could not add their complete names (e.g., *ADHD*, a.k.a. Attention Deficit Hyperactivity Disorder or *DARE*, a.k.a. Drug Abuse Resistance Education), leaving us hoping that anyone who saw those acronyms would know what they meant.

In general, finding the sweet spot between conciseness and understandability is a tricky task and can often create frictions in a semantic modeling project.

Relevancy to Context A Versus Relevancy to Context B

When a semantic model is used in multiple application scenarios, it's quite possible that making it relevant for one scenario actually makes it less useful (or even harmful) for another. This happens when the different scenarios have different and potentially conflicting requirements. For example:

- Application A requires a rich entity lexicalization, without caring so much for ambiguity, while application B wants a minimally ambiguous model
- Client A wants a more accurate model, no matter the completeness, while client B wants a more complete model, no matter the accuracy
- When the model is deployed in region A, it needs to define a single truth for all its statements, no matter the degree of vagueness and inter-agreement, while when it is deployed in region B, it needs to reflect the diversity of opinions and perspectives
- Application A requires the definition of complex inference axioms and rules within the model, while application B cannot handle these elements without sacrificing some of its performance

A particular difficulty with the relevancy trade-off is that, quite often, we don't even know it's there, as we are not aware from the beginning of the different contexts our models are going to be used in. This is to be expected, and the only way to make things more predictable is to have a well-defined semantic model strategy from the beginning. Crafting such a strategy is the topic of the next chapter.

Multiple Models to the Rescue?

Some quality trade-offs can possibly be tackled by creating multiple versions of the same model, each version giving more focus and weight to different dimensions. That will probable save you from having to make some difficult decisions, but it will definitely increase your workload as you will need to maintain and evolve multiple models. For that reason, this approach makes sense when you can actually "outsource" the additional models' maintenance. For example, at Textkernel, we sometimes created custom versions of our knowledge graph for clients with different quality priorities, but we would do that only if the client later assumed the responsibility of that version's maintenance.

Not Linking Quality to Risks and Benefits

So far in this book, I have complained about the quality of many public models but, to be honest, I cannot be sure that all the users of these models will agree with me, not because these complaints are not valid but because they might be completely unimportant and irrelevant to them.

For example, for my work at Textkernel, the fact that ESCO does not have strict synonyms in the lexicalization of its entities is a major problem as I cannot easily link it to my model. But for someone who just wishes to use ESCO for navigation purposes on a job portal, it is probably fine.

Similarly, a biomedical ontology that has 95% accuracy can be very useful to IBM's Watson in its effort to win *Jeopardy!*, yet if this ontology is to be used as part of a medical diagnosis system, the 5% of inaccurate facts might be extremely dangerous.

In other words, treating quality as a mere set of metric values without any concrete reference to benefits and risks, while not technically wrong, can be rather pointless as it won't help you assess the real value of your model, nor will it enable you to prioritize quality improvement work and manage the trade-offs we saw earlier. Just imagine spending a large amount of resources to increase your model's accuracy by 10% and realizing afterward that the contribution to the business's bottom line is zero.

Thus, to properly measure and manage the quality of your semantic model, it's important that:

- *You know what aspects of your model and what quality dimensions contribute to its success or failure, and to what extent.* Ideally this should happen during the strategic planning and specification phase of the model's life cycle.

- *You pick the metrics and measurement processes that reflect these dimensions and risks/benefits.* It can be pretty tempting to use off-the-shelf quality metrics from the literature, yet the important thing is to use metrics that are tailored to the particular characteristics of your model and its context, and which are able to give you reliable and actionable information regarding its quality. In the next section, I discuss in more detail the pitfalls to avoid when selecting such metrics.

- *You connect the potential values of these metrics to some (informed) qualitative or quantitative estimation of the associated risk/benefit.* For example, you decide (through some proper study) that the drug–disease relation statements in your biomedical ontology need to have a minimum accuracy of 80% if the latter is to be deployed in the French pharmaceutical industry. Or that a low coverage in your knowledge graph of historical events that took place during the 15th century in Asia is OK, with any improvements having meager benefits.

 Manage Quality so that Your Model Doesn't Harm Anyone

In 2018, Amazon's machine learning specialists uncovered a big problem in their new recruiting engine, namely that it discriminated against women. That was because Amazon's computer models were trained to vet applicants by observing patterns in résumés mostly coming from men. This problem was enough to warrant the withdrawal of the system and the disbandment of the team, and rightly so. When your semantic model has an impact on real people, failing to spot that it might be biased against any of them in a harmful way is a colossal failure of your quality management strategy.

Not Using the Right Metrics

In the semantic modeling literature, one can find a large pool of metrics that are suggested for measuring semantic model quality [182]. However, not all of them are always useful and/or suitable for what we really need to measure.

One reason for that is that many metrics are defined outside of any application context (especially by academics), trying to capture as many objective quality characteristics as possible. Another reason is that semantic models can be very heterogeneous in their structure, objectives, and level of formality, making the definition of really portable metrics a difficult task.

In all cases, it's important that you scrutinize existing quality metrics and adapt them to your own model's characteristics and context. To help you with that, let's see some of the most common cases of bad semantic quality metrics.

Using Metrics with Misleading Interpretations

One problem with proposed semantic quality metrics is that sometimes they are presented as meaning something that they actually don't. An example of such a metric is *Inheritance Richness*, proposed in the OntoQA framework [183].

Inheritance Richness (IR) applies to the classes of a semantic model and is defined as the average number of subclasses per class. The suggested interpretation is that a model with a low inheritance richness score covers a specific domain in a detailed manner, while a model with a high score represents a wide range of general knowledge with a low level of detail.

To see the problem with this interpretation, assume that we want to create a semantic model in the cinema domain that should describe film entities and the genres they belong to. To do that, we have mainly two options:

1. Define a class `Film` and as many subclasses of it as genres (e.g., `ComedyFilm`, `ActionFilm`, etc.), and link each individual film to the genres it belongs to by making it an instance of the corresponding subclasses (see Figure 9-1).

2. Define a class `Film` and a class `FilmGenre`, instantiate them with individual film and genre entities, and link each individual film to the genre(s) it belongs to via a `hasGenre` relation (see Figure 9-2). Also, organize hierarchically the genre entities via a `narrowerThan` relation.

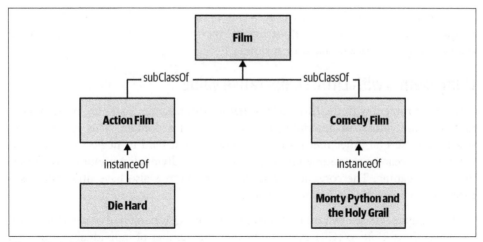

Figure 9-1. Film genres as classes

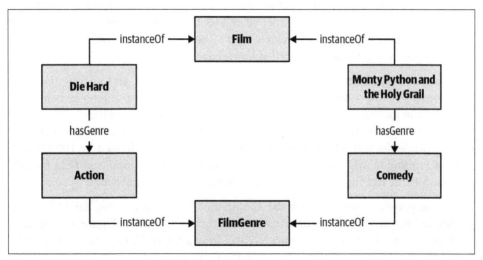

Figure 9-2. Film genres as individuals

Each representation has its pros and cons (see Chapter 12 for more details on that) but, if both are populated with exactly the same individual entities, then their domain coverage will be exactly the same; none will be more detailed or more general than the other. Yet, the second representation will have an IR of zero, while the richness of the first representation will be at least as much as the number of genre entities (since they will all be subclasses of Film). Thus, the suggested interpretation of the metric does not really hold.

In general, you have to be really careful when drawing conclusions about the semantic quality of a model from purely structural metrics, especially when there is more than one way to represent the same meaning.

Using Metrics with Little Comparative Value

The main problem with the IR metric is that it assumes that classes are more important than individuals in describing the semantics of a domain. This is something observed in several other metrics in the literature that tend to neglect the fact that many entities can be represented both as classes and individuals without really changing their meaning. The consequence is that these metrics also have little value as a means to compare the quality of two or more models.

As an example, let's see two other metrics from OntoQA, namely *Average Population* (AP) and *Class Richness* (CR). AP is defined as the number of individual entities in a model divided by the number of classes. If low, this number indicates that the individuals in the model are insufficient to represent all the specified domain knowledge. CR, in turn, is defined as the number of classes that have instances divided by the total number of classes. If the model has a very low CR, then the model does not have elements that exemplify all the specified knowledge in the model.

Now, consider again the two models in Figures 9-1 and 9-2, and assume that they both contain 10,000 individual film entities and 100 genres, the difference being that in the first model genres are class entities, while in the second one they are individuals. The AP of the first model will then be 5,050 (10,100 instances divided by 2 classes), while the second one's will be 100 (10,000 instances divided by 100 classes). Thus, according to this metric, the first model is much better populated than the second, despite the fact that they both contain exactly the same knowledge.

The same paradox happens with the CR metric. If we assume that for half of the genres we have no associated films in our data, then the model in Figure 9-1 will have a CR of 50%, while the one in Figure 9-2 will have a CR of 100%, misleadingly indicating that the second model is better than the first.

Using Metrics with Arbitrary Value Thresholds

Even worse than using quality metrics whose values are not linked to some estimation of the associated risk or benefit is to have such links, albeit arbitrary. A telling example of this is the OQuaRE ontology quality framework [184].

OQuaRE's semantic model quality metrics are adaptations of software quality metrics from the ISO/IEC 25000:2005 standard (also known as SQuaRE). Some of these metrics are:

Class Richness (CROnto)
    Mean number of instances per class

Attribute Richness (RROnto)
    Number of attributes divided by the number of relations and attributes

Weighted Method Count (WMCOnto)
    Mean number of attributes and relations per class

Number of Children (NOCOnto)
    Mean number of direct subclasses

Tangledness (TMOnto)
    Mean number of parents per class

Now, interestingly enough, the potential values of each metric are associated with a set of quality scores in the range from 1 to 5. A score of 1 means that the value is "not acceptable," a score of 3 means that it is "minimally acceptable," and a score of 5 means that it "exceeds requirements." Table 9-1 shows the value-score associations per metric.

Table 9-1. OQuaRE metrics, values, and quality scores

Metric / Score	Not acceptable	Minimally acceptable	Exceeds requirements
CROnto	[0,20]%	(40-60]%	> 80%
RROnto	[0,20]%	(40-60]%	> 80%
WMCOnto	> 15	(8,11]	⇐5
NOCOnto	> 12	(6,8]	[1,3]
TMOnto	> 8	(4-6]	[1,2]

The problem with these associations is that they are given out of context and look completely arbitrary. Even if we all agree that the fewer parents per class a model has, the higher its quality is, agreeing that the maximum acceptable number is eight is pretty unlikely. The same applies for the mean number of direct subclasses and the other metrics.

To be clear, defining a table like Table 9-1 for your model and its quality metrics is absolutely necessary. In fact, you might need to define many such tables for different parts or application contexts of your model. In all cases, though, you need to ensure that the value-score mappings you define are understood, agreed, and accepted by all of the model's stakeholders.

Using Metrics That Are Actually Quality Signals

In the semantic model quality literature, several metrics that are proposed do not really quantify how good or bad a model is in a given dimension, but rather the probability of it being good or bad.

For example, in Zaveri et al. (2015) [182], the authors suggest that a relevant metric for a model's semantic accuracy is the number of outliers it has, namely statements that fall outside of a certain statistical distribution. The problem with this suggestion is that it assumes that all outliers in a semantic model are definitely wrong, something that is not always the case. What is the case is that outliers usually have a high probability of being wrong, depending on the model's structure, content, and domain. As such, they can be used for detecting errors in a model, but not for reporting its quality.

Another example of a quality signal disguised as metric is found in [78], where the authors attempt to measure the trustworthiness of a knowledge graph based on the way the latter's data has been acquired. In particular, they suggest that:

- A knowledge graph whose data has been curated and inserted manually by experts and registered users has a trustworthiness score of 1

- A knowledge graph whose data has been curated and inserted manually by an open community of volunteers has a trustworthiness score of 0.75

- A knowledge graph whose data has been manually curated but automatically inserted from structured data sources has a trustworthiness score of 0.5

- A knowledge graph whose data has been curated and inserted automatically from structured data sources has a trustworthiness score of 0.25

- A knowledge graph whose data has been curated and inserted automatically from unstructured data sources has a trustworthiness score of 0

One problem with this scoring scheme is that it assumes a relative importance of trustworthiness criteria that is not always true. Experts are not always more objective than a community, manual insertion is not always more accurate than automatic insertion, and structured sources can be more unreliable than unstructured ones.

When I develop a semantic model, I never expect that it will be 100% trustworthy just because I built it manually and with experts. Similarly, when I scrutinize a semantic model for reuse, I don't automatically trust it just because it was built by experts (see again my complaints about ESCO). What I do is use these factors as signals that will help me in my work; if my model is built in a semiautomatic way, I know I need to do extra work to convince its users of its trustworthiness, and if I know that a model has never undergone a manual curation, I will be extra thorough when evaluating it.

In short, there is a subtle but important difference between a metric that tells you how good or bad your model is, and a signal that tells you that your model might be bad (or good). Use signals to detect quality problems, but don't use them to report quality.

Measuring Accuracy of Vague Assertions in a Crisp Way

As we saw in Chapter 3, the truth of vague assertions can be subjective and context-dependent, meaning that they may be judged as true and false at the same time, even by the same judge. This means that when we measure the accuracy of a semantic model that contains vague assertions, merely calculating the ratio of the true assertions can be misleading.

In practice, there are four key mistakes we make when measuring the accuracy of vague assertions:

We request judgments without providing any context
Context is always important, but it's even more important when we ask someone to judge the truth of a vague statement. If we don't provide context, it's pretty likely that the judge will think of and use some arbitrary context of their own, without even telling us about it. As such, the judgments we will get will not be aligned to our model's intended meaning.

We use only one judge per assertion
The problem with this approach is that we will have a one-sided subjective evaluation of the model's accuracy and we will never know if there are any disagreements. To avoid that, we should use multiple judges per assertion, making sure that these judges are representative of the model's users.

We use multiple judges but we force them to reach a consensus
This approach is better than the single-judge approach in the sense that it will detect potential disagreements and will make judges think more carefully about borderline cases and align on truth criteria and contexts. In that sense, the final accuracy score will reflect more opinions and be closer to reality. Nevertheless, this approach makes sense only for "light" disagreements that are caused by misunderstandings or unimportant semantic distinctions. If the model's assertions are highly controversial, forcing consensus is risky as it will only make judges susceptible to consensus bias, and the final accuracy score will not reflect reality. To avoid that, it's important to have the judges discuss the assertions they disagree on but, instead of forcing them to a reach a consensus, just use the outcome of these discussions to improve the model (e.g., by contextualizing vague statements).

We report accuracy without reporting disagreement

Even when our judges don't agree, we have many ways to sidestep their disagreements when we calculate an accuracy score. For example, we can consider an assertion true if all judges say it's true (a risk-averse approach), if more than half do (a more risk-prone approach), or if at least one of them does (an even more risk-prone approach). In all three approaches, however, we don't really communicate how small or big the risk is since we don't provide a quantification of the disagreements. This makes the reported accuracy scores less meaningful and actionable than they could be.

It's important to keep in mind that disagreements among judges can be caused by factors other than vagueness, such as ambiguity, lack of knowledge, biases, or even fatigue. It's thus very important to investigate their nature and isolate/quantify only the vagueness-related ones.

Equating Model Quality with Information Extraction Quality

When we develop a semantic model using automatic information-extraction methods or tools, the latter's effectiveness is definitely an indication of how good our model will be. Nevertheless, assuming that our model will be as good or bad as these methods is misleading.

One reason for that is that the model's quality also depends on the quality of the knowledge sources we derive it from; if these sources are inaccurate or irrelevant (see Chapter 8 for examples of that), the model will also suffer, no matter how effective the extraction method we use is.

An example of this pitfall can be found in Zaveri et al. (2013) [89], where the authors performed a user-driven evaluation of DBpedia's accuracy, reporting only 11.93% of inaccurate statements. A closer look, however, at the evaluation methodology they used reveals that the users were not asked whether the statements were correct but whether the statements were correctly extracted from their source (namely Wikipedia infoboxes) [70]. This means that the percentage of incorrect statements can actually be higher than 11.93%, unless we accept that Wikipedia is 100% correct.

A second reason that the model's quality might not be the same as the extraction's quality is the different ways the two are measured. For example, assume that you have at your disposal a Named Entity Recognition (NER) system that has 70% precision and 60% recall in detecting location entities in texts, and you use it to populate your model's Location class. Will your model also have this accuracy and completeness for this class? The answer is not necessarily.

Seventy percent precision means that if, for example, the text contains "Barcelona" 20 times, 14 of these occurrences are expected to be correct and 6 wrong. Yet, for our model, we need just one entity, so it all depends on how many occurrences we are required to find before being confident enough to add the entity to the model. If just one occurrence is enough, then the probability that it is wrong is indeed 70%. But if we require, let's say, 10 occurrences, the probability of error is much lower.

A similar reasoning can be applied for recall; the more occurrences we are required to find before adding the entity, the fewer the chances that we will eventually add it, especially if the entity has low frequency. And, of course, never forget that the recall of an NER system is calculated with respect to the entities contained in the corpus we apply it to, while the completeness of a model is calculated with respect to the entities in the domain. This means that even with a 100% recall NER system, our model will not be complete if the corpus does not contain all the domain's entities.

Summary

Ensuring that a semantic model has the quality we need is not only a matter of not making modeling mistakes or using the optimal tools and resources, but also a matter of using the right methods to measure and manage that quality. In this chapter you have learned how not treating quality as a set of trade-offs, not linking it to concrete risks and benefits, and not using proper metrics to measure it may result into unsuccessful models and wasted resources.

Important things to remember:

- Link quality to risks and benefits, otherwise you only have meaningless numbers
- Treat quality as trade-offs and decide what gives you more benefits
- Gather quality signals but don't use them as metrics
- Use metrics that give you actionable information
- Manage quality so that your model doesn't harm anyone

In the next chapter, we focus less on pitfalls related to the development of a semantic model and more on mistakes we make when we incorporate and use such models within applications.

CHAPTER 10

Bad Application

Computers are useless. They can only give you answers.
—Pablo Picasso

So far we have seen pitfalls mainly related to the development of a semantic model. In this chapter, we switch perspective and we look at a frequent mistake that happens when we apply such a model in an application. The mistake is that we assume that just because the model has been designed for the same domain or kind of data the application operates in, its semantics are directly applicable and beneficial to it. In reality, it can be that:

- The application's semantic needs seem to be covered by the model's elements, yet there are subtle but crucial differences between them that make the model useless or even harmful

- The application's semantic needs are covered by the model's elements, but the model contains additional elements that are not just redundant but actually harmful to the application

In what follows, we see how these two issues can arise in two common applications of semantic models, namely *entity resolution* and *semantic relatedness calculation*, and how we can tackle them in each case.

Bad Entity Resolution

Entity resolution is an information-extraction task that involves detecting mentions of entities within texts and mapping them to their corresponding entities in a given semantic model. For example, consider the following text from an IMDb review of the 1997 film *Steel*:

How's this for diminishing returns? In BATMAN AND ROBIN, George Clooney battled Arnold Schwarzenegger. In SPAWN, it was Michael Jai White versus John Leguizamo. In STEEL, the third and presumably final superhero stretch of the summer, Shaquille O'Neal dons a high-tech, hand-crafted suit of armor to combat the earth-shaking, world-shattering, super-duper-ultra evil menace of…Judd Nelson?

If we apply an entity resolution system to this text that uses DBpedia as a semantic model then, ideally, we would get the entities shown in Table 10-1.

Table 10-1. DBpedia entities in the Steel *review example*

Entity mention	DBpedia entity
BATMAN AND ROBIN	http://dbpedia.org/resource/Batman_&_Robin_(film)
George Clooney	http://dbpedia.org/resource/George_Clooney
Arnold Schwarzenegger	http://dbpedia.org/resource/Arnold_Schwarzenegger
SPAWN	http://dbpedia.org/resource/Spawn_(1997_film)
Michael Jai White	http://dbpedia.org/resource//Michael_Jai_White
Shaquille O'Neal	http://dbpedia.org/resource//Shaquille_O%27Neal
John Leguizamo	http://dbpedia.org/resource/John_Leguizamo
STEEL	http://dbpedia.org/resource/Steel_(1997_film)
Judd Nelson	http://dbpedia.org/resource/wiki/Judd_Nelson

The typical problem in this task is ambiguity, i.e., the situation that arises when a term may refer to multiple different entities (see "Ambiguity" on page 35). For example, in the preceding text, the term "STEEL" can, in theory, refer to the namesake chemical compound [185]. Similarly, the term "SPAWN" may refer, among others, to a comic character [186] or to the biological concept of eggs and sperm released or deposited into water by aquatic animals [187]. Deciding which reference is the correct one is the primary challenge for an entity resolution system.

How Entity Resolution Systems Use Semantic Models

To detect and disambiguate entity mentions in texts, an entity resolution system typically utilizes four types of input:

- A set of texts on which entity resolution is to be performed
- A set of target entities that are to be detected and disambiguated
- An entity thesaurus where each entity has a unique identifier and a set of terms that can be used to express it in natural language
- Some knowledge resource to serve as contextual evidence for the disambiguation of ambiguous entity mentions in the texts

The last input is derived from the strong contextual hypothesis of Miller and Charles, according to which terms with similar meanings are often used in similar contexts [188]. For a given entity, such a context usually consists of the terms that "surround" it in some reference text [189] [174], or the entities that are related to it in some semantic model [173]. For example, the disambiguation context for the film entities Steel and Spawn could include the actors who starred in them, as represented through the DBpedia relation starring [190].

Given these inputs, an entity resolution system works in two steps:

1. The entity thesaurus is used to extract from the texts terms that possibly refer to entities. The result is a set of terms, each associated to a set of candidate entities.

2. The contextual evidence knowledge resource is used to determine for each term the most probable entity it refers to (disambiguation).

In the second step, when the evidence knowledge resource consists of annotated texts, disambiguation is performed by calculating the similarity between the term's textual context in the input text and the contexts of its candidate entities in the annotated texts. When the contextual evidence is a semantic model, then graph-related measures are employed to determine the similarity between the graph formed by the entities found within the ambiguous term's textual context and the subgraphs formed by each candidate entity's "neighbor" entities. In all cases, the candidate entity with the most similar context is assumed to be the correct one.

When Knowledge Can Hurt You

The effectiveness of an entity resolution system is highly dependent on the degree of alignment between the content of the texts to be disambiguated and the semantic data that is used as evidence. This means that the model's elements should cover the domain(s) of the texts to be disambiguated but should not contain other additional elements that a) do not belong to the domain, or b) do belong to it but do not appear in the texts.

To show why this is important, assume that we are back in 2015 and we get the text "Ronaldo scored two goals for Real Madrid" from a news article. To disambiguate the term Ronaldo in this text using DBpedia, the only contextual evidence that can be used is the entity Real Madrid, yet there are two players with that name who are semantically related to it, namely Cristiano Ronaldo (current player) and Ronaldo Luís Nazário de Lima (former player). Thus, if both former and current players are considered, the term will not be disambiguated. Yet, the fact that the text describes a contemporary soccer match suggests that, in general, the relation between a team and its former players is not expected to appear in it. Thus, for such texts, it would make sense to ignore this relation in order to achieve more accurate disambiguation.

As another example, assume that we perform entity resolution on a set of film reviews, targeting mentions of actors and using DBpedia as an evidence semantic model. Since DBpedia contains many person entities that are not actors, it is quite likely that many actor mentions in the texts will be mistaken for other persons (e.g., the actor Roger Moore could be mistaken for the namesake computer scientist [191]). On the other hand, since the input texts are primarily about films, the probability that the term "Roger Moore" actually refers to the computer scientist rather than the actor is pretty low. Thus, if we were to remove from the semantic model all the nonactor person entities, we would most likely increase precision by allowing the system to focus only on the disambiguation of actor entities.

How to Select Disambiguation-Useful Knowledge

Effectiveness of entity resolution systems is typically measured in terms of *precision* and *recall*. Precision is determined by the fraction of correctly resolved terms (i.e., terms for which the entity with the highest confidence is the correct one) to the total number of detected terms (i.e., terms with at least one associated entity). Recall, on the other hand, is determined by the fraction of correctly resolved terms to the total number of existing entity mentions in the input texts.

Thus, a system has low precision if the input texts do not really contain (most of) the system-assigned entities. This usually happens when:

- There is a high degree of ambiguity, i.e., many entities from the thesaurus are wrongly associated to many text terms.
- The contextual knowledge is inadequate to correctly fulfill the disambiguation of terms. For example, if a text contains the term `Page` as a reference to the entity `Jimmy Page` and the contextual evidence knowledge resource has no information about this entity, then the disambiguation will most likely fail.

On the other hand, an entity resolution system has low recall when it fails to detect entities in the texts that are actually there. This may happen in two cases:

- When the thesaurus is incomplete by not containing either several of the target entities or adequate surface forms of them. For example, the thesaurus may not associate the surface form "Red Devils" with the soccer team of Manchester United.
- When the system, in order to be confident about a term's disambiguated meaning, requires a certain minimum amount of contextual evidence to be found in the input texts but fails to do so. This failure may be due to the lack of evidence in the evidence knowledge resource and/or the texts themselves.

Measuring your ambiguity

To effectively troubleshoot the low precision of an entity resolution system we need to assess how well it tackles the following ambiguity types:

Lexical ambiguity
> This is the case when the system mixes target entities with common lexical terms that are not really entities. For example, if the target entities are companies, then the location data services company Factual (*https://www.factual.com*) can be easily mixed in a text with the namesake adjective.

Target to target entity ambiguity
> This is the case when the system mixes target entities with other target entities. For example, if the target entities are locations, then the city of Tripoli in Greece may be mixed with Tripoli in Libya.

Target to nontarget entity ambiguity
> This is the case when the system mixes target entities with nontarget entities from the contextual evidence semantic model. For example, if the target entities are soccer teams and the model also contains locations, then the team of Barcelona may be mixed with the city of Barcelona.

Nontarget to target entity ambiguity
> This is the case when the system mixes nontarget entities from the contextual evidence semantic model with target entities.

Global ambiguity
> This is the case when the target entities can be mixed with entities from other domains, not included in the thesaurus nor in the evidence semantic model. For example, if the target entities are companies, then the company Apple may be mixed with the namesake fruit.

In order to identify which of these five ambiguity types and to what extent they characterize your scenario, you can work as follows. First, consider a representative sample of the texts that you are supposed to perform entity resolution on and manually annotate them with target entities as well as nontarget entities from the contextual evidence model. Subsequently, perform the same task in an automatic way by using the system without any disambiguation. Having done that, you can measure the different types of ambiguity as follows:

Lexical ambiguity
> Measure this as the percentage of terms that i) are common lexical terms rather than entities in the text, ii) have not been manually annotated with any target entity, and iii) have been wrongly mapped by the system to one or more target entities.

Target to target entity ambiguity
> Measure this as the percentage of terms that i) have been annotated with a target entity and ii) have been mapped by the system to this target entity but also to other target entities.

Target to nontarget entity ambiguity
> Measure this as the percentage of terms that i) have been manually annotated with a target entity and ii) have been mapped by the system to this target entity but also to other nontarget entities.

Nontarget To target entity ambiguity
> Measure this as the percentage of terms that i) have been manually annotated with a nontarget entity and ii) have been mapped by the system to this entity but also to other target entities.

Global ambiguity
> Measure this as the percentage of terms that i) are not common lexical terms but actual entities in the texts, ii) have not been manually annotated with any entity, and iii) have been mapped by the system to one or more target entities.

All theses percentages should be calculated over the total number of terms the system has detected in the texts.

Measuring the model's evidential adequacy

Complementary to high ambiguity, a second reason for low entity resolution effectiveness is the inadequacy of the contextual knowledge that is used as disambiguation evidence. When this knowledge has the form of a semantic model, then by *adequacy* we mean two things:

- *How rich is the semantic model in terms of relation/attribute values for its entities?* These values are used as contextual disambiguation evidence, therefore if many entities lack them, their disambiguation will probably fail. For example, if we want to disambiguate film mentions in texts, a potential evidence could be the actors who played in them. If this relation is poorly populated in the semantic model, then the latter may be inadequate for the particular task.

- *How prevalent is the contextual evidence provided by the semantic model in the input texts?* Even if the model is rich, it won't help if the texts do not contain the evidence it provides. Considering the film example, even if we know all the film's actors, this knowledge will not be useful if films and their actors do not co-occur in the texts.

Semantic model richness can be measured in many ways, depending on the desired level of detail. Some metrics that can be useful are:

The percentage of target entities with no related entities at all
> If this number is high, then the semantic model is practically useless for the disambiguation of the particular entities.

The average number of entities a target entity is related to
> If this number is lower than expected (e.g., if films are related on average to only one or two entities when they are typically expected to be related to several actors, directors, producers, characters, etc.), then the model might not be as useful as it could be.

The average number of entities a target entity is related to via a specific relation
> If this number is lower than expected, then this relation cannot really contribute to the disambiguation task even if it is expected to do so. For example, if the "hasActor" relation for films is poorly populated (e.g., only one or two actors per film), then the system is not able to use any actor mentions in the texts as film disambiguation evidence.

These metrics can be easily calculated by merely querying the semantic model. On the other hand, in order to measure the prevalence of the graph's contextual evidence in the input texts, you need to use both the texts and the model. In particular, you can consider again the representative sample of input texts that you used to measure ambiguity in the previous section and which you have already manually annotated with target entities as well as nontarget entities from the contextual evidence model. Then, for each target/nontarget entity pair in the annotated texts, you can derive from the model the relation(s) and/or the relation paths (up to a certain length) through which the entities are linked. This will allow you to calculate the following:

The percentage of target entities for which there is at least one evidential entity in the texts
> If this number is low, then obviously the semantic model is not useful for the given texts.

The average number of evidential entities a target entity is related to in the texts
> If this number is too low, then—again—the model is not appropriate for the given texts.

The percentage of target entities for which there is at least one evidential entity in the texts via a specific relation or relation path
> If this number is low, then this particular relation is not useful for the given texts.

The average number of evidential entities a target entity is related to in the texts via a specific relation (or relation path)
> Again, this number allows you to assess the relative usefulness of the model's relations for the disambiguation task.

Improving your disambiguation capability

If the lexical ambiguity of the entities is considerable, then the word sense disambiguation (WSD) capabilities of the linguistic analysis component of the entity resolution system need to be enhanced. Depending on the existing capabilities of the system and the extent of the problem, these enhancements can range from simple heuristics (e.g., that a company mention in a text typically starts with a capital letter) to complete implementations of WSD frameworks [192].

On the other hand, if global ambiguity is found to be high, then it may be that many of the input texts are not really related to the domain of the target entities. For example, if entity resolution is performed on news articles in order to detect mentions of films (with some film knowledge graph as an evidence semantic model) and most of these articles are not relevant to the cinema domain, then it's quite likely that many nonfilm entities will be mistaken for films. To remedy this situation, you could possibly expand the evidence model to include all the domains the input texts are about; nevertheless, this can be quite difficult and resource-intensive to achieve.

Another, more practical approach, would be to use a domain/topic classifier in order to filter out the nonrelevant texts and apply the resolution process only to the relevant ones. Intuitively, this will boost precision even if some level of recall is sacrificed.

The next two metrics that can lead to action are the target to nontarget entity ambiguity and the nontarget to target entity ambiguity. If the first is found to be high and the second low, then what is most needed is probably the pruning of the evidence model in order to remove parts of it that are not so essential but can still cause noise.

The pruning of the model can be done in two stages. In the first stage, the entities (and their relations) that are not related (directly or indirectly) to the target entities could be discarded. In the second stage, the removed entities would include those that are related to the target entities but via relations that are not prevalent in the texts. For the latter, you can use the average number of evidential entities a target entity is related to in the texts via a specific relation. The pruning should start from the relations with the lowest score.

Of course, this whole exercise is meaningful only if the evidence model has some highly prevalent relations to retain after the pruning. If that's not the case, then the ideal action would be to change/expand the model with different relations than the ones it already has and which are most likely to appear in the texts.

If that's not possible, an alternative action that could be performed in case of low graph prevalence would be the reduction of the minimum evidence threshold that the system uses in the disambiguation phase, provided that target entity ambiguity, target to nontarget entity ambiguity, and nontarget to target entity ambiguity are also low. This action would potentially increase recall (since much fewer nonambiguous entities for which little evidence has been found in the text would be rejected by the system) without decreasing much precision (since for the few entities that are ambiguous there was not much evidence to use in the first place).

Finally, if the richness of the semantic model is low, the obvious thing to do would be to enrich it. Since that may not always be possible due to lack of resources, the relation prevalence metric could also be used here in order to select to enrich only the most useful relations.

Table 10-2 summarizes the key points of the preceding analysis by providing a map between observed metric values, problem diagnoses, and recommended actions. In all cases, it should be made clear that the whole framework I am describing here is characterized by some degree of inexactness, meaning that there's always a possibility that i) a diagnosis is wrong even if the metrics support it and ii) that the execution of a recommended action fails to improve resolution effectiveness even if the diagnosis is relatively accurate. For that, every time you take an action, you need to re-measure precision and recall in order to verify that the system actually performs better. The re-measurement should be done every time with a new test set to ensure that your actions have not introduced any bias to the process.

Table 10-2. Metric values and actions

Metric value	Diagnosis	Action
High lexical ambiguity	The entity resolution system cannot perform WSD well enough	Improve the linguistic analysis component of the entity resolution system
High global ambiguity	Many of the input texts are not really related to the domain of the target entities	Use a domain/topic classifier in order to filter out the nonrelevant texts and apply the process only to the relevant ones
High target to nontarget entity ambiguity and low nontarget to target entity ambiguity	The evidence model may contain several nontarget entities that hamper the disambiguation process rather than helping it	Prune the evidence model in order to remove nonessential, noisy entities
Low semantic model richness	The model is not adequate as disambiguation evidence	Enrich the model starting from the most prevalent relations
High semantic model richness but low text prevalence	The semantic model is not adequate as disambiguation evidence	Change or expand the model with entities that are more likely to appear in the texts
Low semantic model text prevalence, low target entity ambiguity, low target to nontarget entity ambiguity and low nontarget to target entity ambiguity	The system's minimum evidence threshold is too high	Decrease the threshold

Two Entity Resolution Stories

Several years ago, I was working at iSOCO, a semantic technology company in Spain, and my team there had developed *Knowledge Tagger*, an in-house entity resolution system that was designed to use semantic models as disambiguation evidence. We had the chance to apply this system to a number of projects and, whenever its effectiveness was low, we would use the diagnostic framework I just described to increase it. Let's see two characteristic cases.

Resolving players in soccer texts

In this case, we had to semantically annotate a set of textual descriptions of soccer match highlights from the Spanish Liga, like the following:

> It's the 70th minute of the game and after a magnificent pass by Pedro, Messi managed to beat Claudio Bravo. Barcelona now leads 1-0 against Real.

The descriptions were used as metadata of videos showing these highlights and our goal was to determine, in an unambiguous way, which were the players mentioned in each video. The annotated descriptions were then to be used as part of a semantic search application where users could retrieve videos that showed their favorite player, with much higher accuracy.

Our first attempt at performing this task involved using Knowledge Tagger with DBpedia as both an entity thesaurus (as it included all soccer players we were interested in) and an evidential knowledge graph. The result of this was a precision of 60% and a recall of 55%, measured against a manually annotated set of one hundred texts. For comparison purposes, we also applied the AIDA system (that used the YAGO knowledge graph) on the same texts and we got similar figures (precision 62% and recall 58%).

To diagnose the reasons for this rather mediocre performance, we calculated the ambiguity and evidential adequacy metrics using a one hundred–text diagnostics dataset. As shown in Table 10-3, the main types of ambiguity that characterized our case were target entity ambiguity (several players with similar names) and target to nontarget entity ambiguity (several players in the text sharing similar names with other DBpedia entities). On the other hand, nontarget to target entity ambiguity (actual nonplayers mixed with players) was low. This was rather expected as the input texts were very domain-specific and thus unlikely to contain many person entities that are not soccer players.

Table 10-3. Ambiguity metric values for soccer case

Metric	Value
Lexical ambiguity	1%
Target entity ambiguity	30%
Target to nontarget entity ambiguity	56%
Nontarget to target entity ambiguity	4%
Global ambiguity	2%

Given these metric values, we went on to prune the DBpedia by removing most of the non-soccer related entities as well as several player relations that had no evidential value. To determine the latter, we calculated the text prevalence of the player relations in the knowledge graph. As Table 10-4 shows, the most prevalent (and thus useful for disambiguation) relations were those between players and their current team, current co-players, and current managers; so we kept those and discarded the rest.

Table 10-4. Text prevalence of semantic model relations and relation paths in the soccer case

Relation	Prevalence
Relation between soccer players and their current club	85%
Relation path between players and their current co-players	95%
Relation path between players and their current managers	75%
Relation between players and their nationality	10%
Relation between players and their place of birth	2%
Relation between players and their spouse	0%

Then we applied Knowledge Tagger again, but with the pruned semantic model, and this time precision and recall were found to be 82% and 80%, respectively.

Resolving companies in news articles

In this case, our task was to detect and disambiguate mentions of technology startups within news articles coming from a variety of news sources (newspapers, blogs, specialized websites, etc.). For that, we had at our disposal a thesaurus of four thousand company entities as well as a custom-built knowledge graph that contained useful knowledge about each company, like its founders, investors, competitors, and business areas. Running Knowledge Tagger with this knowledge graph as disambiguation evidence gave us a precision of 35% and a recall of 50%, both of which, of course, were rather low.

To identify the underlying reasons for this low effectiveness, we applied our diagnostic framework again, starting with the identification of the ambiguity types we were up against. As Table 10-5 shows, contrary to the soccer case, our main problem in this scenario was not the ambiguity between startups and/or other related entities in the knowledge graph, but the global ambiguity, i.e., the ambiguity between startups and entities outside our domain. In hindsight, this was somewhat expected as the news articles we were analyzing were not necessarily related to startups or technology. Moreover, there was a considerable lexical ambiguity as several companies had names like "Factual," "Collective," and "Prime."

Table 10-5. Ambiguity metric values for companies case

Metric	Value
Lexical ambiguity	10%
Target entity ambiguity	4%
Target to nontarget entity ambiguity	4%
Nontarget to target entity ambiguity	3%
Global ambiguity	40%

Given the high global ambiguity, we built and applied a simple binary classifier to filter out news articles that were not related to our domain. The classifier was trained on a set of 400 news articles (200 within the domain and 200 outside), achieving an accuracy of 90%. Running Knowledge Tagger only on the news articles classified as domain-specific resulted in a substantially increased precision of 72%, while recall stayed roughly the same (52%).

At the same time, in order to deal with the considerable lexical ambiguity, we incorporated some heuristic rules into the linguistic analysis component of our system like, for example, the rule that text terms that refer to startups should start with a capital letter. This increased precision to 78% and recall to 57%.

To see if any more improvements were possible, we measured the knowledge graph's prevalence in the texts, which turned out to be low. In fact, almost 40% of the texts contained no evidential entities at all, while most of the graph's relations had small prevalence (see Table 10-6). Based on this fact and the low scores for target entity ambiguity, target to nontarget entity ambiguity, and nontarget to target entity ambiguity we ran Knowledge Tagger again, but with a reduced minimum evidence threshold; this increased recall to 62%.

Table 10-6. Text prevalence of knowledge graph relations and relation paths in the companies case

Relation	Prevalence
Relation between companies and the business areas they are active in	50%
Relation between companies and their founders	40%
Relation between companies and their competitors	35%
Relation between companies and their CEO	20%
Relation between companies and their investors	15%
Relation between companies and their CFO or CMO	6%

Bad Semantic Relatedness

Another common usage of semantic models is the calculation of the semantic related-ness (or similarity) between terms and entities. For example, in Sharma et al. [193] the authors use WordNet and a network of Wikipedia links in a patent search system to expand user queries with semantically related terms. For similar purposes, in papers by Lord et al. [194] and Caviedes et al. [195], the authors define semantic relatedness measures over the Gene Ontology (*http://geneontology.org*) and the Uni-fied Medical Language System (UMLS) ontology (*https://oreil.ly/zj4gB*), respectively.

If you want to use a semantic model for calculating semantic relatedness, you have the following options:

- *Reuse some existing relatedness relation that the model already provides.* Many models already contain a `related to` or `similar to` relation between their enti-ties. WordNet, for example, links many of its adjectives to semantically similar ones (e.g., "banal" is considered similar to "unoriginal" [196]). Similarly, the Eurovoc taxonomy defines semantically related terms for most of its concepts (e.g., "civil law" is related to "civil code" and "private law" [197]).

- *Apply some existing semantic relatedness measure on the model.* In the past deca-des, several methods and measures for determining semantic relatedness in tax-onomies, ontologies, and other types of semantic models have been developed [198] [199] [200]. A pretty simple approach, for example, is to calculate the relat-edness between two entities based on the length of the shortest path that links them in the model (the shorter the path, the higher the relatedness) [201].

- *Define and apply your own semantic relatedness measure, based on the existing model's elements (relations, attributes, etc.).* This approach involves defining cus-tom semantic relatedness measures and rules that make sense and are effective in your particular model and/or application scenario [194] [195]. For example, given a taxonomy of entities, you might want to define a rule saying that every entity is similar to its broader entity but dissimilar to its narrower entities.

- *Extract your own semantic relatedness relation from text and/or other, external to the model, data sources.* This approach involves extending the model with a custom semantic relatedness relation that you define and populate from external sources, using information-extraction methods and techniques we saw in Chapter 5 [202] [203].

- *Any combination of the above.*

No matter what option you choose, there is one major pitfall you need to avoid: calculating a different relatedness than what your applications and their users need.

Why Semantic Relatedness Is Tricky

Semantic relatedness is tricky because it's a vague relation for which it's relatively easy to get agreement outside of any context, but hard within one.

For example, if I ask you whether Prolog and Python are semantically related, you will probably say yes because they are both programming languages. If, however, I ask you whether you would hire someone with experience in Prolog as a Python programmer, you will most likely say no, as Prolog is pretty different in philosophy than Python. Similarly, if you ask a linguist which languages are closer to German, they will most probably mention Dutch, Danish, or Swedish, based on their linguistic similarities. But if you ask the same question to a recruiter who works in the German market, they might suggest English and French, as these are the languages that most of their German-speaking clients speak as a second language.

In other words, in specific situations and contexts, people tend to have specific interpretations of semantic relatedness in their minds that can be quite different from what a semantic model already contains or a typical context-independent relatedness measure can give.

To exemplify this context dependence further, assume that you are applying the same semantic model in two different semantic search systems. The first system is part of an online bookstore where users can look for history books to buy, while the second system is part of a university library where students can look for history books to borrow and use for their papers and studies.

The semantic model is a history ontology that describes entities and relations regarding historical events, periods, personalities, etc. The ontology is to be used by both systems to semantically tag and index the books with the entities they talk about, as well as to expand a user's query with semantically related entities. Thus, for example, if a user searches for books about a particular historical event (e.g., the Battle of

Waterloo), the system should also return books about entities related to this event (e.g., Napoleon Bonaparte).

Your challenge is to determine which semantically related entities these should be. There's not an easy answer, and you will probably need to experiment with different relatedness measures and methods before you find the optimal one. Nevertheless, I can already tell you this: whatever approach will work in the bookstore system won't work in the library one (and vice versa).

To see why this is the case, just think about the different search goals of each system's users. When a library user searches for a particular historical event, they are actually on the hunt for any information that could be useful for their paper or exam. Thus, for example, if they're doing research on the Battle of El Alamein, they won't mind getting books about more generic events that contain this battle (e.g., the Second World War), especially since they won't need to pay for them. On the other hand, a bookstore user who wants to buy a book about the Battle of El Alamein might not be so willing to pay for a book that merely dedicates a chapter or section to it.

How to Get the Semantic Relatedness You Really Need

To get the semantic relatedness that an application actually requires, you need to apply the "semantics-first" approach that we saw in Chapter 8. That means you should start by identifying and making explicit, in as detailed and clear a way as possible, the assumptions, requirements, and expectations of the application's users with respect to semantic relatedness.

In most cases, these requirements will be implicit and hidden behind a generic "should be related" or "should be similar" characterization. One way to uncover them is to give people examples of entities that you think can be related, ask them to judge them as related or not, and then challenge them to justify their decisions. When you do that you should avoid the temptation of micro-arguing over isolated examples and focus instead on identifying patterns and rules that characterize these decisions.

Your goal should be to transform the "should be related" specification to something more concrete and context-specific. For example, a more appropriate definition of semantic relatedness for the history bookstore and library example can be the following:

History bookstore
> An entity A is semantically related to entity B when a user who is interested in *buying books* about A is also interested in buying books about B.

History library
> An entity A is semantically related to entity B when a user who is interested in *finding information* about A will also find books about B useful.

With such definitions at hand, you can then move on and decide which of the options we saw earlier for calculating semantic similarity are more applicable to your case. For that, you can work in the following order:

1. *First check if the model you have at your disposal already has a relatedness relation that expresses your target relatedness.* This may require some investigation, especially if it's not you who has developed the model.

2. *If there's no such relation or it's not compatible, then see if your target relatedness is available in some other existing model that you could easily reuse.* Again, this will probably require some digging and scrutinization as most models will lack an accurate description of their elements' semantics (see Chapter 6).

3. *If you cannot find what you need elsewhere, start testing different standard semantic relatedness measures on your model to see if any of these can effectively approximate the relatedness you need.* In many cases, such measures can prove surprisingly effective, especially if the target relatedness is not too specific and context-dependent.

4. *If that fails, start considering custom metrics and rules applied on your model.* Pretty often, basic rules or minor adjustments of existing metrics do the trick.

5. *If this customization is not enough, then you will need to mine the target relatedness from scratch, considering corpora, user logs, and other data sources external to the model.* For techniques and guidelines on how to best do that you can revisit Chapters 5 and 8.

Feel free to change this order in any way you see fit, but never forget that if you are targeting the wrong relatedness, anything you do will most likely fail.

A Semantic Relatedness Story

In 2008, I worked on a project that involved developing a semantic information access system for the Hellenic Transmission System Operator S.A. (HTSO),[1] a governmental organization responsible for the management and operation of the Greek electricity network and market. The system provided the public with access to documents that described the operation principles, processes, and rules of the Greek electricity market, and had two main components:

- An ontology that described the Greek electricity market domain, modeling entities and relations about processes, participants, systems, and other market-related knowledge

---

1 Now called Independent Power Transmission Operator S.A.

- A semantic search engine that used the ontology's entities to semantically tag and index the documents, parse user queries, and expand them with semantically related entities.

In Tables 10-7 and 10-8, you can see the main classes and relations of the ontology.

Table 10-7. Classes of the electricity market ontology

Class	Description
Market Process	Refers to any process or procedure that is part of the overall operation of the electricity market
Market Participant	Refers to individuals and organizations that play some role within the market
Market Action	Refers to actions performed by market participants in the context of specific market processes
Market Right	Refers to rights of the market participants in the context of the market operation
Market Obligation	Refers to obligations of the market participants in the context of the market operation
Market Rule	Refers to rules that govern the operation of the market
Market System	Refers to equipment, facilities, and systems that are used in the context of the market operation

Table 10-8. Relations of the electricity market ontology

Relation	Description
isImportantPartOfProcess (MarketProcess, MarketProcess)	Links processes with other processes that are important parts of them
isImportantPartOfAction (MarketAction, MarketAction)	Links actions with other actions that are important parts of them
participatesInProcess (MarketParticipant, MarketProcess)	Links participants with the processes they participate in
performsAction (MarketParticipant, MarketAction)	Links participants with the actions they perform
isPerformedByParticipant (MarketAction, MarketParticipant)	Links actions with the participants who perform them
isPerformedInTheContextOfProcess (MarketAction, MarketProcess)	Links actions that are needed to complete a process
isInterestedInProcess (MarketParticipant, MarketProcess)	Links participants with processes they are interested in
hasObligation (MarketParticipant, MarketObligation)	Links participants with obligations they have in the context of the market's operation
hasRight (MarketParticipant, MarketRight)	Links participants with rights they have in the context of the market's operation
isRightOf (MarketRight, MarketParticipant)	Links participants with rights they have in the context of the market's operation

To enable query expansion we worked with a representative group of the system's future users to elicit their interpretation of semantic relatedness that we needed to implement. After lots of discussions and debates, we agreed that queries should be expanded with entities that give the users as much information as possible about everything they needed to do to participate in the electricity market, but in some order of importance.

For example, if a user searched for documents regarding a particular kind of market participant, they should first get all documents that describe the processes this participant is typically interested in, and then information about relevant actions or rights and obligations. Similarly, if a user searched for a particular action, they should definitely get information about the important subactions involved but not so much about the kinds of participants this action is performed by.

To enable this kind of behavior, we implemented a custom semantic relatedness measure that was based on manually defined weights on each of the ontology's relations. The values of these weights ranged from −1 to 1, with −1 denoting that the relation should not be considered at all in measuring relatedness, and 1 denoting the exact opposite, namely that two entities connected with this relation should be considered identical. Any weight between −1 and 1 denoted an intermediate situation. A sample of these weights (as finalized after several rounds of tuning) is shown in Table 10-9.

Table 10-9. Relatedness weights of the electricity market ontology relations

Relation	Weight
isImportantPartOfProcess	1
isImportantPartOfAction	1
isInterestedInProcess	1
performsAction	0.8
isPerformedByParticipant	−0.5
hasObligation	0.5
hasRight	0.5

To test whether these weights and custom relatedness had any meaningful impact in the effectiveness of the search engine, we measured the latter using two versions of the system, one with a standard distance-based semantic similarity measure, and another with our custom measure. For our experiment we used a golden set of 25 queries together with their corresponding ideal system responses (ground truth). The results indicated that the customized relatedness increased the precision and recall of search by approximately 8%.

Summary

This chapter described and showcased a major pitfall of using a semantic model in our applications, namely assuming that just because the model has been designed for the same domain or kind of data the application operates in, its semantics are directly applicable and beneficial to it. You have seen how this may happen when using a semantic model for disambiguating entities and for calculating semantic relatedness, and you have learned how to adapt/optimize the model for different contexts and scenarios.

Things to remember:

- Not all relations or other aspects of a semantic model are helpful to an entity disambiguation system; some can actually harm it.

- To improve the usefulness of a semantic model as disambiguation evidence you need to measure this usefulness, but also to identify and measure the different types of ambiguity that appear in the data. The values of these measurements will point you to the actions you can take to improve things (see Table 10-2).

- Semantic relatedness is tricky to use or calculate, because it's relatively easy to get humans to agree that two concepts are semantically related outside of any context, but hard within one.

- To get the semantic relatedness that an application actually requires, aim to transform the "should be related" requirement to something more concrete and context-specific.

The next chapter concludes the "Pitfalls" part of the book by looking the broader strategic and organizational context where semantic data modeling takes place, and examining relevant pitfalls and bad practices that may prevent an organization from successfully executing semantic data initiatives.

CHAPTER 11

Bad Strategy and Organization

Strategy 101 is about choices: You can't be all things to all people.
—Michael Porter

Every time a general goes to battle they first draw a strategy on how to beat their opponent and communicate this strategy to their troops. If they don't have a strategy they will be defeated. If this strategy is not tailored to the circumstances of the battle (terrain, weather, etc.) and strengths and weaknesses of the opponent, they will also be defeated. And if the composition and organization of their troops cannot support the strategy, they will, again, fail.

Well, the same applies more or less to semantic data modeling projects and initiatives. No matter how knowledgeable and savvy we might be in semantic modeling frameworks, knowledge mining methods and techniques, or other relevant aspects, without the right strategy and organization the initiative will most probably fail.

With that in mind, in this chapter we'll see some common strategy- and organization-related pitfalls we fall into when designing semantic modeling projects and initiatives, and discuss some possible ways to avoid them.

Bad Strategy

There are two main strategy-related pitfalls to avoid when you contemplate and plan a semantic modeling initiative. The first is not to include any strategic and organizational aspects in your plan and focus instead merely on technical and procedural issues. The second is to include such aspects, but for the strategy you draw to be incompatible with the context where it will be executed.

In my career I have drafted several such plans and proposals that, unfortunately, were accepted by the organizations I submitted them to. And I say "unfortunately" because most of these plans proved to be inadequate to effectively deal with all the nontechnical nuances and complexities of a real-world semantic modeling project.

What Is a Semantic Model Strategy About?

A semantic model strategy is essentially about three things: the model's goals, the high-level approach to achieve these goals, and the decision-making mechanisms to execute this approach.

Strategic goals are the result of asking questions like:

- Why are we building the model?
- What products or processes do we want to power/enhance?
- Who is going to use it, and for what purpose?
- What value do we expect the model's users to derive from it?
- What happens if we don't build the model?

If you don't have a concrete enough answer to these questions, it can be very hard to specify and develop the model you actually need, as well as foresee the challenges and difficulties that you will face. For example, the approach you will need to follow if your goal is to develop an ontology that will become the de facto semantic data interoperability standard in a given industry is very different than the one you will need if your model's goal is to improve the precision and recall of a product recommendation engine.

What I cannot stress enough is the need for the goals to be as concrete as possible. The worst goals are the ones that use buzzwords and overloaded generic terms. Telling me, for example, that you need an ontology in order to make your search engine semantic rather than keyword-based is meaningless. Telling me, instead, that you need an ontology in order to increase the precision of your search engine in a given subdomain or for a category of users is much better.

A strategic goal should also not be about the approach you intend to follow for the model's development. Telling me, for instance, that your goal is to develop a knowledge graph using deep learning doesn't convey any useful information about who needs this model and why. Choosing to trust and invest in deep learning as your main approach for building the knowledge graph can indeed be a strategic decision (and a source of competitive advantage), but it shouldn't be a goal in itself.

The second thing a semantic model strategy is about is the high-level approach by which the model's goals are to be achieved. By "high-level" I mean that this approach does not need to be an exhaustive list of model requirements accompanied by a detailed plan with concrete actions and methods, but rather an overall philosophy, set of principles, and strategic directions and priorities on which the model's development will be based.

As an example, let's juxtapose two existing semantic models, namely the ESCO classification (that we've seen in previous chapters) and the Diffbot knowledge graph [204].

If we look at ESCO carefully, we can identify at least three strategic choices its creators have made. First, they decided to represent and enable access to the model using open standards, namely RDF(S) and SKOS. Second, they exclusively used domain experts as knowledge sources. And third, they decided to create new releases of the model pretty infrequently. Diffbot, on the other hand, has developed its own representation and query language (called *Diffbot Query Language*) and has been populating its graph by crawling and mining web resources. Moreover, it provides a new version of the graph every four to five days. Table 11-1 shows additional examples of typical questions a semantic model strategy needs to provide answers for.

Table 11-1. Sample what and hows of a semantic model strategy

Questions about the model and its usage	Questions about the model's development
What knowledge domains do we want the model to cover?	Are we going to use open semantic modeling standards or develop our own?
What parts of the model will the users pay for and what will be free?	Will the model's content be primarily provided by domain experts, or will it be mined from data?
What is the minimum level of accuracy the model should have?	How often are we going to be updating the model?
Are we going to have a single model for all customers or customized ones per customer?	Will we maintain control of the model's maintenance and evolution, or will we allow anyone from the public to contribute to it?

Finally, a semantic model strategy is about tackling dilemmas and making decisions, not only during the initial stages of a model's development but throughout its life cycle. Therefore, more than the decisions themselves, a strategic plan should define the criteria and mechanisms by which these decisions should be made.

For instance, I can wake up tomorrow morning, go to my work, and contemplate what new domain to add to my model or what quality aspect of it to improve. If I don't have concrete criteria and processes to determine these things, I will either spend my time agonizing over the best choice without doing anything, or I will make some decision that might end up adding little or no value to the model.

The Importance of a Product Owner

In my first year at Textkernel, the knowledge graph we were building did not have a dedicated product owner to define its roadmap and strategic directions and priorities. As a result of that, much development work went unexploited as it had no immediate value for our clients, and important features the graph needed to have were not developed as they were not identified or prioritized in time. When the graph was assigned a proper product owner, its value for the company significantly increased.

In a nutshell, a semantic model strategy is about avoiding running in too many different directions, wasting resources and accomplishing little, and building something that nobody likes or needs.

Buying into Myths and Half-Truths

To craft an effective strategy for your semantic model, you first need to have a good and realistic knowledge of the general landscape of semantic data modeling, and understand what is possible, feasible or even desirable given the current state of technology. Some myths and half-truths that I have come across during my career (and already identified in earlier chapters) are the following:

- *You can only build semantic models using Semantic Web languages, standards, and technologies.* This is not true, and the living proof is many ontologies, taxonomies, and knowledge graphs that are not represented according to RDF or OWL (e.g., Cyc, LinkedIn Knowledge Graph). We can always debate the merits and flaws of different representation approaches, but it's important to keep in mind that there are more options than some community or vendor might make you think.

- *You can populate your semantic model automatically from data with little human intervention—so many organizations have done it.* Indeed, there are many semantic models out there whose generation is primarily automatic, such as DBpedia, Diffbot, LinkedIn Knowledge Graph, and others. Are you sure, though, that your model's requirements in terms of structure, content, quality, and usage are the same as the requirements of these models? Is it possible that your target entities and relations are nowhere to be found in the data you have available, or are they pretty hard to accurately extract with the methods and algorithms you have available? Unless your answers to these questions are "Yes" and "No," respectively, you can't really base your model's development on what these organizations have done.

- *You can easily reuse publicly available semantic models and standards.* As we've seen in Chapter 8, many public semantic models contain information that is semantically inaccurate, or information that is accurate but not exactly what your model requires. Therefore, while it makes sense to try to exploit such models, you can't rely on them to provide everything your model needs.

- *Semantic interoperability is a matter of using the same representation language.* While a common formalism definitely helps, it's not a sufficient condition for your model to be semantically interoperable with other models. What you actually need is agreement and consensus on the meaning of things.

- *Uncertainty, vagueness, and other non-boolean phenomena are noise that need to be left out of the model.* A keynote speaker in a Semantic Web conference explicitly told me that when I asked him how the Semantic Web world should address these phenomena. Consume at your own risk.

- *You can just use the methodology/algorithm/tool described in paper X.* Have you ever tried to reproduce or apply an academic or industrial paper's suggested solution for a given problem in your own context? If yes, you know how hard it can be to achieve the outcomes the paper promises, both from an implementation and methodological perspective. If no, I encourage you to do it; it's a frustrating but eye-opening experience. This is not to say that research papers are not important and useful—quite the opposite. However, you need to approach them with a healthy skepticism, and don't expect them to immediately give you the solution you are looking for.

Underestimating Complexity and Cost

Another common problem when crafting a semantic model strategy is underestimating the complexity of the whole endeavor. This is a relatively well-studied problem in the world of software engineering, where many projects end up costing much more than originally budgeted and taking much more time and resources than originally allocated. In semantic data modeling, though, there's little research or reference data that could help estimate the cost of developing a model.

An attempt to estimate the typical cost of semantic model development is described in "How Much Is A Triple?" [115], where the author analyzes publicly available information about manually created knowledge graphs (Cyc and Freebase) and automatically created ones (DBpedia, YAGO, and NELL). His methodology is approximate and not complete (e.g., it excludes the cost of providing the knowledge graphs) but ends up suggesting that the cost of generating a semantic triple (i.e., a subject-predicate-object statement) in a manual fashion was between $2 and $6, while in an automatic one it was between $0.0083 and $0.14. He also shows that the statements created at higher cost have a higher likelihood of being correct.

Even if its reported numbers are not fully accurate, this analysis indicates two important complexity and cost factors for a semantic model's development, namely the degree to which this development is automated and the desired level of the model's accuracy. Some additional factors that typically increase costs are:

The diversity and nuance of the domains you want to cover
The more heterogeneous and nuanced these domains are, the more effort and domain expertise you need to detect and make explicit subtle meaning distinctions.

The complexity of the model's desired elements
It's generally much harder to define complex relations, rules, and axioms than terms, entities, and simple relations.

The degree of abstractness of the entities
Abstract entities are more difficult to rigorously define than concrete ones (see Table 8-3 for how DBpedia struggles to define the correct type of such entities).

The degree and intensity of vagueness
The more vague the desired elements of your model are, the more effort you need to make their meaning explicit and commonly accepted among their users.

The desired level of applicability and reusability of the model
The more applicable and reusable across different languages, cultures, applications, or other contexts you want your model to be, the more development effort and maintenance overhead you will have.

The appropriateness, degree of structure, and semantic explicitness of available data sources
DBpedia and LinkedIn extract their knowledge graphs from data with some degree of explicit and controlled structure (infoboxes and user profiles, respectively). If instead they had to use more unstructured and unpredictable data (e.g., Wikipedia articles and CVs), they would need more sophisticated tools to achieve the same quality.

The maturity of infrastructure, technology, and processes available to develop and/or apply the model
To support the complete life cycle of a semantic model you typically need a variety of methods, systems, tools, and processes available (e.g., information extraction tools, data processing pipelines, model-editing user interfaces, model editing guidelines and rules, etc.). Thus, if you are in an organization that has never done such a thing before, odds are that you will need to develop or set these up from scratch.

Not Knowing or Applying Your Context

A third strategy-related pitfall is basing our model's characteristics and development approach on what other models and organizations have been doing, without investigating and applying our own context. Sure, model X covers the same domain as ours, but do we really need all the relations it defines in our model as well? Sure, company Y has been developing its knowledge graph fully automatically, but is the quality it achieves acceptable by our standards? And sure, company Z has been using its semantic models to enhance its search engine, but is doing the same for our search engine equally important and beneficial?

Such questions can only be answered if we have a broad and deep understanding of our model's context and of what is possible, feasible, and desirable within it. "Broad" in the sense that we need to consider not only the domains, semantics, and usages of the model, but also the organization, its clients, its people, its competitors, its technology, etc. And "deep" in the sense that we need to actively look for the devil that lies in the context's details and who might knock our strategy off track.

Knowing your model's context, in the end, is knowing your strengths and weaknesses and using this knowledge to make strategic decisions. For example:

- If product A generates more revenue than product B, you might choose to optimize the model for A
- If your model's semantics are highly vague and cause disagreements, you might need to support multiple truths
- If the best extraction system for relation X is only 50% accurate, you will probably need manual curation
- If you can't find an effective entity disambiguation system in the market, you might need to invest in developing one
- If your competitor's model covers many domains but in a superficial way, you might choose to provide a model on a niche complex domain
- If there is already a non-RDF semantics management infrastructure in the organization, it may not be worth replacing it with an RDF one

Why I Have Been Using Neo4j for the Textkernel Knowledge Graph

Whenever I tell Semantic Web people that in Textkernel we have been using Neo4j to represent and store our Knowledge Graph, they look surprised and try to convince me of the merits of RDF and the Semantic Web stack, without even asking me about the graph's or the company's context. My answer to them is simple: if you can make a convincing business case to my boss that throwing away all the development work that the company has been doing around Neo4j since before I even joined the company (and which has covered our needs just fine so far) is a good idea, I will be happy to take it to him.

A final note: just as a semantic model is susceptible to change, so is its context. For that, crafting a model strategy is not a one-time thing but a continuous process of forming, applying, monitoring, and revising.

Bad Organization

Just as a bad semantic model strategy will most likely lead to failure, a good one will also fail if it's not well executed. And good strategy execution relies on, among other things, ensuring you have the right people in place with the right skills and attitudes, as well as the processes that will enable them to collectively do their best work. Let's see why this often does not happen.

Not Building the Right Team

There are numerous books and articles out there discussing what skills and structure an ideal data science team should have. But what about a semantic modeling team? Should it mainly consist of hardcore ontologists and analytical philosophers who would define the most rigorous and realistic formal definition of each concept and entity? Should it include logicians who would ensure that the models and their reasoning behavior are always logically consistent? Should linguists have a say since a semantic model is tightly coupled with the way human language works? Or is this just another typical data mining and storage/access problem that any competent data engineering and science team could handle?

The answer to this question lies in the fact that semantic data modeling is as much about data as it is about semantics, and neglecting either dimension over the other is highly likely to lead to failure. A team consisting only of formal ontologists might be able to give you the most accurate definition of a concept's meaning, but only after spending on it more time and resources than you can afford. A team of logicians might come up with perfectly logical axioms and rules that, however, do not work when applied on real-world data that is rife with ambiguity, uncertainty, and vagueness. But also, a team of statistical savvy data scientists might help you automatically derive from data a 90% accurate semantic model, only to realize later that the extracted semantics are not the ones you actually wanted.

In practice, for your semantic modeling team to succeed, you need a variety of people with complementary skills and, most importantly, the right attitude toward data semantics. Let's see what these skills and attitudes are.

Skills you need

The fundamental skill any semantic modeling team needs to have is *conceptual and semantic thinking*. This is not so much about having knowledge of a specific modeling language or framework like SKOS or OWL (which are important, of course), but rather being able to understand and correctly use any such framework. For that to happen, you need people who:

Can understand, identify, and make explicit the different semantic phenomena that they come across when they develop semantic models
> For example, understanding ambiguity is crucial for ensuring that an element's name or definition conveys a unique meaning. Similarly, understanding vagueness is crucial for anticipating and mitigating disagreements about the entity's intended meaning. And, most importantly, understanding the difference between ambiguity and vagueness is important for selecting the right approach to tackle each of them.

Can understand and use correctly the modeling elements they have available
> For example, understanding that the `owl:subclass` relation in OWL should not be used for representing part-whole relations is important to avoid getting nonsensical inferences. For the same reason, it's important to understand that the `rdfs:domain` and `rdfs:range` axioms do not behave as constraints but as inference rules.

Are skilled in observing and deciphering the terminology people use
> As we saw in earlier chapters, people use the same terms for different things and different terms for the same thing. A good semantic modeler is able to detect when this happens and make explicit these differences and similarities throughout the semantic model's life cycle.

Are able to put themselves in the shoes of the model's users and think of all the possible ways the latter may (mis-)interpret and (mis-)use its different elements
> This is about anticipating the biases and diverse viewpoints and perspectives of the model's stakeholders, but also about suppressing their own biases as semantic modelers. If that doesn't happen, the model's applicability will be extremely narrow.

This kind of thinking is necessary no matter what semantic model development strategy you have decided to pursue. Even if, for example, you are building your model completely automatically from data, you still need to select the right data sources for your target semantics, and that's going to be problematic if you have got these semantics wrong.

At the same time, of course, semantic thinking is not enough on its own; depending on your semantic model's goals and strategy, you might need:

Skills and experience in information extraction, natural language processing, and machine learning

> The more reliant your model's development is on extracting semantics from unstructured and heterogeneous data, the more expertise you will need to develop and use sophisticated extraction algorithms and methods.

Skills and experience in data engineering and management

> Both the data you derive your model from and the model itself need to be stored, processed, and made available to different systems and applications. The bigger and more complex the data, the more expertise you will need to develop efficient and scalable data pipelines.

Skills and experience in UX/UI design and development

> The more you need non-technical people to interact with your model, either as contributors or users, the more you will need to invest in building intuitive user interfaces.

Domain expertise

> The more specialized and complex the domains your models need to cover, the more domain knowledge you will need in order to drive development and ensure quality.

Expertise and experience in applying semantic models

> For example, information professionals such as librarians and taxonomists can influence models for the better by understanding user warrant, translating requirements, and understanding the wider social contexts of how the model will be used.

Attitudes you don't need

Something more important (and difficult) than finding people for your team who have one or more of the preceding skills is to ensure that these people will work well together. In my experience, one condition for that to happen is to avoid, or at least moderate, the following behaviors and attitudes:

Being pedantic

Some people, in their effort to define the meaning of terms and concepts in a rigorous way, end up being excessively concerned with valid but insignificant or too-theoretical details and arguments. For example, as we will see in Chapter 13, it's almost always possible to find a semantic distinction between two or more terms that we typically consider synonyms, and that's actually a good skill for a semantic modeler. Insisting, though, to always include that distinction in the model independently of whether, and to what extent, it's used in practice can be counterproductive.

Being a semantics nihilist

The flipside of being pedantic is not seeing or caring about obvious and important semantic distinctions, as well as not pushing for specificity and clarity of the things that we include in a semantic model. We have already seen the consequences of such behavior in the previous pitfall chapters.

Believing everything is boolean

As comforting and convenient as it is to model a domain with true and false statements, the real world is uncertain and vague. Failing to see or accept that fact may lead to useless semantic models.

Being a data, expert, or crowd fanatic

When it comes to choosing knowledge sources for building a semantic model, people have their favorites. Some believe that only domain experts can be trusted to provide accurate and complete facts. Others do not trust these experts and believe in the "wisdom of the crowd." And others believe that any claim that is not empirically supported by data is not correct or useful. However, as we saw in Chapter 8, experts can be wrong, the crowd can be wrong, and data can be wrong, meaning that being a blind supporter of one of them at the expense of the others is counterproductive.

Seeing everything as a nail just because a cool hammer is available

This is a common phenomenon among technologists, and it has to do with not fitting the solution to the problem but the problem to the solution. If, as we saw in Chapter 10, some application requires a particular type of semantic relatedness from your model and all you do is reuse some existing relatedness relation without questioning its compatibility, you are mistaking the solution for the problem.

In the end it's all about finding the optimal balance between these attitudes, and this is admittedly not easy. That's why you need to constructively combine them, hoping that one counterbalances the other.

Underestimating the Need for Governance

I mentioned earlier that an important aspect of a semantic model strategy is the mechanisms by which decisions about the model and its development, application, and evolution are made and executed. More than a strategic problem, this is an organizational issue that involves establishing, as much as possible, a system of clear rules, roles, decision rights, processes, and accountabilities that bring everyone in the organization on the same page.

This is admittedly not an easy task, and it can be tempting to avoid it altogether by adopting a laissez-faire attitude. The risk of having such an attitude, however, is semantic divergence and waste of resources.

A semantic divergence story

In early 2019, my team at Textkernel started working on expanding our knowledge graph with a new set of skill concepts based on a client's request. During the same period, another team started doing the same thing for another client. Despite the fact that they were expanding the same part of the knowledge graph, the two projects started independently and ran in parallel for some months without much exchange of information.

When at some point the two teams got together to discuss how to merge our expansions, we realized that that was not so easy because the two models differed in a fundamental aspect, namely the required granularity. The second client had a more relaxed attitude toward synonymy and would not accept the same semantic distinctions that the first client made. Conversely, the first client would not accept many of the synonyms that the second client had demanded.

As a result, we spent another two to three months working on negotiating and implementing a middle ground between the two clients so that the two graph expansions could be merged into one. Much of this additional work could have been avoided if the two teams had started working together from the beginning and had communicated to each other the different requirements.

Preventing semantic anarchy

The reason you need some form of governance for your semantic model is to minimize risks, reduce costs, and ensure the continued existence and evolution of the model. There is much literature on the subject of data governance, but for me the main questions any semantic model governance framework needs to answer are the following:

- *What kinds of changes are allowed to be made in the model, and under what circumstances?* For example, you might want your model's classes and relations to be static and only allow changes at the individual entity level. Or, you might suggest that the model can be expanded to cover a new domain only if there is a critical mass of explicit requests by users or customers. The goal in all cases is to avoid unexpected and undesired changes in the model, no matter how correct they are.

- *Who is allowed to make these changes?* If your model is about a highly specialized domain and accuracy is a critical requirement, you might decide to restrict edit rights only to a few verified and trusted domain experts. If the model contains complex axioms and inference rules, you might want these to be editable only by people trained in knowledge representation. And if some part of the model is country- or culture-specific, allowing it to be changed only by natives of that country or culture might be a good idea.

- *How should these changes be made?* A change in the model can be as simple as just filling up an attribute value of an entity in a graphical editor, or as complex as making a business case for the need of this value, getting it approved by some authority, and performing extensive testing to ensure it does not introduce any unexpected side effects to the model or its applications. In all cases, the processes, rules, guidelines, and best practices that need to be followed when making changes to the model should be well defined, documented, and communicated to all the relevant contributors.

- *Who owns the model and is responsible/accountable for it?* If as a user of your model I have a question, complaint, or request, who is the go-to person or team that I can contact and be sure that I will get a response? Who is responsible for driving the model's development and evolution and ensuring its quality continuously improves? It can be a single person, a team, an organization, a community; anything is acceptable as long as there is someone.

- *Who makes decisions and resolves conflicts and disagreements, and in what ways?* What happens if two editors of the model disagree on the veracity of a statement? Does the more senior editor prevail? Or, does the decision to expand the model in a new domain need to be unanimous by the community members, or is a majority vote is enough? Wikipedia, for example, defines a quite detailed and comprehensive process for building consensus among its editors [205]. In general, the more diverse the people and parties involved are in the model's development and evolution, the clearer, more formal, and perhaps more sophisticated the decision-making processes need to be.

- *How are principles, rules, and decisions enforced?* Defining rules and making decisions is only half the work; the other half is enforcing them. What happens if some contributing party routinely violates some content or conduct rule (e.g., adding copyrighted content or harassing someone for their different perspective)? The FIBO community, for example, permanently bans anyone who "demonstrates a pattern of violation of community standards, including sustained inappropriate behavior, harassment of an individual, or aggression toward or disparagement of classes of individuals" [206].

Summary

In this chapter we concluded the "Pitfalls" part of the book, having focused on two very important aspects of a semantic model's life cycle, namely its strategy and organization. You have seen what aspects a semantic model strategy needs to minimally cover, and what mistakes you should avoid while defining these aspects. You have also learned the key skills and attitudes that a semantic model development team needs in order to successfully execute such a strategy.

Important things to remember:

- When you define a semantic model strategy, make sure you include the model's goals, the high-level approach to achieve these goals, and the decision-making mechanisms to execute this approach.
- Define a strategic goal by asking questions like "Why are we building the model?" and "What will happen if we don't build the model?"
- There are more technological and framework options to build a semantic model than some community or vendor might make you think.
- Semantic interoperability is not merely a matter of using the same representation language; you actually need agreement and consensus on the meaning of things.
- The cost of a semantic model is proportional to the diversity and nuance of the target domains, the abstractness and vagueness of the target entities, and the desired level of applicability and reusability of the model.
- Knowing your model's context is knowing your strengths and weaknesses; use it to guide your strategy.
- Semantic data modeling is as much about data as it is about semantics; don't neglect either dimension over the other.
- Make sure your semantic modeling team is able to think semantically.

Now it's time to move to the "Dilemmas" part of the book, where you will learn how to tackle semantic model development situations in which you have to choose between different courses of action, each with its own advantages and disadvantages.

PART III

The Dilemmas

CHAPTER 12

Representation Dilemmas

Design is the method of putting form and content together. Design, just as art, has multiple definitions, there is no single definition. Design can be art. Design can be aesthetics. Design is so simple, that's why it is so complicated.
—Paul Rand

When developing a semantic data model, it is often the case that a particular piece of information can be represented in more than one legitimate way, even within the same representation language (e.g., deciding whether an entity should be represented as a class or an individual). Each way has different strengths and weaknesses that you need to be aware of, both as a creator and a user of a semantic model. As a creator because you will need to pick and implement the way that is best for your case, and as a user because it will help you select between semantically equivalent models that don't have exactly the same capabilities.

This chapter covers some common representation dilemmas, with particular focus on when and how you should represent vague elements by fuzzifying them.

Class or Individual?

In Chapter 2 we saw that, in some cases, the modeling language you use obliges you to decide whether an entity should be modeled as a class or an individual (i.e., as an entity that has no instances). We also saw that one problem with having to do such a selection is that there are several entities that can be legitimately modeled as both a class and an individual (e.g., `Eagle` and `Data Scientist`).

A second problem is that, in most cases, the modeling framework does not give you the same modeling and expressivity freedom for classes as it does with individuals. For example, in OWL-DL, you cannot define a class as an instance of another class, nor can you define direct relations between classes and other entities other than some predefined ones. Thus, if you want to say at the same time that John is an instance of Data Scientist, and Data Scientist is an instance of Occupation, you just can't.

So, the dilemma we have here can be expressed as follows: "Given a modeling framework that requires the crisp separation of classes and individuals, and an entity that can be legitimately modeled as both, how should we model that entity?"

To tackle this dilemma, you need to consider the following questions:

What instances does (or can) the entity have?
> As we discussed in Chapter 2, the only criterion that matters when determining if an entity can be a class or not is whether there are other entities that can be instances of it. So, can you actually find (convincing and not artificial) instances for your entity?

Do you care to describe these instances in your model and define relations and attributes for them?
> Even if your entity has potential instances, it doesn't mean that they are necessarily important for your model. For example, let's say that your model is about video games and you want to include the game *Assassin's Creed Odyssey* in it [207]. A possible instance of this entity could be the particular copy of this game that I bought last month, with attributes like serial number, price, or production date. Do you actually want to include this information about my copy in your model, or do you merely want to talk about the game in general, perhaps defining relations and attributes about its producers, writers, and the consoles it is available in?

Are there facts about the entity that you cannot easily express if you model it as a class?
> For example, let's say you want to state in OWL-DL that an essential skill for the profession Data Scientist is Data Mining and the average salary it commands is $150,000. One way to do the first is to link the two entities via a direct relation hasEssentialSkill just like ESCO does, but then you would be treating Data Scientist as an individual entity instead of a class. To treat it as a class you could perhaps define an axiom saying that all instances of Data Scientist need to be linked via the hasEssentialSkill relation with the entity Data Mining but that would have ramifications: in a closed-world setting, your reasoner would not accept individual data scientists that do not have this skill, while in an open-world setting it would always infer that they have it. Similarly, it would be quite difficult to define an attribute averageSalary that is applicable to the class Data Scientist but not its instances, since class attributes are not allowed in OWL-DL (apart perhaps from annotation properties, which are not considered a formal part of the model, but merely documentation).

If your answer to the first question is negative, you definitely should not model your entity as a class. And just because other models may have modeled it as a class doesn't mean that they are right, or that they mean the same thing as in your model (see "Giving Bad Names" on page 87).

If your answer to the first question is positive but negative to the second, then you also don't really need to represent your entity as a class, especially if the answer to the third question is positive. In other words, there's no reason to make your life harder than it is, and your model unnecessarily complex, just to accommodate in it entities that you will never have. On the other hand, if your answer to questions one and two is positive but negative to question three, then you are OK with modeling your entity as a class. Just remember, as we discussed in Chapter 6, to name and describe your class in a way that makes it clear what instances it should have.

The really difficult scenario is when the answer to all three questions is positive; namely, you want to represent direct information for both the entity and its instances. For such a case, there are a couple of workarounds you can implement, each with its own trade-offs.

One workaround is to model your entity as an individual and, instead of the language-provided instantiation relation (e.g., rdf:type), use a custom binary relation to link the entity to its instances. For example, instead of saying that the entity John is an instance of the class Data Scientist, you can say that John is related to the individual Data Scientist via the relation hasProfession. Or, instead of saying that Harry Potter's owl Hedwig is an instance of the class Owl, you can relate it to the individual entity Owl via the relation belongsToSpecies.

The advantage of this approach is that you get the freedom to use the entity in any relations you like, not only instantiation, keeping at the same time its instances in short reach. Moreover, you can still position the entity into a hierarchy of similar entities (e.g., saying that a Data Scientist is a kind of Information Technology Professional) by using, for example, the skos:narrower relation or similar.

On the other hand, you cannot use the entity in class-related axioms, thus losing standard inference capabilities that the modeling language provides. For example, in OWL, without the owl:subclassOf relation you cannot expect your reasoner to infer by default that any person who is a Data Scientist is also an Information Technology Professional, unless you define a custom rule for that. Similarly, if you want to state that the attribute hasCompletedMilitaryObligations is applicable to male persons and Male is not a class but an individual, then you cannot use the rdfs:domain element that OWL provides.

A second workaround is to model the entity as two entities, one as a class and one as an individual, using different names for each (see approach 3 in [208]). Here are some examples of how this could happen:

- Data Scientist becomes Data Scientist (Profession) as an individual and Data Scientist (Professional) as a class

- Pneumonia becomes Pneumonia (Disease) as an individual and Pneumonia (Incident) as a class

- Eagle becomes Eagle (Species) as an individual and Eagle (Animal) as a class

- Samsung A8 becomes Samsung A8 (Mobile Phone Model) as an individual and Samsung A8 (Mobile Phone Device) as a class

The advantage of this approach is that you can state almost anything you like for your entity without caring if these statements apply only to classes or individuals. Moreover, having to name your entity in a way that makes explicit its role as a class helps avoid the naming pitfalls that we saw in Chapter 6. On the other hand, you still cannot link the two variations of the entity to each other (since one is a class and the other an individual), thus making it harder to keep them in sync with each other.

A third option, which is applicable for OWL modelers, would be to use OWL2 and *punning*, a feature that allows you to use the same entity in your model as both a class and an individual. The trick with punning is that the reasoner decides at runtime whether the entity should be interpreted as a class or individual, based on the entity's context. Thus if, for example, the entity is linked to a class via an instantiation relation, it is treated as an individual, while if it is related to it via a subclass relation, it is treated as a class. In other words, even though the entity has one single identifier, depending on its context, it is evaluated by the reasoner as a different thing.

Keep in mind that, while punning can be a useful technique, it's not a free ticket to treating all entities as both a class and an individual. As Michael Uschold rightly argues in [209], punning is more syntactic trickery than an actual solution to the semantic problem of metaclasses, because the only thing it does is raise an invisible wall between the two interpretations of the entity. This wall may relieve you from having to use different names for the same thing, but it can also confuse your fellow modelers and users of your model if you are not careful.

To Subclass or Not to Subclass?

Another difficult decision to make during semantic modeling is how to specialize the meaning of a class, namely by introducing a new subclass or by representing the distinction through different relation or attribute values. For example, assume you have the class Restaurant and you want to specialize it so that you can distinguish its instances based on the cuisine served (e.g., Asian, fusion, French, etc.). For that you can implement at least two models:

- For each cuisine, create a subclass of `Restaurant` (e.g., `AsianRestaurant`, `Fusion Restaurant`, etc.) and have each individual restaurant instantiate the class it corresponds to its cuisine (see Figure 12-1).

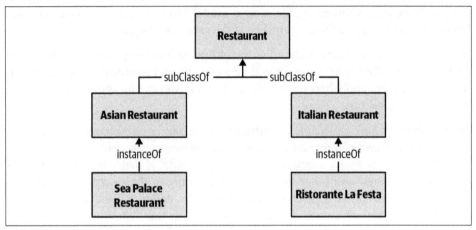

Figure 12-1. Example of subclass-based distinction

- Create a class `Cuisine` with instances of particular cuisines (e.g., `AsianCuisine`, `FusionCuisine`, etc.) and a relation `hasCuisine` to link individual restaurants to these cuisines (see Figure 12-2).

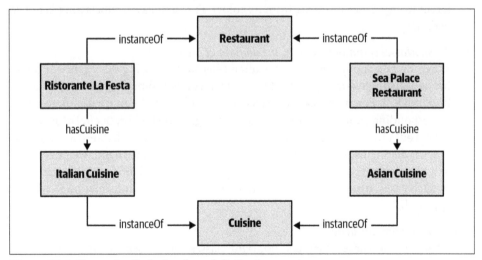

Figure 12-2. Example of relation-based distinction

The advantage of the first model is that it's simpler, more intuitive, and it allows you to exploit the reasoning capabilities of the subclass relation (e.g., any instance of a

`ChineseRestaurant` will be automatically inferred as an instance of `AsianRestaurant`). On the other hand, having the different cuisines embedded within the restaurant class can make it hard to talk directly about them (e.g., you cannot easily say that one cuisine is influenced by another) or link them to other entities (e.g., with recipes). Conversely, the second model allows you to talk about cuisines but takes away from you the convenience of the subclass relation.

In practice, this is the same trade-off as the one we saw in the previous section when contemplating whether an entity should be a class or an individual, so the questions we discussed there apply here as well. In addition, however, you should also consider the following questions:

Do the subclasses have any additional attributes, relations, or restrictions compared to their parent class and siblings that you want to include in your model?
> The key ability that a subclass gives you in a model is that you can define relations, attributes, and other axioms that apply only to the instances of that class and not those of its superclass. For example, by defining the class `mammal` as a subclass of `animal` we are able to state the axiom that "all mammals are vertebrates," something that is not true for all animals. The same applies for siblings of the subclass, namely classes that inherit the same parent class. For example, mammals can produce body heat, while reptiles need some external heat source to stay warm. Without subclassing, it's not so easy to make these distinctions. On the other hand, a human's left lung does not really have any distinguishing characteristics from their right lung (apart from its position), nor is a red car very different from a blue car (apart from its color). For such cases, subclassing is not so necessary.

Are the subclasses commonly used in the domain of discourse?
> When we talk about films, we very often refer to them using their genre or director as a distinguishing qualifier (e.g., "I love comedy films," or "This is a Tarantino movie"). For such cases, it makes sense, and might be more useful, to create corresponding subclasses of the class `Film` (e.g., `ComedyFilm`, `QuentinTarantino DirectedFilm`, etc.), even if you don't intend to be very detailed in your model as to what distinguishes a comedy from a drama. On the other hand, we rarely refer to a film using its duration or the languages it has been dubbed into as qualifiers. In such cases, using an attribute or relation to model this information is a better approach.

How rigid are the subclasses?
> As we saw in earlier chapters, nonrigid classes are classes whose instances can stop belonging to them without ceasing to exist. Yet, some classes are less rigid than other classes in the sense that their instances are more volatile. For example, `AsianRestaurant` is nonrigid since a restaurant can always change the cuisine it serves, yet this is something that does not happen very frequently. On the other

hand, the (also nonrigid) class `RestaurantWith50Employees` is much more volatile as the personnel needs of the culinary business can be quite seasonal. In general, the low rigidity of a class should make you rethink its importance and value to the domain, but also consider its maintenance overhead compared to having an attribute or relation for representing the same information.

A final note about ambiguity: when we name subclasses it's pretty tempting to use shorter and less descriptive names than necessary so that we don't get too verbose. For example, to represent films directed by Quentin Tarantino, we might define a class `TarantinoFilm` rather than `QuentinTarantinoDirectedFilm`, assuming that `Tarantino` can be disambiguated and `Directed` inferred. The same applies for the `AsianRestaurant` example I used earlier; most users would understand that the characterization `Asian` refers to the restaurant's cuisine and not, for example, its ownership. So, this is not necessarily a problem, but you have to be careful as to the extent of these assumptions.

Attribute or Relation?

In Chapter 2, I defined an attribute as a characteristic of an entity that we choose not to represent as a relation with another entity, and instead we use literal values (i.e., numbers, strings, dates, etc.). I used the term "choose" deliberately as, in my view, there's not really a strict and conceptual distinction between attributes and relations that you should always apply in your models. What ultimately matters, as in the previous dilemmas, is the extent to which you care to semantically describe the values of your entity's characteristic in your model.

As an example, let's revisit Table 2-3 from Chapter 2, which contains some attributes and relations that DBpedia defines for the class `Film`. According to DBpedia, a film's original language is defined as a relation `originalLanguage` [210] that links film instances with instances of the class `Language` [211]. This class, in turn, semantically describes individual human languages, with attributes and relations like `iso6391Code` or `languageFamily`. On the other hand, the color type of a film [212] is defined as an attribute that can take some string as a value for which we don't get to know anything else.

Now imagine that you are modeling the same information in your own Film ontology and you don't care so much about the semantics of human languages, but it's important for you to model everything you know about the different color types a film can have. Then it makes more sense to define `originalLanguage` as an attribute and `filmColourType` as a relation.

In practice, there are some characteristics that we almost never model as relations, like those that take as values numbers or dates. In theory, we could do it by defining specific numbers as entities, like DBpedia does in some cases [213] [214], and use them as relation objects. However, that would be rather strange and highly impractical, especially for characteristics that can take an infinite number of possible values.

To Fuzzify or Not to Fuzzify?

In Chapter 6 we saw how ignoring the vagueness that characterizes a semantic model can cause problems to the latter's development, application, and evolution. We also saw how we can identify and document our model's vagueness in an effort to prevent misunderstandings and misuses of it by humans. Now we will see if we can represent vagueness in a way that makes it more machine-processable via a technique commonly known as *fuzzification*.

The idea of *concept fuzzification* was first advanced by Dr. Lotfi Zadeh of the University of California at Berkeley in the 1960s [215]. Its basic premise is that we can assign a real number to a vague statement, within a range from 0 to 1. A value of 1 would mean that the statement is completely true, a value of 0 means that it is completely false, and any value in between that is "partly true" to a given, quantifiable extent. Thus, for example, whereas in a classical semantic model we would say that "John is an instance of YoungPerson" or that "Google hasCompetitor Microsoft," in a fuzzy one we could say that "John is an instance of YoungPerson to a degree of 0.8" or that "Google hasCompetitor Microsoft B to a degree of 0.4."

While it can be hard to philosophically ground the nature of fuzzy truth degrees, it is important to understand that they are not probabilities. A probability statement is about quantifying the likelihood of events or facts whose truth conditions are well defined to *come true* (e.g., "it will rain tomorrow with a probability of 0.8"), while a fuzzy statement is about quantifying the extent to which events or facts whose truth conditions are undefined can *be perceived as true*. That's the reason why they are supported by different mathematical frameworks, namely probability theory and fuzzy logic, that treat probability degrees very different from fuzzy ones.

While different, probabilities and fuzzy degrees have one thing in common: they both try to reduce the undesired effects of their underlying phenomenon, namely uncertainty and vagueness. Thus, in the same way that a probability, if calculated correctly, can effectively reduce the uncertainty about a certain outcome, a truth degree, also if calculated correctly, can effectively reduce the disagreements around the truth of a vague statement.

What Fuzzification Involves

Before we see under what circumstances fuzzification is a good choice to tackle vagueness, we need first to understand the tasks and challenges it involves. Given a semantic model that may have vague elements, here are the main steps needed for its fuzzification:

1. *Detect and analyze all vague elements.* In this step you need to identify which of your model's elements have a vague meaning, as well the type (qualitative or quantitative), potential dimensions, and applicability contexts of their vagueness.

2. *Decide how to fuzzify each element.* Depending on the outcome of step 1, you will have different options for how to fuzzify each vague element of your model, so you will need to pick one that serves you best.

3. *Harvest fuzzy degrees.* In this step you need to set up and apply some mechanism or process for acquiring fuzzy degrees for each vague element.

4. *Assess fuzzy model quality.* In this step you need to evaluate the model with respect to the quality dimensions we saw in Chapter 4, but with a focus on its fuzziness.

5. *Represent fuzzy degrees.* In this step you need to come up with a way to incorporate the fuzzy degrees in your model's representation.

6. *Apply the fuzzy model.* In this step you need to enable the systems and applications that (are meant to) use the model to take advantage of the fuzzy degrees and improve their effectiveness.

We have already discussed step 1 in "Detecting and Describing Vagueness" on page 100; let's see now what the rest of the steps are all about.

Fuzzification options

The number and kind of fuzzy degrees you need to acquire for your model's vague elements depend on the latter's vagueness type and dimensions.

If your element has quantitative vagueness in one dimension, then all you need is a fuzzy membership function that maps numerical values of the dimension to fuzzy degrees in the range [0,1]. For example, let's say you have the classes YoungPerson, MiddleAgedPerson, and OldPerson that are quantitatively vague in the dimension of age. Then, for each of them you can define functions like the ones in Figure 12-3, which will give you a fuzzy degree for every possible age a person has.

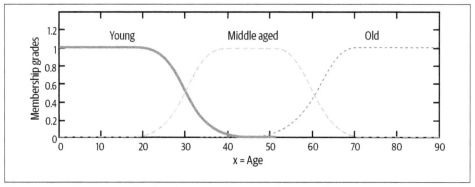

Figure 12-3. Fuzzy membership functions for age-related predicates

Thus, for instance, if Maria is 30 years old then, according to these functions, she will be considered an instance of YoungPerson to a degree of 0.5, of MiddleAgedPerson also to a degree of 0.5, and of OldPerson to a degree of 0. Similar functions can be defined for other quantitatively vague predicates like Tall (as a function of height), Fat (as a function of weight or body mass index), or Expensive (as a function of price). Some commonly used fuzzy membership functions are shown in Figure 12-4.

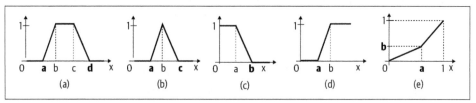

Figure 12-4. Commonly used fuzzy membership functions: (a) trapezoidal function, (b) triangular function, (c) left-shoulder function, (d) right-shoulder function, and (e) linear function

Now, if an element has quantitative vagueness in more than one dimension, then things become a bit more complicated. One option is to define a multivariate fuzzy membership function like the one in Figure 12-5, i.e., a function with one variable for each dimension. For example, if you have the class CompetitorCompany that you have identified as quantitatively vague in the dimensions of revenue and employee count, then you could define a two-variable function based on these dimensions. Obviously, as the number of dimensions increases, the complexity becomes higher.

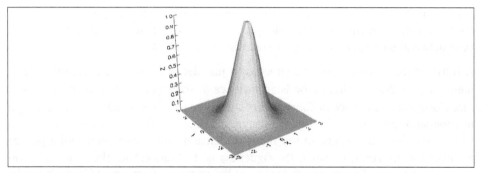

Figure 12-5. Example of a two-variable fuzzy membership function

Another option is to define one membership function per dimension and then combine these via some fuzzy logic operation, like fuzzy conjunction or fuzzy disjunction [216]. These two operations are implemented in fuzzy logic via *t-norms* and *t-conorms*, namely functions that take two truth degrees and combine them into one, preserving the behavior of classical conjunction and disjunction on the values 0 and 1.

The most popular t-norms in the fuzzy logic literature are:

- The minimum t-norm T(a,b) = min(a,b), also called the Gödel t-norm, that gives as output the minimum of the two degrees
- The product t-norm T(a,b) = a · b that gives as output the product of the two degrees
- The Łukasiewicz t-norm T(a,b) = max(0, a+b-1)

Accordingly, the most popular t-conorms are:

- The maximum t-conorm max(a,b), which is dual to the Gödel t-norm, and gives as output the minimum of the two degrees
- The probabilistic Sum t-conorm sum(a, b) = a + b − a · b, which is dual to the Product t-norm
- The bounded sum t-conorm min(a+b,1) which is dual to the Łukasiewicz t-norm.

For example, considering again the class CompetitorCompany, you could define the classes SimilarRevenueCompany and SimilarEmployeeCountCompany with their respective membership functions, and define CompetitorCompany as the fuzzy conjunction of them. Then, for a given company you could determine the degree to which it is an instance of each of these two classes and get the degree to which it is an instance of CompetitorCompany by applying to them the t-norm of your choice.

Unfortunately, there are no hard-and-fast rules for selecting the optimal t-norm for your domain or application scenario [217] [218], so you need to experiment with your data and with experts or users to see which works best.

A third option to define fuzzy degrees is to just define one direct degree per statement, i.e., say directly that Maria is an instance of `YoungPerson` to a degree of 0.5 or that Google is an instance of `CompetitorCompany` to a degree of 0.3, without having a membership function on the age or revenue dimensions. This approach makes sense when your element is vague in too many dimensions and you cannot find a proper membership function, or when its vagueness is qualitative and, thus, you have no dimensions to use. The drawback is that, as the number of statements in your model grows, you will have to harvest degrees for them instead of just generating them from some already defined membership function.

Harvesting truth degrees

Now, let's see how we can harvest truth degrees and membership functions. Remember again that vague statements are characterized by the existence of blurry boundaries and by a high degree of subjectivity, therefore they are expected to provoke disagreements and debates among people or even among people and systems. For example, it might be that two product managers disagree on what the most important features of a given product are or that two salesmen cannot decide what amount of sales is considered to be low. Similarly, it might be that the user of a recommendation system does not agree with the system's classification of "expensive" and "non-expensive" restaurants. To generate fuzzy degrees for these statements you need to *capture and quantify* these disagreements.

For the capturing part, you need to design and deploy an appropriate mechanism that allows you to gather vague assertions, both positive and negative (e.g., "A budget of €100,000 is low," "John is not expert in ontologies," etc.). This mechanism can take many forms, depending on the available resources and application context of your model, but here are some ideas:

Ask people directly
The idea here is to directly ask human judges about the truth of a vague statement. This can be done through a workshop, a survey, or even a crowdsourcing campaign, depending on the number of statements and the number/type of people you need. The benefits of this approach are structure and control, as it's easier to select your judges, ensure they understand the questions, and gather/process any additional feedback they may have. On the other hand, it's an approach that does not easily scale and, depending on the people involved, can be way too slow. For example, you can't expect to ask a philosophy expert whether Socrates influenced Plato and receive a simple yes/no answer. In all cases, remember from Chapter 7 that vagueness is noncomplementary (i.e., that "not tall" is not

necessarily the same as "short"), so you have to be careful how you pose your questions (i.e., if you want to get the degrees for tall, don't ask "Is John short?").

Ask people indirectly

The idea here is to ask human judges about the truth of a vague statement, but in an indirect way, typically in the context of an application. For example, if your model is used by a restaurant recommendation system and you want to harvest a fuzzy membership function for the `ExpensiveRestaurant` class, you can have your system accompany each recommendation with a relevant explanation (e.g., "I recommend this restaurant because its average price is $50 per person and you prefer expensive restaurants") and ask the users whether they agree with this explanation. The advantage of this approach is that it feels more natural, takes context in mind and, in theory, provides a good incentive to the user to give this information, namely to receive more accurate recommendations. In that sense, it's more scalable than the direct approach. On the other hand, it's less predictable, reliable, and controllable, and requires a smart design and incorporation of the harvesting mechanism into the overall system so that the latter is effective without being overbearing.

Mine them from data

The idea here is to take advantage of large pools of controversial information that you may have available, such as discussions, debates, or reviews, and extract from them vague statements by using natural language processing and other knowledge extraction techniques (see Chapter 5). For example, you could use restaurant reviews to identify what prices are typically perceived as expensive, or film reviews to see what films people characterize as comedies. The obvious advantage of this approach is scalability and complete automation. The disadvantage, though, is the high level of noise that the data may have (comments and reviews can be notoriously polarized and badly structured) and which can lead to highly inaccurate extracted assertions.

As soon as you have vague assertions for your model's elements, you can transform them into truth degrees and membership functions using a variety of techniques found in the literature [219] [220] [221]. In general, it is quite difficult to come up with a single fuzzification method that will work for most applications; instead, you will most likely need to use several of them in tandem, depending on your domain, target elements, and data or people available.

Fuzzy model quality

As with crisp semantic models, it very important that you measure the quality of a fuzzy model. Here are the main questions you need to ask yourself:

Have I fuzzified the correct elements?

In Chapter 3 we saw how vagueness is often confused with other phenomena like uncertainty or ambiguity. So it's pretty important that all the elements of your model that you have fuzzified can indeed have borderline cases.

Are the truth degrees accurate?

It's hard to talk about accuracy in the presence of borderline cases and disagreements, but remember that the whole goal of truth degrees is to smoothen these disagreements. So, the truth degrees of a vague element can be considered as accurate not when they have specific golden values, but rather when their values are perceived as natural and intuitive by those who use the model. For example, the fuzzy statement "*Monty Python and the Holy Grail* is an instance of Comedy Film to a degree of 0.2" is highly unintuitive (and therefore inaccurate), while the statement "Sergey Brin is an instance of RichPerson to a degree of 0.8" makes more sense. Someone might argue that the degree of the second statement should be 0.85 instead of 0.8, but even if that were the case, 0.8 is still a pretty close approximation (as opposed to 0.3, for example). Therefore, the accuracy of fuzzy degrees is best captured via some fuzzy distance metric [222] [223].

Are the truth degrees consistent?

As with a crisp model, a fuzzy model can also contain contradicting information. For example, the fuzzy statements "*Monty Python and the Holy Grail* is an instance of ComedyFilm to a degree of 0.9" and "*Monty Python and the Holy Grail* is an instance of ComedyFilm to a degree of 0.3" are inconsistent. As with accuracy, it's best to treat inconsistency in truth degrees not as a binary metric but rather as a distance.

Is the provenance of the truth degrees well documented?

As we saw in Chapter 6, knowing the provenance of a semantic model is pretty important for its understandability and reusability, and that's even more important in the presence of vagueness and truth degrees. For example, if your model suggests that "Hadoop is an essential skill for a Data Scientist to a degree of 0.9," I want to know the data and process by which you ended up with this degree.

Pay Attention to Fuzzification Bias

As any semantic modeling decision, fuzzification can be susceptible to bias and might have a negative impact on certain people and social groups if we are not careful. Determining, for example, the degree to which a particular age classifies a person as "old" can have important ramifications for persons of that age if this degree is used by an insurance company to decide their premiums.

Representing fuzzy models

No matter how good the fuzzy degrees and membership functions that you have managed to harvest are, they are not of much use if they are not effectively incorporated into your model. Unfortunately, most of the current semantic modeling languages and frameworks do not inherently support the representation (and reasoning with) fuzzy degrees; there have been several efforts to create fuzzy extensions of frameworks like OWL [224] [225] [226] or E-R models [227], but these have been mostly academic approaches rather than industry-strength ones. In any case, should you decide in favor of fuzzification, you can either pick and use one of these academic frameworks or develop your own fuzzy extension on your framework of choice.

The latter option makes more sense when your fuzzy model is not too complex. For example, to represent a truth degree for a relation you simply need to define a relation attribute named "truth degree" or similar. This is straightforward if you work with E-R models or property graphs, but also possible in RDF or OWL, even if these languages do not directly support relation attributes. Figure 12-6 shows how the fuzzy statement "Jane is expert in Data Science to a degree of 0.6" can be represented without the need for a relation attribute by modeling the expertise relation as an entity.

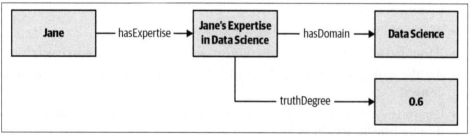

Figure 12-6. Representation of a fuzzy relation when relation attributes are not allowed

On the other hand, things can become more difficult when you need to represent fuzzy membership functions like the ones in Figure 12-3 or more complex fuzzy rules and axioms, along with their necessary reasoning support; in such a case it might be worth reusing some existing framework, albeit academic.

Applying a fuzzy model

This last step might not look like a semantic modeling task, yet it is a crucial one if you want your fuzzification effort to pay off. As we saw in Chapters 8, 9, and 10, unless your model is simply meant as a description of a domain without being used by any specific application, it's imperative that you work together with the application developers to ensure that your model is used in the most effective way and manages to improve the application's quality. The same applies for fuzziness, in the sense that a semantic application is not always capable of processing and benefiting from truth degrees without additional research and development.

In my experience, a fuzzified model can be helpful in tasks like semantic tagging and disambiguation, or semantic search and match, though with proper design and adaptation of the underlying algorithms. In the next sections I describe a couple of fuzzification stories that illustrate exactly this point.

When to Fuzzify

Considering the steps involved in the fuzzification of a semantic model, you can see that is not an easy task to carry out. The main reason for that is the difficulty and cost of acquiring and maintaining truth degrees; a task that, unless you manage to effectively automate it, can be pretty hard to scale. Also, the lack of standard fuzzy semantic modeling frameworks can be a hurdle. So, before you embark on a fuzzification journey, you need to assess whether it makes sense for your model, domain, and context. For that, you need to have answers to the following questions:

- Which elements in your model are unavoidably vague?
- How severe and impactful are the disagreements you (expect to) have on the veracity of these vague elements?
- Are these disagreements caused by vagueness or other factors?
- If your model's elements had fuzzy degrees, would you get less disagreement?
- Are the applications that use the model able to exploit and benefit from truth degrees?
- Can you develop a scalable way to get and maintain fuzzy degrees that costs less than the benefits they bring you?

The first three questions are about sizing the vagueness problem. Question one is important as there's no point in considering fuzzification for a model without vagueness. Therefore, you first need to ensure that you have vague elements in your model, being careful not to detect vague elements that are actually crisp, just described in a vague way (see "Detecting and Describing Vagueness" on page 100).

The second question, in turn, reflects the fact that, while we can all agree that vagueness can be a problem, in practice we don't really know how much of a problem it actually is until we measure its consequences. For example, if different people keep disagreeing in a severe way on what constitutes a "LargeBudget," and this disagreement significantly slows down the decision-making process, then truth degrees may be helpful.

To measure the level of disagreement, all you need to do is give the same set of statements to different people, ask them to characterize them as true or false, and then apply some statistical inter-agreement measure or other, like Cohen's Kappa [228]. On the other hand, to measure the impact of these disagreements you need to monitor closely how the model is used in practice and how it affects applications and processes.

For example, assume that you have a semantic model about films that contains a (vague) relation between individual films and the genre(s) these belong to. Assume also that this relation is used as a feature in a machine learning–based film recommendation system. You can always measure the disagreement intensity of the relation by asking different people whether they believe that particular films belong to particular genres. But you will not be able to know if this intensity has an impact on the effectiveness of your recommendation system until you apply a feature engineering process to it and assess the effect of the vague relation.

In all cases, remember that the existence of vagueness in your model does not exclude the existence of uncertainty or ambiguity. That's why, in the third question, you need to ensure that the root of your disagreement problems is not caused by uncertainty or ambiguity, otherwise fuzzification will neither be appropriate nor helpful.

The next two questions are about examining whether, and to what extent, fuzzification can actually tackle the vagueness problem. The fourth question highlights the fact that even with fuzzy degrees you may not really get reduced disagreement on your model's veracity. This can be for many reasons, from not having the ability to generate the right degrees, to vagueness being so intense that even the degrees cannot tame it.

The fifth question, in turn, suggests that even with less disagreement, the applications that use your model may not be able to really improve their effectiveness. This can be for technical reasons (the application might need a major refactoring to be able to accommodate fuzzy degrees), for algorithmic ones (the application's algorithms might need a major redesign to use the fuzzy degrees in any useful way), or even because you had miscalculated the vagueness impact in the first place.

The best way to answer questions four and five is through A/B testing, i.e., creating two versions of your model, one with truth degrees and one without, and comparing them. For question four, you would need to compare the inter-agreement scores of the two models, while for question five, you would need to compare the effectiveness of the end system or process when using the one model and when using the other. In the film recommendation example, this would translate into testing whether a fuzzified version of the film-genre relation results in higher recommendation accuracy.

Finally, the sixth is the most important question of all: if you cannot develop a scalable and cost-effective way to acquire (and maintain) fuzzy degrees for your model, then any benefit you may get from their potential usage may just not be worth it.

Fuzzification Is Not an Excuse for Not Documenting Vagueness

Fuzzifying a vague semantic model does not reduce the need for documenting the characteristics of the model's vagueness (types, dimensions, applicability contexts, provenance); it actually increases it. Not only do you need this information to guide the definition and harvesting of fuzzy degrees and membership functions for your vague elements, but you also need to complement it with information about the sources and methods you used to perform the fuzzification.

Two Fuzzification Stories

Now let's look at two cases where the fuzzification of a semantic model managed to improve the effectiveness of the application it powered.

Fuzzy electricity

In Chapter 10, I mentioned a project I worked on in 2008 involving the development of a semantic information access system for the Greek electricity market domain. A core component of that system was a domain ontology representing semantic information about processes, actions, participants, and other entities related to the electricity market.

If you revisit the main relations of the ontology as shown in Table 10-8, you will notice that three of them were actually vague (`isImportantPartOfProcess`, `isImportantPartOfAction`, and `isInterestedInTheProcess`). During the design of the ontology with the help of domain experts, we didn't really manage to make them crisp and reach a consensus on their applicability criteria. For that, we decided to fuzzify them by asking our domain experts which entities should be linked through these relations, and transforming their disagreements into fuzzy degrees. From this exercise we derived, for example, that the process "Issuing of Distribution Orders" is an important part of "Distribution Process" to a degree of 0.5, while the participant "Producer of Distributed Unit" is interested in the process "Issuing of Distribution Orders" to a degree of 0.9.

To test whether this fuzzification had any meaningful impact on the effectiveness of the search engine, we measured the latter using two versions of the ontology, the non-fuzzy one and the fuzzy one. For our experiment, we used a golden set of 25 queries together with their corresponding ideal system responses (ground truth). The results indicated that the fuzzified version of the ontology increased both the precision and recall of search by approximately 7%.

Fuzzy actors and fuzzy warriors

In "Two Entity Resolution Stories" on page 178, I mentioned Knowledge Tagger (KT), an entity resolution system that I had developed while working at iSOCO. In addition to entity resolution, KT was also performing *thematic scope resolution* in texts using relevant domain ontologies and semantic data as background knowledge. The thematic scope of a document can be defined as the set of semantic entities the document actually talks about. For example, the scope of a film review is typically the film the review is about, while a biographical note's scope includes the person whose life is described.

KT was useful in application scenarios where the documents' domain(s) and content nature were a priori known (or could be easily predicted) and comprehensive semantic models covering these domain(s) were available (either purposely built or from existing sources such as Linked Data). By content nature, I mean the types of semantic entities and relations that are expected to be found in the documents. For example, in film reviews one can expect to find mentions of films along with the directors and actors who have directed and appeared in them, respectively. Similarly, in texts describing historical events one will probably find, among other things, military conflicts, locations where these conflicts took place, and people and groups that participated in them. Documents with known content nature can be found in many application scenarios where content is specialized and focused (e.g., reviews, scientific publications, textbooks, reports, etc.).

Given such scenarios, KT targeted the task of thematic scope resolution based on the following intuition: a given entity is more likely to fall within the thematic scope of a text when the latter contains several additional entities that are semantically related to it. These related entities can be seen as *evidence* whose quantitative and qualitative characteristics can be used to determine the most probable thematic scope of the text.

To see why this assumption makes sense, assume a cinema-related text like so:

> *Annie Hall* is a much better movie than *Deconstructing Harry*, mainly because Alvy Singer is such a well-formed character and Diane Keaton gives the performance of her life.

In this text, the evidence provided by the entities `Alvy Singer` (a character in the movie *Annie Hall*), and `Diane Keaton` (an actress in the movie *Annie Hall*) indicates that *Annie Hall* is more likely to be the movie the text is about rather than *Deconstructing Harry*.

While developing KT, we performed several evaluations of it, using publicly available crisp semantic models as background knowledge. At some point we wondered what would happen if these semantic models were fuzzy, i.e., whether the quantification of the vagueness that characterizes the semantic models could increase the evidential power of their entities and consequently KT's entity and scope resolution effectiveness.

For example, in the film domain, instead of having just the relation `hasPlayedInFilm` that linked actors and films, it may be more useful to have the fuzzy relation `wasAnImportantActorInFilm` and relate specific actors to film using fuzzy degrees (e.g., "Robert Duvall was an important actor in *Apocalypse Now* to a degree of 0.6"). To see why this can possibly work, consider the following text:

> Robert Duvall's brilliant performance in the film showed that his choice by Francis Ford Coppola was wise.

If Duvall and Coppola have collaborated on more than one film, but Duvall had a major role in only one of them (as captured by the fuzzy degree of his relation to the film), then this film is more likely to be the subject of this text.

To answer this question, we performed two comparative experiments with KT in two different scenarios [229]. In the first scenario we focused on tagging film review texts with the film their review was actually about. Although we had available a set of 25,000 IMDb reviews to use as data, the need to have a comprehensive fuzzy ontology for them made us select only a small subset, consisting of 100 reviews in the end. These reviews contained about 20 distinct films that were similar to each other in terms of genre, actors, and directors, and thus more difficult to distinguish between them in a given review. For these films we derived a crisp ontology from Freebase and we created, in a manual fashion, a fuzzy version of it that comprised the following elements:

Classes
- `Film`
- `Actor`
- `Director`
- `Character`

Fuzzy relations
- `wasAnImportantActorInFilm(Actor, Film)`
- `isFamousForDirectingFilm(Director, Film)`
- `wasanImportantCharacterInFilm(Character, Film)`

Using this fuzzy ontology within KT (after slightly modifying its scope resolution algorithm to be able to take advantage the ontology's fuzzy degrees) we used the latter to determine for each review a ranked list of possible films it may refer to and we measured the effectiveness of the process by determining the number of correctly tagged texts, namely texts whose highest ranked films were the correct ones. For comparison purposes, we performed the same process using the crisp version of the film ontology (i.e., all fuzzy degrees were equal to 1). The results showed that by using the fuzzy ontology, KT improved its accuracy by 10%.

As a second experiment we used KT to tag a set of one hundred texts describing military conflicts with the conflicts they were actually about. This time, the fuzzy ontology we created was based on DBpedia and comprised the following elements:

Classes
- `Location`
- `Military Conflict`
- `Military Person`

Fuzzy relations
- `tookPlaceNearLocation(Military Conflict, Location)`
- `wasAnImportantPartOfConflict(Military Conflict, Military Conflict)`
- `playedMajorRoleInConflict(Military Person, Military Conflict)`
- `isNearToLocation(Location, Location)`

Following the same comparative evaluation process as with film reviews, we measured an improvement in accuracy of 13%.

Summary

This chapter kicked off the "Dilemmas" part of the book by describing cases where the same semantic information can be modeled in more than one way, even within the same modeling language. As with any dilemma, there is not a clearly correct or wrong way to do things and, in order to decide what's best for you, you really need to analyze your context. For that, you can use the questions I have provided for each dilemma and, based on the answers you get, decide what is best for your context.

Important things to remember:

- Useful subclasses are those that have additional attributes, relations, or other characteristics compared to their parent class, and these characteristics are commonly used in the domain of discourse
- Avoid subclasses with low rigidity as they are harder to maintain
- Choose to represent an entity's characteristic as a relation instead of an attribute if you care to semantically describe the meaning of this characteristic's values
- Fuzzy degrees are not probabilities

- Truth fuzzification makes sense only when it manages to reduce disagreements over the validity of a model's vague statements, and the benefits of this reduction outweigh the fuzzification effort and cost
- Truth fuzzification increases the need for documenting the vagueness of a model

The next chapter continues in a similar fashion to this one but with dilemmas about what should be included in a semantic model and what should be left out, so as to achieve the right balance of expressivity and content you need, without wasting effort and resources.

CHAPTER 13

Expressiveness and Content Dilemmas

I don't know how much more expressive you can get than being a rock and roll singer.
—Robert Plant

In this chapter, we deal with dilemmas about what should be included in a semantic model and what can (or should) be left out. As a model creator, this will help you achieve the right balance of expressivity and content that your model needs without wasting effort and resources. As a model user, on the other hand, you will be able to better understand the rationale behind certain expressiveness and content choices that different models make (e.g., not having complete lexicalizations of entities, or representing multiple truths) and adjust your expectations accordingly.

What Lexicalizations to Have?

Some 30 years ago, when I was a kid, I used to watch a sportscaster on a Greek TV station who would routinely refer to the English Premier League soccer clubs by their nicknames: "the Gunners" for Arsenal F.C., "the Citizens" for Manchester City, "the Magpies" for Newcastle United. I had no idea why he did that and, in the beginning, I was annoyed because I couldn't understand him. After several viewings of his sportscasts, though, I also started calling these teams by their nicknames instead of their formal names, and I bet I wasn't the only one to adopt these nicknames. Thirty years later, every time I build a semantic model and I need to provide lexicalizations for its entities, I can't help but think: What would this sportscaster call them?

As we saw in Chapter 2, lexicalizations of a semantic model element are terms that can be used to refer to the element in natural language. There are mainly two reasons we need such terms in our models:

- *To clarify further the meaning of the elements.* No matter how clear and unambiguous an element's name may be, complementing it with some of its most common synonyms helps make its meaning clearer and more explicit.

- *To enable applications to detect the elements in textual resources.* An application that would try to analyze the aforementioned sportscaster's transcriptions for mentions of soccer clubs without the knowledge of the clubs' nicknames would most likely fail.

Now, do these two reasons mean that we should strive to have in our models as many lexicalizations as possible? Well, in theory yes, in practice no. Why? Because of ambiguity.

Let me explain. Assume that we have a semantic model of technology concepts that is used by an application to detect mentions of them in news articles. If we decide to use the term *Tomcat* as a lexicalization of the entity "Apache Tomcat" then we increase the likelihood that mentions of other entities with the same lexicalization (e.g., the namesake animal) are erroneously detected. The same will happen if we use the term *NLP* for "Natural Language Processing" as the particular acronym may also refer to the concept of "Neuro-Linguistic Programming."

In other words, as we keep adding lexicalizations to an element, the probability that we add ambiguous terms increases. And if the applications that use these lexicalizations cannot handle their ambiguity very well, they will suffer from low precision.

Thus, the dilemma we have here can be expressed as follows: "Given a semantic model element (entity, relation, or other) and one or more possible lexicalizations of it, which of these lexicalizations should we keep?"

To tackle this dilemma, you first need to consider how the model will be used. If it's just for browsing or reference, you don't need a lot of lexicalization; the element's name plus one or two common lexicalizations will suffice. But even if you add ambiguous lexicalizations this won't be a problem, provided, of course, that you have additional names and descriptions that make it unambiguous for a human user.

On the other hand, if you want to use your model as part of a semantic tagging detection and resolution system (just like we saw in Chapter 10), then you need to consider and assess the impact of adding a candidate lexicalization. The ideal way to do this is as follows.

First, create two versions of your semantic tagging system, one where the model does not include the candidate lexicalization and one where it does. Then run both versions of the system on the same data and derive the subset of them where the second system's tagging is different from the first one's. Then evaluate the difference to see if it is positive or negative and by how much. If the difference contains more correct taggings than wrong ones, then it's probably safe to keep the term. Of course, you might want to assess the difference in a qualitative manner as the introduced wrong taggings may be more important than the correct ones. In any case, knowing the impact of the added lexicalization will help you decide what to do.

Now, if you need to add lexicalizations to your model in large batches, or very frequently, assessing their potential ambiguity by manually checking their tagging difference can become too cumbersome and resource-intensive. To accelerate the process, there are a number of things you can do:

- *Evaluate only the quantitative characteristics of the tagging difference.* Instead of looking one by one at the different taggings that the addition of the lexicalization has produced and judging whether or not they are correct, you can just consider their numbers and look for any abnormal or unexpected patterns. For example, let's say that you are detecting technology entities in news articles and you know that roughly 30% of these articles are about technology. Let's also say that your current system detects such entities in around 15% of these articles. If by adding some lexicalization, this number skyrockets, to let's say, 40% of the articles, then most likely your added lexicalization is ambiguous. The inverse is not necessarily true; the absence of such an increase does not mean that you haven't introduced ambiguity, just that, if you have, it's not that obvious.

- *Look for already known ambiguity in existing semantic models.* The lexicalization terms you are introducing might already be lexicalizations of other elements, both in your own model and external ones, like WordNet or DBpedia. The higher the number of these elements is, the higher the probability that your added lexicalizations will negatively affect the effectiveness of your tagging system. Of course, it all depends on the quality (accuracy and coverage) and scope of the external semantic models with respect to your target data, as it might be that highly ambiguous terms in these models are unambiguous in your data, and vice versa. For that, you need to be careful what external models you use.

- *Look for ambiguity using some word sense induction method.* Word sense induction (WSI) is the task of automatically discovering multiple senses of a word (e.g., discovering that the word *pen* can mean the ink-based writing instrument or be short for the word *penitentiary*, which is a correctional institution for those convicted of major crimes). For this purpose, several methods and techniques have been proposed in the research literature [230] [231] [232] [233]. Applying such a method to your target data can potentially give you an idea of how many different meanings your candidate lexicalizations may have. In case you don't have any data or external semantic models available, you can still get an idea of the probability that a lexicalization will be ambiguous, through some simple heuristics.

- *Check if the term is a shorter version of the element's name (or other lexicalization of it) with fewer words.* Elements with multiword names are often expressed in natural language with fewer words (e.g., Apache Hadoop is just referred to as

"Hadoop," or Microsoft Excel as "Excel"). In some cases, these mentions are not ambiguous (e.g., "Hadoop" is pretty unambiguous), but in many others they are (e.g., "Excel" can also mean "doing extremely well"). In general, the removal of one or more words from a term is more likely to broaden/alter its range of meanings than keep it the same. These additional words are usually there for a reason.

- *Check if the term is an acronym of the element's name (or other lexicalization of it).* Acronyms are notoriously ambiguous so unless your data's domain is very narrow, you need to be extra careful with them.

- *Check if the term is a translation of the element's name (or other lexicalization of it) in some other language.* Pretty often a term that is unambiguous in one language ends up being ambiguous when it is translated in another. For example, the English term *data retrieval* is translated into Spanish as *recuperación de datos*, yet the latter term can also mean *data restoration*. Similarly, the Italian term *commercio elettronico* can mean both *electronic commerce* and *electronic trading* in English, which are different concepts.

- *Contemplate the different parts of speech the term can assume in a sentence.* Several terms can be both verbs and nouns (e.g., watch, sail, damage), nouns and adjectives (e.g., light, fine, fair), or other combinations. You should expect that these terms will be highly ambiguous unless your tagging system has a very strong part-of-speech disambiguation capability.

- *Check the number of words the term has.* In general, the more words a term has, the less likely it is that it has multiple meanings.

Beware of Controversial, Insulting, or Discriminatory (Lack of) Lexicalizations

Apart from ambiguous lexicalizations it might be risky to have in your model lexicalizations of entities or other elements that are highly controversial, politically, socially, or otherwise. Many events, like the Armenian genocide of the 1920s, for example, are not recognized as "real" by certain countries. At the same time, not having certain elements in your model might be considered discriminatory, like not having gender-neutral lexicalizations of occupation concepts.

A final question is what you do with the lexicalizations you decide you don't want in your model; do you do something with them or just ignore them? My recommendation is keep them, just don't use them yet because these lexicalizations will come in handy when you have (or decide to develop) a semantic tagging system with better disambiguation capabilities.

Lexicalizations You Can Live Without

If, for any reason, you need to limit the number of lexicalizations in your model, you can probably omit those that do not appear very frequently in your target data or those for which you already have a shorter version (e.g., keep the term `PowerPoint` and ditch the term `Microsoft PowerPoint`). You need to be careful, though, as some of these "redundant" terms might actually have some value. For instance, keeping the lexicalization `Microsoft PowerPoint`, even though `PowerPoint` is unambiguous enough, can help the tagging system avoid matching the term `Microsoft` to some other concept every time it encounters `Microsoft PowerPoint` in a text.

How Granular to Be?

In Chapter 7, I mentioned that we often define incorrect synonyms in a semantic model because we need to include certain terms that we don't want to model as distinct entities or other elements, so we add them as lexicalizations of existing ones. I also suggested that when we consciously do that we should make it explicit that our model's lexicalizations are not synonyms. However, I didn't say that we shouldn't do that at all; while defining incorrect synonyms is a pitfall to avoid, not making certain semantic distinctions is actually a choice, albeit difficult.

Let me explain. In an ideal semantic model all distinct meanings of a term should be modeled as different elements, and the same should be the case for two or more terms that have different meanings. In a real-world model, however, this may be too difficult and impractical, for several reasons:

Semantic distinctions can be complex and expensive
    Depending on the complexity and specifications of your model, defining a new element may mean having to define several additional other elements (entities, lexicalizations, attributes, axioms, etc.). Moreover, the more subtle or less known a semantic distinction is, the more research and additional information you need in order to make it explicit in your model and to your users. If, for example, you want to model the terms `violin` and `fiddle` as distinct entities (even though in most dictionaries they are considered the same), you will need to somehow express in your model that their difference is their playing style (folk for `fiddle` and classical for `violin`). Similarly, if you want to distinguish between a `Data Scientist` and a `Data Analyst` you will need to determine and represent the skills and activities where they typically differ.

Semantic distinctions can be subjective
    As a practitioner of semantic data modeling, I can be pretty conscious of (and sensitive to) the nuances of different semantic artifacts, like an *ontology* and a *taxonomy*. On the other hand, I am not a hardcore fan of the science fiction

genre, so I wouldn't know (or care about) the differences between some of its subgenres, like *Biopunk* and *Nanopunk*. The opposite probably applies for a science fiction film expert. Thus, it can be that the very detailed and granular semantic model that we try hard to build might not be of much use to its users.

Semantic distinctions can make disambiguation harder

The more meanings a term might have, the more challenging its disambiguation can be, especially when the differences between these meanings are too subtle. For example, determining whether the term *apple* in a text refers to the fruit or the company is relatively easy as the two meanings are very different and typically appear in very different contexts. On the other hand, determining whether the term *fabrication* refers to "the act of making something (a product) from raw materials" or "the act of constructing something as a piece of machinery" is much more difficult. Moreover, semantic distinctions that are unambiguous in one language can be ambiguous in another. *Welding* and *soldering*, for example, are both translated as *soudage* in French.

Semantic distinctions can make semantic matching harder

Another reason why we may not want a semantic distinction is that it makes the process of semantic matching easier. Assume, for example, that a violin player is looking for a job and a music band is looking for a fiddle player. In order for a system to semantically match the player's résumé with the band's vacancy, it needs its underlying semantic model to contain a semantic relatedness relation between the concepts of *fiddle* and *violin*. If, instead, the two concepts were one, then there wouldn't be a need for such a relation.

Thus, the dilemma we have here can be expressed as follows: "Given one or more terms that have very similar yet different meanings, should we model these meanings as distinct semantic model elements or as the same?"

To tackle this dilemma, you need to consider the following questions:

- *Are the differences in meaning substantial and pragmatic, or benign and theoretical?* If you look hard enough on the web for differences in the meanings of very close terms, you will almost always find some. Thus, the real question is whether these differences are important and applicable enough to justify a distinction in your model. For example, if you look on Google for the differences between a software engineer and a software developer, you will get that "Software Engineer is a professional who applies the principles of software engineering for designing, development, maintenance, testing, and evaluation of computer software" whereas "Software Developer is a professional who builds software which runs across various types of computers" [234]. For me this difference is benign (if not a bit artificial) and I wouldn't care to represent it in my model. What do you think?

- *What are the consequences of (not) making the distinction?* It might be that if you don't make the distinction between `Software Developer` and `Software Engineer`, an angry mob of the latter will come to you to complain. It might also be that if you make it, the analytics you run on labor market data will give you distorted or strange insights. And it might be that whatever you do nobody will notice. In other words, you need to have a way to assess the potential impact of your decision and preserve your energy and resources for the distinctions that really matter.

- *Can you support the distinction?* The less obvious a semantic distinction between two or more elements is, the more specialized information about them you need to include in your model (names, textual definitions, relations, attributes, or axioms) that makes their differences more explicit than their similarities. Moreover, you might need particular knowledge acquisition sources that you don't have, complex elements that your modeling framework doesn't support, or advanced features that the applications that use your model don't yet provide. All these are factors that should ultimately weigh in on your decision.

In the end, the odds are that your model will be imbalanced in terms of granularity; some parts will be more granular and others more coarse. This is to be expected, and it won't be so big of a problem as long as the different granularity levels are aligned with what the model's users and applications can tolerate and handle. And, in all cases, you need to make sure that these different levels are clearly communicated via your model's documentation.

How General to Be?

In Chapter 2, we saw the distinction between concrete and abstract entities, based on whether an entity has a physical existence in space and time, or not. A second interpretation of abstractness is related to the generality or specificity of an entity, i.e., the quantity of domain-specific information contained in it. Some entities are more general than others, in the sense that their meaning is pretty broad, usually spans across multiple domains, and is specialized by many more specific entities.

The entity `Analysis`, for example, as "the detailed examination of the elements or structure of something" [235] is quite general and gives rise to several narrower entities in different domains, such as `Chemical Analysis`, `Data Analysis`, `Historical Analysis`, and others. The same happens for concepts like `Management` (in the sense of "the process of dealing with or controlling things or people"), `Operation` (in the sense of "the action of functioning or the fact of being active or in effect"), or `Technology` (in the sense of "the application of the knowledge and usage of tools and techniques to control one's environment"). Table 13-1 contains additional examples of some very general concepts.

Table 13-1. Some very general entities

Entity	Meaning
Technology	The application of the knowledge and usage of tools and techniques to control one's environment
Design	The act of working out the form of something
Acquisition	The act of contracting or assuming or acquiring possession of something
Diagnosis	The identification of the nature or cause of some phenomenon
Dilution	The action of making something weaker in force, content, or value
Engineering	The practical application of technical and scientific knowledge to commerce or industry
Science	The intellectual and practical activity encompassing the systematic study of the structure and behavior of the physical and natural world through observation and experiment
Security	The state of being free from danger or threat

A common mistake is to call an entity ambiguous just because it is very general. For example, if I tell you that I am an engineer, you will most likely ask me what kind of an engineer I am (e.g., a civil engineer or a software engineer). But even if I don't give you that information, you will still get to know that I am "a person who uses scientific knowledge to solve practical problems," as WordNet suggests [236]. In other words, highly general entities are not necessarily ambiguous.

On the other hand, very generic entities have a very interesting and potentially problematic characteristic: their generic meaning is often forgotten or ignored, and their lexicalizations tend to refer to narrower entities when used in natural language.

For example, if you are at a dinner party and you say "My work is related to technology," most people around you will think you work in the electronics or software industry, even though your assertion would be correct if you worked in a company producing agricultural technology. Similarly, if the same people hear you talking on the phone saying "The diagnosis was good," they will immediately think that you just got the results of some medical exams.

This behavior seems to indicate that when the meaning of an entity is too broad, its informational value might be too low and its usage might make disambiguation harder. Moreover, defining and using very general entities can be quite difficult for both semantic modelers and domain experts.

One piece of evidence of that difficulty is the fact that there is currently no generally accepted and standardized upper ontology in use. Another one is an experiment reported by Stevens et al. [237] where the authors asked eight BFO experts to classify 46 commonly known entities from the domain of travel with BFO entities. The resulting classification was highly inconsistent, with the mean agreement of the participants with the classification decisions of an expert panel being only 51%, and the inter-rater agreement (using Fleiss Kappa) being a mere 0.52.

Thus, the dilemma we have here is whether it's worth including very general entities in our model. To tackle this, I have two pieces of advice:

Evaluate the informational value and potential ambiguity of your general entities
When asked about a general entity, do people immediately think something more specific of it? If you give it to them in an application, do they suggest it's of no use to them? If yes, then the entity does not really have an informational value and it's pretty likely that will cause high ambiguity at natural language level. For example, if your semantic search users write *analysis* in a search query, it's actually more useful to ask them what kind of analysis they want rather than giving them all results related to this entity. Similarly, if these users always have a particular kind of analysis in mind when making this query, giving them all kinds because you could not disambiguate well enough, is actually something they won't appreciate! In such cases, you may want to have this entity in your model but exclude it from particular usages.

Add general entities to your models "on demand" and only when it's actually necessary and useful
If, for example, you have a taxonomy whose root concept is `Civil Engineering`, don't add `Engineering` on top without good reason. If you are building a model for a specific domain, don't do it by taking an upper ontology and start specializing its entities. And if you want to interlink your model with other models, find the minimum generalization that will do the trick.

How Negative to Be?

If you go to Wikidata and look for the famous philosopher and mathematician Bertrand Russell [238], you will find a lot of information about him, including where he was born, where he died, who his spouses were, and which other philosophers influenced his work. On the other hand, you will not find any information about where he was not born, where he did not die, which people he didn't marry, or which philosophers he was not influenced by. Similarly, if you go to DBpedia and look for the entity `Data Science` [239], you will find the entities that have the same meaning as it in other semantic models (through the relation `owl:sameAs`), but not the entities that do not. In other words, in both cases, you won't find any *negative assertions* that explicitly state that something isn't true.

Now, I am not saying that this is necessarily a bad practice. For example, it would be totally absurd for Wikidata to define all the places Bertrand Russell was not born, not only because they are too many, but also because it already contains the place he was born in, and we all know that a person can be born into exactly one place. Similarly, it would be an overkill for DBpedia to state all the external entities `Data Science` is different from. I can't refrain from thinking, though, that it would be extremely useful if

DBpedia explicitly listed those external entities that seem to be the same as its own `Data Science` but are actually not.

In practice, negative assertions in a semantic model can give us information that positive assertions (or the lack of them) cannot. If we want to state that someone is not tall we can't just say that they are short, nor if a person has lived in Canada can we infer that they haven't lived elsewhere. On the other hand, it's completely impractical to add to our model all the possible assertions that are not true, plus it might be that the modeling framework we need to use does not support negation, so we want to avoid it as much as possible. So, how can we decide what negative knowledge to add and what to leave out?

From my experience, it makes sense to explicitly add negative assertions in your model when:

They cannot be inferred or replaced by means of other elements
> For example, if your modeling language allows you to define that the relation `is born in` can only relate a person to exactly one location, then you don't need to add all the locations a particular person wasn't born in, just state their actual birthplace. Similarly, if you want to state that John is not alive and you have defined `LivePerson` and `DeadPerson` as complementary classes in your model, then you can just assert he is an instance of `DeadPerson` without also saying that he is not an instance of `LivePerson`. But you cannot do the same with the classes `TallPerson` and `ShortPerson` as vague classes are not complementary (see Chapter 7 for this pitfall).

They are an important part of some element's meaning
> For example, it might be that in an ontology about political philosophy it's important to state for Karl Marx that he did not believe in the elimination of most physical labor and for Friedrich Hayek that he did not believe that all taxation was incompatible with freedom. Similarly, in a semantic model that describes educational courses, you might want to explicitly state what learning outcomes a particular course does not cover.

They refute common beliefs or assumptions that many people or other models mistakenly consider to be true
> For example, you might want to explicitly state that "Earth is not flat," "Agnosticism is not a religion," "A data scientist is not the same as a data engineer," or "Parkinson's disease is not fatal."

They help you improve information extraction systems or other applications
> For example, you might have a supervised entity recognition system that erroneously suggests particular terms in a text are `Organization` entities. You can then use explicit assertions in your model that this is not the case to reject the same

suggestions the next time they appear, as well as to retrain and improve the system.

In other words, you should treat negative knowledge with the same care and consideration as you do with positive knowledge.

How Many Truths to Handle?

As we learned in earlier chapters, the truth of a vague statement can be highly subjective and context-dependent. Stephen Curry's height of 191 cm (6′2″), for example, makes him short by NBA standards but tall with respect to the general population. An annual income of $25,000 classifies a person as middle class in some countries, but as lower class in others. And a behavior that is interpreted as rude in some cultures (e.g., not tipping) is considered perfectly normal in others.

Now, in theory, a semantic model that contains context-dependent statements should explicitly represent all the contexts in which these statements are true (or false in the case of negative knowledge). In practice, however, such a task might be quite difficult for the following reasons:

The contexts might be too many
Imagine that every single statement in your model has to express its truth for 10, 100, or even more contexts. Unless you are able to do this completely automatically, the creation and maintenance overhead can be too much.

The contexts might be unknown or hard to identify and express
In some cases the contexts that your model needs to keep in mind will be easily identifiable and discernible, but in others they won't. Try asking a board of directors in a large corporation what different contexts they have in their mind when they evaluate a business strategy and see if you get a crisp and consensual answer. Or a group of diners what contexts affect their judgment of a restaurant as expensive or not. In both cases, you might need considerable effort to identify and rigorously define these contexts.

The applications that consume the model might not be able to work with contexts
Imagine an application that merely wants to know what skills a data scientist needs to have. If your model defines different skill sets per industry, location, or other context, which set should this application use?

To determine whether and to what extent you should contextualize your semantic model, you can use a similar set of criteria as those we saw in Chapter 12 for deciding whether or not to fuzzify a model. That is, it's worth contextualizing when:

- The level of disagreement on the veracity of your model is high and consensus is difficult to achieve

- You are able to identify truth contexts in a cost-effective way
- The applications that use the model can actually handle and benefit from contextualized elements
- Contextualization actually manages to reduce disagreements and have a positive effect on the model's applications
- The benefits of contextualization outweigh the context management overhead

Should you decide to contextualize, my advice is to start simple and aim for the minimum viable number, granularity, and complexity of contexts. If, for example, you decide to contextualize based on location, try first to see if using continents or countries does the trick, before you consider cities or postal codes. Similarly, if your contexts are the business functions of an organization, start with the core functions (e.g., finance, R&D, operations) before diving into the detailed structure of the organization.

The problem with more complex context models (e.g., a taxonomy of locations or an ontology of business processes) is that, apart from representing them, you will also need to reason with them. If, for example, a statement is true in Europe, then you want to be able to infer that it is also true in all European countries. Conversely, if a statement is true in some European countries and false in others, you will need a way to infer the truth of the statement in Europe. Can you think of a formula for that?

A final note: truth contextualization and truth fuzzification are complementary approaches rather than alternative ones. Even with contextualization you still may be getting disagreements within the same context, so you might need to fuzzify. And even with fuzzification you still may be getting disagreements on the fuzzy degrees and membership functions of your elements, so you might want to contextualize these as well.

How Interlinked to Be?

In 2006, Sir Tim Berners-Lee, the inventor of the World Wide Web, published an influential note suggesting four rules for the publication of data on the (semantic) web [240]:

1. Use Uniform Resource Identifiers (URIs) as names for things
2. Use HTTP URIs so that people can look up those names
3. When someone looks up a URI, provide useful information about it using relevant standards (e.g., RDF)
4. Include links to other URIs so that they can discover more things

Now, as Berners-Lee admits, these rules are best seen as recommendations and best practices rather than something to be enforced, the idea being that the more people follow them, the more their data will be usable by others. With all due respect, I disagree; my data and semantic models (and most likely yours) won't automatically become more valuable just by interlinking them with other external data. In fact, the opposite may happen. Therefore, a careful risk-benefit analysis of the interlinking is important.

Let me explain. If you come to me and tell me that my semantic data model should be interlinked with yours, I will immediately do the following:

- *Scrutinize your model's quality and compatibility with my own.* As it may have become obvious from all the previous chapters in this book, my a priori trust toward existing semantic models is pretty low, not because my models are necessarily better, but because their goals, strategy, and quality requirements are most likely different (to refresh your memory, see "Bad Mapping and Interlinking" on page 113 and "When data is wrong" on page 135). And if I cannot trust your model, I won't invest in interlinking with it.

- *Demand to know your model's management and evolution strategy.* Interlinking my semantic model to yours means that every time you change something in it, the interlinking might need to be updated (e.g., if you decide to split an entity into two new entities). Moreover, this change may affect my model in a negative way (e.g., introduce ambiguity that I am not able to handle). For that, I need to know how often you are expected to change your model, and what kind of changes you are expected to make. I know I will have no control and/or opinion on how you manage your model (and that's fine), but if the latter changes too often in unpredictable and potentially harmful ways for me, I will just not interlink with it.

- *Assess the cost and effort of interlinking.* Merging, mapping, or interlinking two or more different semantic models can be a difficult and costly process that requires substantial human labor despite the promises of automatic approaches. The reason for that is not so much that the different technology or modeling languages of the different models, but rather that the different contexts in which they have been created and are being used and evolved. If our models are relatively compatible and cost-effective to interlink (and maintain this interlinking), then I probably won't object to moving forward.

- *Assess the benefits of interlinking.* The ultimate question is what benefit I get from interlinking to your model. For me, the main reason to do it is if your model is a widely adopted standard in my domain or industry, which means that by ignoring it, my applications and services will not be able to easily interoperate with other important systems and organizations. If I am merely interested in your model's content, I prefer to merge it with my model whenever and however I choose, rather than tying the two together.

A case that exemplifies this attitude and approach is the work my team at Textkernel did in 2017 when we faced the dilemma of whether we should interlink our labor market knowledge graph with the ESCO classification for occupations and skills that was officially released in October of that year.

On the surface, the two models had pretty similar structure and content; a taxonomy of profession concepts with lexicalizations in multiple languages, a similar taxonomy of skill concepts, and relations linking professions to semantically related skills. On closer inspection, however, several key differences were revealed.

For starters, the granularity of different subdomains in the two models was pretty different. ESCO, for example, did not make a distinction between a `Data Scientist` and a `Data Engineer`, nor between `Finance` and `Economics`, while the Textkernel knowledge graph did. On the other hand, ESCO made a distinction between speaking, understanding, and writing a particular language, while the Textkernel knowledge graph did not. That meant that finding exact matches between concepts was not a straightforward task.

Second, lexicalizations of ESCO entities were not optimized for detecting and disambiguating the latter in texts in the way the Textkernel entities were (see Chapter 10 for ways to do that). As such, we couldn't just accept them in our graph as is. The same was the case for the essential/optional relations that ESCO defined between professions and skills; they seemed pretty arbitrary, not well documented with respect to the criteria used to populate them, and quite inaccurate when benchmarked against our data.

On the other hand, ESCO was set to become a shared standard among public employment agencies in Europe, so business-wise it was pretty important for Textkernel to support it. Also, it contained useful lexicalizations in languages that were missing from our graph. And, evolution-wise, it was a pretty stable model; changes would happen once a year, typically affecting a very small part of it.

Based on all these, we decided on a middle-ground interlinking approach: we linked our model's entities to the ones of ESCO's, but we explicitly disallowed any additional information about these entities that ESCO provided (lexicalizations, attributes, related entities, etc.) to automatically enter our model. Instead, we carefully selected whatever ESCO information we thought was useful, correct, and compatible with our model's semantics, and incorporated it.

Summary

This chapter made clear that what elements we put into a semantic model do not depend merely on the data and domain(s) we wish to model, but also on our ability to manage and apply these elements in an effective and efficient way. When the resources and technology you have at your disposal are limited, you need to make conscious and informed choices about how elaborate and rich your models can realistically be. To that end, the questions, techniques, and guidelines I described in this chapter can help you make such choices for a variety of semantic expressivity dilemmas.

Important things to remember:

- The lexicalizations of a semantic model's elements are useful to the extent their ambiguity does not cause problems to the model's applications and users. Add them with care.
- Semantic distinctions can be complex and expensive; focus on those that matter.
- Very general concepts can be problematic and not so useful; use them carefully.
- In presence of intense vagueness, contemplate truth contextualization.
- Truth contextualization is orthogonal to truth fuzzification.
- Don't neglect negative knowledge; it can be more useful and reliable than positive knowledge.
- Interlinking is not always beneficial; do it when it provides value, and with care.

The next chapter shifts the discussion from dilemmas related to content and expressivity to dilemmas related to the evolution and governance of semantic models.

CHAPTER 14

Evolution and Governance Dilemmas

It is not the strongest or the most intelligent who will survive but those who can best manage change.
—Leon C. Megginson

Semantic models are dynamic artifacts that need to evolve over time if they are to maintain and improve their quality and usefulness. Typical model evolution tasks include fixing quality issues, adding structure and content to cover additional domains or applications, or removing elements that are no longer valid due to semantic change.

Moreover, as we saw in Chapter 11, it's very important that this evolution is done in a controlled and strategy-compatible way, meaning that an effective model governance system needs to be in place. In this chapter I describe some key dilemmas related to these two major tasks and discuss ways to tackle them.

Model Evolution

Evolution is a very important aspect in the life cycle of a semantic model that you can only avoid caring about if:

The model's first version has the quality you need/want in all the relevant dimensions
If this first version has quality problems in one or more relevant dimensions (accuracy, completeness, etc.), you will need to fix these problems in subsequent versions.

There are no external forces that may cause this quality to deteriorate
Such forces include changes in the model's existing domains (e.g., new knowledge being added or existing knowledge becoming invalid), scope (e.g., new

domains or applications to support), and/or quality requirements (e.g., need for higher accuracy).

If at least one of these conditions is not met, then it's imperative that you have in place an evolution strategy for your model that will define, among others, how often will it be updated, in what ways, and to what extent. Let's see some key dilemmas to consider when crafting such a strategy.

Remember or Forget?

A semantic model's evolution includes not only adding new statements to it, but also removing ones that are either not valid or relevant anymore, or that should not have been there in the first place. A question that arises when we perform such removals, though, is what we should do with the removed statements; should we just delete them and forget they ever existed (or leave them be in previous versions of the model), or should we somehow "recycle" them and also keep them in the updated version of the model, in one form or another?

To answer this question, you need to assess whether the removed statements have any usefulness and value in the updated model. This can be the case when:

The statements have a high risk of reappearing
> If certain erroneous statements that you remove keep making their way back into the model because you have no way (yet) to fix their root cause (e.g., by improving the automatic knowledge acquisition system you use), it makes sense to explicitly represent and use their negative version in the model to keep them out (see Chapter 13 for the value of negative knowledge).

The statements have value as historical knowledge
> Certain statements that used to be correct but are not anymore can potentially be useful in the updated model, especially if the latter is to be used for processing historical data. For example, if at some point in time the capital city of a country changes, it makes sense to keep this city in the model as a former capital, as it will still appear in older documents referring to that country. Similarly, a company's current headcount will change over time, yet it might be useful for the HR department to keep the older values in a time-contextualized form (e.g., state in the updated model that the company's headcount at the end of 2019 was 250 people).

Run or Pace?

A second important question your model's evolution strategy needs to answer is how often a new version is going to be created, and how much different it should be from the previous version. That is, is it better to have very frequent but small releases, or infrequent but bigger ones?

As with all dilemmas, the answer is "It depends." Different semantic model producers follow different release patterns. EMSI, for example, a labor market analytics firm, releases a new version of its Skill Taxonomy every two weeks [241], while the EDM Council releases a new version of FIBO every quarter [242]. I don't know exactly how they have decided on these particular frequencies but, in general, the factors that affect a model's evolution pace include:

The pace at which changes in the model are actually needed

> If the model's quality is satisfactory, its domains are relatively static, and no strong business or other forces call for it to change, its evolution pace doesn't need to be high.

The pace at which you are actually able to implement needed changes

> If your model needs regular changes, yet you don't have the time or resources to continuously work on these, then promising short release cycles is not a good idea.

The change value/overhead ratio

> If the release of a new version takes a considerable amount of time and resources, it's probably better to do it only when the changes in your model are significant enough to justify this effort (e.g., a critical quality fix or a substantial number of new entities).

The pace at which changes in the model can be absorbed by the applications or other models that depend on it

> A change in the model does not only affect the model itself, but may also have consequences in all its related artifacts and processes. Imagine, for example, a semantic search system that uses a model to semantically annotate and index a large number of documents. If with every new version of the model the system needs to reindex the documents and this reindexing takes, let's say, three weeks, then weekly model releases might be problematic.

So, how can you determine the optimal evolution pace for your model? Well, first you need to define some minimal criteria and conditions that determine the release-worthiness of a model change. These criteria might be model related, time related, business related, or other. You might say, for example, that any accuracy fix in the model's statements regarding a particular subdomain or element needs to be released as soon as possible. Or that the updated model needs to contain at least 20% additional statements compared to its last version in order to be released. Such rules will help you avoid wasting time on unnecessary releases.

Second, you need to know all your models' dependent artifacts and assess how change-friendly or change-averse they are; that is, what types and amounts of changes they can actually accept and how fast they can respond to them. If two or more artifacts are dependent on the same or overlapping parts of the model but have different change tolerance and responsiveness, then the least tolerant and least responsive will dictate the model's maximum release frequency.

A way to avoid this, and be able to provide more frequent model releases for more responsive applications, is to make your model "skip-safe"; that is, to make it possible for an application to skip some intermediate version of your model without risking not being able to use future ones. At Textkernel, for example, we had to do that when an important client wanted a maximum of one update per quarter of our knowledge graph, while all the others wanted biweekly ones. For that to work, though, we made sure that the biweekly releases were still compatible with that client's application, even if the latter wouldn't use them.

Respect, as Much as Possible, the Unknown Dependents

If your model is a public one (like DBpedia or SNOMED), it will probably have many applications and other models that use or map to it, without you being necessarily aware of them. That means that you may not be able to adjust your model's evolution pace to the needs of all these dependents. That's to be expected and it's not necessarily your responsibility to accommodate all of them. What you can do to make their lives easier, though, is to have a transparent and well-documented evolution strategy for your model that you share with them. This is a good practice not only for public models, but also for commercial ones, as no model user likes unpredictability.

React or Prevent?

Another important question to ask yourself when crafting a model's evolution strategy is whether and to what extent updates will be the result of feedback from the model's users and other stakeholders regarding its quality and features (reactive approach), or of your own efforts and actions to "guess" that feedback before you actually get it (preventive approach).

Being reactive looks like the easy and probably more cost-effective choice, yet it can be risky if you don't have mechanisms in place that are able to capture a comprehensive amount and range of feedback in a reliable and timely manner. *Comprehensive* means that there are no important model aspects for which you are unable to get adequate feedback. *Reliable* means that the feedback you get is noise-free and can be trusted. And *timely* means that this feedback reaches you before it's too late to act on it.

Designing an effective feedback elicitation mechanism for your semantic model is not an easy task. Among others, you need to make sure that:

The feedback you receive is about the model rather than the application that uses the model
Assume, for example, that your model is used in a film semantic search engine and the users of this engine can give feedback regarding the relevance of the results they get for their queries (e.g., with a thumbs up-thumbs down button). If this feedback is negative, it might be because there is something wrong with your model, but it can also be that the problem lies with the engine's results ranking algorithm. Thus, you need a feedback mechanism that is able to separate the two.

The feedback you receive is compatible with the semantics of your model
As we saw in Chapter 8, it's very important that the knowledge sources and acquisition methods you use to develop your model are compatible with its intended semantics. Well, the same applies for the sources and methods you use to get feedback.

You make it easy and worthwhile for people to give you feedback
You might assume that anyone who interacts with your model will be willing to give you feedback, but that's not true. In my career I have used several models, directly and indirectly, but I haven't always given feedback to their creators. Sometimes this was because there was no well-defined and easy procedure to do that; providing an email address or contact form asking people to send you anything they think is wrong with the model does not work. Other times it was because I had the feeling that my feedback would not be considered, at least within a reasonable amount of time. This was especially the case with models that had infrequent or unpredictable updates. I am not saying that all people think like me, just that it's crucial that you understand how your potential feedback sources think and behave, and design your feedback elicitation methods accordingly.

How I Stopped Giving Feedback to Amazon's Recommendation Engine

With regard to the easiness of giving feedback, I have a personal experience to share. Until recently, I was a keen user of Amazon's book recommendation functionality as a way to discover new books to read. A feature that I really liked, and frequently used, was that every recommended item was accompanied by a justification of the form "Item A was recommended to you because you purchased item B," and I was able to tell the system whether it should continue using item B for future recommendations or not.

At some point, though, Amazon changed this. Now in order to give this kind of feedback I need to proactively go to "Improve my recommendations" and choose there what items from my purchase history the engine should use, outside of any concrete context. I am sure Amazon had its reasons for that change, but for me it was so impractical that I haven't given any feedback to them ever since.

While a reactive model evolution strategy requires good feedback mechanisms, a preventive one requires effective tools and processes that can tell you in a timely manner if and what kinds of updates your model might need. For example, either manually or automatically, you could periodically check if:

- The average number of entities your semantic tagging system manages to detect per document has fallen below a certain threshold (evidence that your model's completeness might have decreased)

- The percentage of entities that have no lexicalizations in a given language has fallen below a certain threshold (evidence of linguistic divergence within your model)

- The number of entities that are statistically outliers has increased (evidence that your model's accuracy might have decreased)

- The number of wrong links from third-party models to your model has substantially increased (evidence that your model's understandability might have decreased)

- The number of your model's downloads (paid or free) within the last month has fallen below a certain threshold (evidence that your model's overall value has decreased)

Of course, your proactive inspections might still miss important issues or features that direct feedback could give you. For that you need a healthy balance of proactive and reactive behavior.

To strike such a balance, there are four actions you can take:

1. Consider the different parts of your model and assess how susceptible they are to quality deterioration. For example, you should know if your domain experts have trouble in instantiating a particular vague class and end up providing inaccurate statements. Or if a given relation is so volatile that half of its statements become invalid every month. The more resilient your model is to decay, the more reactive you can afford to be.

2. Assess the importance of your model's different parts and their quality in terms of risks and benefits (see Chapter 9). If the vague class that is prone to wrong instantiations is critical for the effectiveness of an important application, you

need to proactively make sure that its accuracy stays high enough. If, on the other hand, the highly volatile relation is not used that much, you can probably afford to wait until someone complains about it.

3. For each of these parts assess the effectiveness of the feedback mechanisms you have available; the less effective these mechanisms are, the more proactive you need to be.

4. Make sure that you use whatever feedback you can get to fix the underlying issues this signifies, as well as to improve and expand your automatic error detection and quality monitoring capabilities.

Knowing and Acting on Your Semantic Drift

In order to effectively plan and prioritize the maintenance and evolution of a semantic model, it is quite important to have identified the aspects of it that are most volatile and in need of more frequent updates. A key way to do that is by defining and measuring the model's semantic drift, i.e., how and to what extent the model's elements change their meaning over time.

To properly do that, you need to be aware of two things:

The definition of semantic drift for a given model should take into account the latter's content, domain, and application context, and adapt accordingly

While generic formalizations of semantic drift are very useful (like modeling drift in terms of label, intension, and extension), these are not necessarily directly or completely applicable to all domains and/or models. The reason is that not all aspects of a model element's meaning contribute to its drift in the same way and to the same extent.

There is not a unique optimal way to measure semantic drift for a given model, but rather multiple ways whose outcomes can have different interpretations and usages

Indeed, the values one gets when measuring semantic drift can be quite different, depending on the metrics, data sources, and methods/algorithms used for the measurement. Therefore, it is important that a) for a given drift measurement approach, the drift values it produces can be clearly interpreted and used, and b) for a desired interpretation/usage, an appropriate drift measurement method can be selected.

To see why this is the case, let's consider the labor market domain and a (fictional) corresponding knowledge graph, and contemplate how we could model and measure the latter's drift.

Drift modeling

Let's assume that this graph defines and interrelates entities such as professions, skills, and qualifications, for multiple languages and countries. Using the graph, an agent (human or computer system) can answer questions like:

- What are the most important skills for a certain profession?
- What professions are specializations of profession X?
- What qualifications do I need in order to acquire skill Y?

More specifically, let the graph consist of the following entity types:

Professions
> Entities that represent groupings of jobs that involve similar tasks and require similar skills and competencies.

Skills
> Entities that represent tools, techniques, methodologies, areas of knowledge, activities, and generally anything that a person can "have knowledge of," "be experienced in," or "be expert at" (e.g., economics, software development, "doing sales in Africa," etc.). Also, entities that represent personality traits, including communication abilities, personal habits, cognitive or emotional empathy, time management, teamwork, and leadership traits (usually referred to as soft skills).

Qualifications
> Entities that represent "formal outcomes of assessment and validation processes which are obtained when a competent body determines that an individual has achieved learning outcomes to given standards" [243].

Organizations
> Concepts that represent organizations of different types, including public organizations and institutes, private companies and enterprises, educational institutes (of all educational levels), and others.

Industries
> Concepts that represent industrial groupings of companies based on similar products and services, technologies and processes, markets, and other criteria.

The different ways an entity can be expressed in a text (lexicalizations) are represented in the graph via the SKOS relations `skos:prefLabel` and `skos:altLabel`. Moreover, entities can be taxonomically related to other concepts of the same type via the SKOS relations `skos:broader` and `skos:narrower` (e.g., `Software Developer skos:narrower Java Developer` and `Economics skos:narrower Microeconomics`).

Additional relations are defined per concept type. In particular, professions are linked to skills and activities they involve, qualifications that are (formally or informally) required for their exercise (e.g., the bar exam for practicing law in the United States), and to other professions that are similar to them. Skills, in turn, are linked to similar skills and activities, professions they are mostly demanded by, and qualifications that develop and verify them. Finally, qualifications are linked, apart from skills, to organizations that provide them as well as the educational levels they cover.

Assume also that most of the preceding relations are extracted and incorporated into the knowledge graph in a semiautomatic way from a variety of structured and unstructured data sources, such as CVs, job vacancies, or Wikipedia. Moreover, many of these relations are vague, such as the similarity between different skills or the importance of a skill for a profession. As we saw in previous chapters, the problem with vague relations is that their interpretation is highly subjective, context-dependent, and usually a matter of degree, thus making it hard to achieve a global consensus over their veracity. For this reason, in the graph, such assertions could have the following three attributes:

Truth degree
    A number (typically from 0 to 1) indicating the degree to which the assertion is considered to be true (see "To Fuzzify or Not to Fuzzify?" on page 212)

Applicability context
    The contexts (location, language, industry, etc.) in which the assertion has been discovered and considered to be true

Provenance
    Information about how the assertion has been added to the graph (source, method, process)

These properties do not remove vagueness, but they can play an important role in the measurement of semantic drift.

Given all these things, semantic drift is mainly observed in professions, skills, and qualifications. Take journalists, for example. Before the proliferation of the internet and social media, a reporter would have to research stories mainly through contacts, speaking to people, door knocking, and visiting the local library to consult past publications. They also most likely would not know how to do their own video production editing, but would rely on experts to do that for them. Nowadays, however, reporters are more technology savvy, and are able to handle (some of) their own production, expand their research in social media, public databases, and other modern information channels, and analyze/visualize data to make their story more reliable and compelling.

Similar arguments can be made for other professions but also for qualifications and skills. A contemporary degree in finance, for example, definitely has different content and even somewhat different learning objectives than it had 30 years ago. Similarly, being expert in marketing nowadays is highly associated with being expert in search engine optimization and social media.

Now, as we saw in Chapter 3, semantic drift in the semantic modeling literature is usually modeled (and measured) with respect to three aspects of an entity's meaning, namely its lexicalizations (i.e., the terms used to express the concept), its intension (i.e., the concept's characteristics as expressed via its properties and relations), and its extension (i.e., the set of the concept's instances). For this knowledge graph, however, it's not so useful to consider extensions as part of its entities' meaning and drift.

One reason for that is that both skills and professions are rather abstract and they do not have straightforward instances that affect their meaning. One could consider as profession instances the people who exercise them, but then a change in the work-force size does not alter the profession's meaning. Instead, it's the qualitative charac-teristics of this workforce that signify a change, and that's exactly what the entities' intension captures.

Nevertheless, not all attributes and relations of the entities have equal contribution to their meaning and drift. In particular:

- Changes in an entity's lexicalizations do contribute to drift, yet only when they are not merely additions or removals of spelling and/or morphosyntactic varia-tions of existing labels (e.g., part-of-speech or plural form). Moreover, changes in preferred labels could perhaps be considered slightly more important than alter-native labels, as the former are typically more suggestive of the concept's meaning.

- Changes in an entity's `skos:broader` and `skos:narrower` relations also contrib-ute to drift, with `skos:broader` changes suggesting in general a more fundamen-tal drift in the entity's meaning than the `skos:narrower` ones.

- For profession entities, meaning is primarily defined by the skills and activities they involve (see the example of journalists mentioned earlier). Essential skills for a profession are more important than optional skills, though that can be hard to distinguish. Profession meaning also changes, though to a lesser extent, when the industries it is found in change (e.g., journalists start working in the tech sector). On the other hand, a profession entity does not drift when the locations or com-panies it is most popular in, change.

- For skill concepts, meaning is primarily defined by their similar skills and activi-ties, as these describe for what tasks and in what contexts a skill is used. It also changes, though to a lesser extent, when it starts being applied in different pro-fessions and industries, as part of possessing a skill includes having experience in its application contexts.

- For qualification entities, meaning is primarily defined by the skills they develop and/or verify. Secondarily, by the professions they regulate and/or are useful for (especially in some countries, qualifications are the main criterion for entering a profession).

Drift measuring

Now, as we saw in Chapter 3 semantic drift of an entity is typically detected and quantified by measuring the difference in meaning between two or more different versions of the same entity in different points in time, and the more dissimilar the two versions are to each other, the greater the drift is.

Measuring concept meaning similarity is obviously dependent on how meaning is modeled. Thus, for example, in papers by Wang et al. [56] and Stavropoulos et al. [57] where the authors consider as meaning the concept's intension, extension, and lexicalization, they define corresponding similarity functions for each of these aspects. In particular, they employ string similarity metrics for measuring lexicalization drift, and set similarity metrics for measuring intension and extension drift. For the particular labor market graph, we could follow a similar approach, but with some important differences.

First, for lexicalization we shouldn't use string similarity to measure change, one reason being that we don't consider spelling or morphosyntactic change as a drift. Instead, we consider labels as part of the concept's intension and we use set similarity metrics to measure the difference between a concept's changing lexicalization sets.

Second, since many of the entity relations are vague and their validity quantified by some fuzzy degree, when we calculate similarity based on them we should use metrics that can take into consideration this degree. One approach that we can use, for example, is as follows: Given two versions of the same concept and a (vague) relation that influences drift, we can derive the top N related concepts for each version (based on the strength score), and calculate their similarity using a metric that can measure distance between rankings (such as the Kendall Rank Correlation Coefficient [244]). In that way, for example, if the Data Scientist profession continues having the same top 10 related skills but differently ranked, a drift will be detected.

Third, in order to be able to understand and interpret semantic drift better, we need a versatile measurement framework that enables the dynamic and highly configurable measurement and presentation of drift. Such a framework should take as input a set of parameters, specifying the scope, type, and other characteristics of the drift we want to measure, and generate corresponding output. Examples of parameters we can consider are:

- Target concept types (professions, skills, etc.)
- Time scope (either as a specific time period or as specific releases to be included)

- Relations and properties to be included
- Relation applicability context and provenance

The reason we need all these parameters, is that different values of them can yield different drift, not only in terms of intensity, but also in terms of interpretation. For example, if we calculate a concept's drift using only CVs as a data source, then the drift we will measure will reflect the change in the way the workforce side of the labor market interprets and uses the concept. On the other hand, if we use only vacancies, we will get an idea of how the same concept changes from the industry's perspective. Similarly, if we use news articles, we will measure the change in the general perception of the concept, while the usage of more encyclopedic and definitional data sources (e.g., Wikipedia or specialized dictionaries) may indicate changes in more core aspects of the concept's meaning.

Finally, as suggested in the previous section, different relations have different influence to concept drift, and that difference needs to be considered when relation-specific drifts are aggregated. A similar argument can be made for other drift aspects like provenance or context (e.g., the change of a profession concept in a country with a more advanced economy may be more important/crucial than the change in a less developed country). For that reason, the drift framework should support the definition of drift aspect importance weights that are used for combining and aggregating partial drift scores.

Semantic Drift from a User's Perspective

While measuring a model's semantic drift can help its developers determine its evolution strategy, it can also be useful to the model's users. For example, the drift in the preceding labor market knowledge graph could indicate to a large extent the changes that take place in the labor market, especially if the graph's entities are derived from CVs and vacancies. These changes can then be communicated to job seekers, candidate seekers, education and training providers, policy makers, and generally anyone who can gain advantage from knowing the dynamics of the labor market.

For instance, most job holders have a narrow perception of what their profession entails and to what extent and rate it evolves over time, as they usually operate in a narrow context. As a result, when these people become job seekers, they have to change this perception, otherwise they may fail to secure a new job that may have the same title but quite different content. The same applies for organizations that need to hire people but fail to do so, mainly because their job definitions are too restrictive and not in sync with the supply side of the market.

All this illustrates how not all aspects of a semantic modeling element's meaning contribute to its drift in the same way and to the same extent, thus requiring a careful analysis and selection for the domain and semantic model at hand. It also shows how versatile the outcome of measuring drift can be (depending on the metrics, data sources, and methods/algorithms used for the measurement), and how this versatility can actually be useful and, therefore, in need of proper management.

Model Governance

A proper evolution strategy is necessary for ensuring that your semantic models maintain and improve their quality and value, but it's not enough. As we saw in Chapter 11, you also need a model governance system, namely a set of agreed-upon principles, processes, and rules that ensure this strategy's effective and efficient execution.

A fundamental dilemma when designing such a system is deciding how centralized or decentralized it should be. In a completely centralized system the model is governed by a small, relatively homogeneous team of people who are the sole editors of the model and decision makers on what goes into it and what does not. In a completely decentralized system, on the other hand, editing, planning, and decision making are collective activities performed by multiple heterogeneous groups of people, without a central authoritative location or group. Let's see how to determine which approach makes sense for your model.

Democracy, Oligarchy, or Dictatorship?

Both proponents of centralized and decentralized governance have arguments to support their views. Here are some of them:

- Semantic modeling requires technical and domain expertise that only few people can reliably provide. DBpedia's quality problems are caused by its collaborative development.

- Without large-scale collaboration, it's pretty hard or too expensive for a semantic model to evolve fast enough. DBpedia's coverage is the result of Wikipedia's collaborative editing strategy.

- Without diverse opinions and perspectives, a model will definitely contain biases.

- With too many opinions, it's hard to steer the model toward achieving specific goals.

These arguments are valid but they do not necessarily apply to all domains, models, and situations. There are circumstances under which a stricter, more controlled governance approach works better, and circumstances under which a looser and more inclusive approach is preferable. To diagnose your own situation you need to assess the following factors:

The automation degree of your model's development
> The more aspects of your model you develop without human input, the fewer contributors you need.

The modularity of your model
> The more distinct and independent components your model has whose quality does not depend on or affect other parts, the more decentralized you can afford to be.

The automation degree of your quality management and monitoring processes
> The more quality dimensions and metrics you can automatically monitor and measure, the more decentralized you can afford to be.

The (required) breadth, diversity, and vagueness of your model
> The more domains you need to support, the more difficult it is to do it with a handful of experts. Also, the more vague and subjective your elements' meaning is, the more perspectives you need to encompass.

The quality priorities you have
> If completeness is more important than accuracy or conciseness, then you can have more people contributing to the model with more relaxed quality controls.

The expected impact of the changes
> What might seem to be a small change inside the model could have a large impact downstream on consuming applications. An example might be in an ecommerce site where a small class change suddenly makes it harder for end users to find what they want to buy. In such cases, stricter governance may be warranted.

The existence, acceptance, and adoption of shared goals, principles, and practices regarding your model and its development
> If your model's contributors do not share the same goals and priorities, or don't adhere to a common development philosophy, practices, and standards, a more centralized approach might be necessary.

The complexity of your model
> The more advanced modeling skills or domain expertise your model requires, the more difficult it is to have many people contributing to it.

The effectiveness and efficiency of the available conflict resolution and decision-making mechanisms
> The smoother and faster you can resolve conflicts and make collective decisions about your model without sacrificing quality, the more decentralized you can be.

The organization's existing structure and data governance culture

If your model is going to be maintained and evolved in an organization that already has a decentralized data governance culture, there might be a significant resistance to centralization, and vice versa. This is especially the case if the organization or the different stakeholders do not really see a reason to change.

Knowing where you stand with respect to these factors will allow you to define different degrees of (de-)centralization for different governance tasks and aspects of your model.

Clean Slate Versus Legacy

If you are in a situation where you are building a semantic model from scratch, with little legacy to uphold (clean slate), it makes sense to start with a central governance approach and start decentralizing in a gradual and controlled way. If, on the other hand, you are integrating multiple existing models, each with its own governance system, ignoring these systems might not be such a good idea.

A Centralization Story

When I joined Textkernel and started building a team to develop their knowledge graph, the company had already been developing, using, and maintaining several semantic models. These models were mostly disconnected (hence the need for the knowledge graph), but their governance was also rather informal and somewhat problematic.

The main issue was that there were four different teams that had the right to edit these models (apart from mine), though without shared practices and clear guidelines on how to do that. For example, the meaning of certain entity types and relations (e.g., what is a skill, or when are two skill terms synonymous with each other?) was interpreted differently per team, leading to accuracy mistakes. Pretty often, too, people would harm a model's conciseness by adding some new element to it without checking first if this element existed already in some other form. And it was not an uncommon habit for some teams to create a custom version of some model, for a given client or specialized application scenario, without considering the maintenance overhead this customization would bring.

As we were integrating these semantic models to a single knowledge graph, it was pretty obvious that these issues had to be tackled. For that, my team worked closely with all the other teams, initiating the following key changes:

- *We reduced the number of teams that were responsible and accountable for developing and maintaining the knowledge graph from five (mine and the existing four) to two.* Other teams could still contribute to the graph but in less direct and more limited ways.

- *We defined different processes and rules for different parts of the graph and different types of changes.* For example, changes in the graph's schema (a new entity type or a new attribute) required more deliberation, consensus, and good documentation than changes in a particular entity's attribute value.

- *We worked on harmonizing and centrally documenting the definitions of key elements of the knowledge graph, especially when these were vague (such as the definition of a skill).* That included also changing the names of certain elements to make them less ambiguous and vague (see Chapter 6 for that).

- *We increased the number and frequency of (automated) quality controls and alerts.* That allowed for more people to be able to contribute to the graph without the fear that they would "break" something.

- *We established stricter criteria and processes for deciding when the graph should be customized for a particular case or client.* In that way, we ensured that the graph's maintenance overhead would not increase without a good reason.

These changes were not easy and, as I am writing these lines, many of them are still in progress. However, they have already helped make the governance of the Textkernel knowledge graph much smoother and more efficient than before.

Summary

In this chapter we concluded the "Dilemmas" part of the book, having focused on another two very important aspects of a semantic model's life cycle, namely its evolution and governance. You have seen some key dilemmas that model creators face when crafting a strategy for these two aspects, and you have learned what information you need to gather and assess in order to solve them.

Things to remember:

- To effectively plan and prioritize the maintenance and evolution of a semantic model, you need to understand the nature and intensity of its semantic drift and act accordingly

- To model and measure the semantic drift of a model you should take into account the latter's content, domain, and application context, and adapt accordingly

- Centralized model governance is not inherently better or worse than decentralized model governance. Use the modularity of the model, the automation degree of its development, and other factors, to define different degrees of (de-)centralization for different governance tasks and aspects

The next chapter is the final one of this book, wrapping up the key points and insights that you should keep from all the previous chapters, and shifting the discussion to the future of data semantics and, in particular, the things we could/should do in order to tackle the challenges that lie ahead.

CHAPTER 15

Looking Ahead

It's supposed to be automatic, but actually you have to push this button.
—John Brunner, *Stand on Zanzibar*

And so, here we are. You have walked with me on a journey in the world of data semantics, examining many of the quirks and challenges that make it a difficult yet worthwhile world to be part of and work in. Along the way, I hope that you've learned a few tricks that can help you avoid critical pitfalls and break key dilemmas that may otherwise prevent you from building and using high-quality and valuable semantic representations of data.

In this last chapter, I would like to bring together some of the recurring themes of this book, and build on them to envisage the future.

The Map Is Not the Territory

The main reason why I have structured the book around pitfalls and dilemmas and haven't given you a set of recipes for building the perfect semantic model is that I have no idea what such a model looks like for your domain, data, and application context. In other words, my map does not necessarily reflect your territory.

Unless we sit together and do all the work I described in Chapter 11 to craft a tailored strategy for your semantic model and its context, my telling you that you should use one modeling language instead of another, or optimize one quality dimension at the expense of another, is not only ineffective but also irresponsible. Instead, I have chosen to tell you what potential dangers your context might contain and how to avoid them, and what risks you might be taking by making certain choices and decisions and how to mitigate them. In that way you will be able to not only carve your own path, but also effectively navigate it.

Being an Optimist, but Not Naïve

The key premise of this book is that the goal of semantic data modeling is creating descriptions and representations of data that convey—in a clear, accurate, and commonly understood way—those aspects of the data's meaning that are important for their effective interpretation and usage by humans and machines. What the numerous pitfalls and dilemmas we saw throughout the book indicate is that this is still a challenging problem that is nowhere near solved, despite all the developments in semantic technologies, big data processing, natural language processing, and machine learning.

This is not pessimism, but realism. Something we data people tend to forget (or downplay) is the fact that semantics is almost always consensus-based and that building consensus is hard. Yet, a semantic model is only as valuable as the scope of the underlying consensus, and its (correct) usage cannot be guaranteed by parties who disagree with it. And as knowledge graphs and other types of semantic models become larger in size and scope, and are used by bigger and more diverse audiences, their ability to represent consensual information is stressed.

It is thus naïve to start a semantic model initiative without contemplating how to tackle the problem of consensus, and much of the criticism that the Semantic Web has received in the past years is exactly about this. Clay Shirky, for example, a well-regarded thinker on the social and economic effects of internet technologies, published an essay in 2003 where he suggested that the problem with the Semantic Web vision is that "it takes for granted that many important aspects of the world can be specified in an unambiguous and universally agreed-on fashion, and spends a great deal of time talking about the ideal XML formats for those descriptions" [245]. And sixteen years later, in 2019, two prominent Semantic Web researchers from Ghent University wrote an article called "The Semantic Web Identity Crisis: In Search of the Trivialities That Never Were" where, among other things, they stated that "while the call for Linked Data has brought us the eggs, the chickens that were supposed to be hatching them are still missing, partly because making sense of others' data remains hard" [246].

This does not mean that semantic technologies have no value, or that developing semantic models is a futile endeavor; quite the opposite. It means, though, that you should be immune to vendors and consultants claiming that they can build for you a semantic model overnight, with minimal effort, that will make all your organization's data and applications semantically interoperable. Even in small organizations, complexity of domains, data, processes, and systems can be quite high, and expecting that all this complexity will be seamlessly taken care of by a couple of existing semantic models and some software platform, no matter how sophisticated it is, will not serve you well.

Avoiding Tunnel Vision

When I was working as a researcher, my job was to consider a very specific, challenging semantic modeling task, come up with a creative and original method to tackle it, prove somehow that this method works, publish it, and then move on to a new problem. Because of the difficulty and intensity of this kind of work, I rarely had the luxury to think whether, and under what conditions, my solution could actually be applied in a real-world setting. Only when I worked on my first end-to-end industrial semantic modeling project did I realize how one-dimensional and incomplete many of my "innovative" methods were, and how many critical dependencies and prerequisites I had missed or ignored.

This is not to say that research work and specialized methods and tools for particular semantic model development tasks are not important; in our battle to tame semantic heterogeneity, we need the best weapons we can get. At the same time, though, we need to be aware that this battle won't be won by tackling semantic modeling tasks in isolation, but combined as a whole.

You can have, for example, the most expressive semantic modeling language that you could ever wish for, yet this won't be any good if your semantic modelers keep using it incorrectly. You can have an infrastructure that allows you to store and reason with billions of semantic statements, yet this won't be good if you have no efficient way to acquire these statements in an accurate manner. And you can build the most accurate, complete, concise, and relevant semantic model for your organization, yet this model will sooner or later decay if you don't also develop and put in place a proper evolution strategy.

Avoiding Distracting Debates

When we were kids and quarreled with other kids, many of us would say something along the lines of "My dad can beat your dad." Well, things haven't changed much now that we are grown ups; the difference is that now we say things like "My RDF-based model is semantic, but the one you built using property graphs is not," or "My data-driven machine learning–based inference is truer artificial intelligence than your handcrafted concepts and axioms." I find both these debates meaningless and counterproductive because the main thing they manage to achieve is inflexibility and lack of collaboration. Let's see why.

Semantic Versus Nonsemantic Frameworks

If you wear your semantic modeler's hat, you will realize that in order to be able to characterize some data modeling frameworks as semantic and others as not, you need to define the class `Semantic Modeling Framework` in a nonvague way. And something that I hope you have learned from this book is that in order to do this you need to clearly define the necessary and sufficient conditions for an entity to belong to this class. If you cannot find such conditions, then you are not in a position to claim that framework A is definitely semantic and framework B is definitely not.

Another key lesson of the book is that semantic distinctions should be made insofar as they provide some value. Well, for me, trying to prove that a given data modeling framework is not semantic has little to no value. What has value is determining to what extent the features and capabilities the framework provides can help me build the semantic model I need. If, to exaggerate a bit, my needs can be satisfied with a CSV file, why should I be worried that I am not being semantic enough?

To be sure, some modeling frameworks have built-in features that make certain aspects of the semantic model development effort easier and more straightforward than other frameworks. But they also have features and limitations that make other aspects more difficult.

For example, a nice feature of RDF(S) and OWL is that the URI can be used to unambiguously identify a particular entity on the web, similarly to how URLs identify web pages. This makes it easier to publish your semantic model on the web and interlink it to other models that also support URIs. On the other hand, as we saw in Chapter 7, RDF(S) and OWL are implemented with the open-world assumption in mind, making it quite hard to control and reason about your model's contents and structure in isolation from whatever other models it is interlinked to.

Similarly, building a knowledge graph using Neo4j (which implements the labeled property graph paradigm), has its pros and cons. For instance, as we saw in Chapter 2, in a property graph there's no formal distinction between a class and an individual since everything is a node, and while one can use labels as classes, there's no way to define relations between these labels. On the other hand, it is relatively straightforward to add attributes to relations without the need for modeling workarounds like the one shown in Figure 5-3.

A feature that could possibly justify calling a modeling framework more semantic than another is the support of predefined semantic modeling elements with standardized meaning and usage (such as the `rdfs:subClass` and `rdf:type` elements of RDF(S)). There is a caveat, though: these elements are valuable and important insofar as they are correctly interpreted and used as intended by everyone. Otherwise, the ad hoc elements I define and use in my models can be just as good.

In short, obsessing over whether a given modeling framework is semantic or not is not productive. What is productive is taking the time to determine which framework is best for the semantic model you want to build, as well as learning how to use this framework correctly.

Symbolic Knowledge Representation Versus Machine Learning

Knowledge graphs, ontologies, and other types of semantic models represent knowledge and data meaning by means of explicit symbols and logic-based axioms and rules that are first comprehensible to humans, and then to machines. Machine learning models, on the other hand, operate at the subsymbolic level, inducing latent representations of meaning that are first comprehensible to machines and then to humans.

Historically, these two paradigms have often clashed. Proponents of machine learning would dismiss symbolic methods because of their inability to generalize beyond what is known explicitly, as well as their difficulty to scale. Symbolists, in turn, would suggest that machine learning approaches are not able to capture nuanced meaning distinctions and reasoning patterns, but also that they are not trustworthy because their latent representations are not easily interpretable and explainable by humans. So, which paradigm should prevail?

The answer is neither, and the reason is that they both have merits and limitations that make them more appropriate and effective for some applications rather than others. It can be very hard, for example, to build a purely symbolic movie recommendation system that explicitly encodes and applies all the criteria and domain knowledge that film viewers use in their heads when they choose what movie to watch tonight; hence the best-performing of such systems are based on machine learning. On the other hand, in a medical diagnosis or legal decision-making scenario, it can be critical that an automated system is able to distinguish between very similar but ultimately different concepts, and also explain its reasoning process.

In practice, the two approaches should complement each other. As we saw in Chapter 5, if we want to automate and scale the development and evolution of semantic data models, we need to develop and apply machine learning–based knowledge mining methods and tools. Conversely, semantics and deductive reasoning can pre-label data to improve the accuracy of machine learning models, as well as generate explanations for the latter's behavior and output. Moreover, the combination of induction from machine learning and deduction from semantic models can enable systems to deal with types of situations that do not appear in the training data.

Who knows, perhaps 10 to 20 years from now this book will be obsolete as machine learning will have eradicated the need for symbolic representations. Till then, it's more useful to make the best of both worlds.

Doing No Harm

Semantic data models are symbolic abstractions of what humans believe and how they think and, as such, are susceptible to human biases. As semantic modelers we can be tempted to think that the ontologies and taxonomies we build are less biased than machine learning models, because the latter are statistical in nature with obscure reasoning rules, while the former contain only crisp and explicit facts. Yet, this is not necessarily true.

Much of the conceptual knowledge that goes into a semantic model is abstract, vague, and context-dependent, and seemingly neutral debates about the semantic difference between a `Data Scientist` and a `Data Engineer`, or the age threshold that classifies a person as `Old` or `Young` can lead to unintended consequences—whether these are false information being disseminated from a trusted source, or marginalized groups being erased from datasets. Imagine your model's definition of `Old Person` being used by an insurance company to adjust the premiums someone has to pay; how confident would you be that it is correct and objective?

Biases may originate in the very specification of a semantic model, in the algorithms and (human and data) sources that we use to (semi)automatically construct it, in the way we measure quality and the priority we give to certain quality dimensions over others, or even in the strategy we follow for its evolution. And depending on the ways and the scale at which the model is used, these biases may become magnified and spread through different systems. It is therefore crucial that we acknowledge and address the various types of bias in semantic data modeling, and do our best to prevent and reduce their negative effects.

As creators of semantic models that means that for every model-related decision we make, smaller or bigger, we should think (and test) whether someone is harmed. It's also very important that we scrutinize the methods, sources, assumptions, and design decisions we use to develop our models, and that we are transparent and meticulous in documenting them. Conversely, as users of semantic models we should not take them at face value, but actively seek to identify any biases they might contain.

In the end, it's all about transforming the vicious bias cycle into a virtuous one, with well-designed and bias-aware semantic models helping machine learning systems be less biased, and vice versa.

Bridging the Semantic Gap

This book argued that there is a semantic gap between the data practitioners who work on the data supply side and those who work on the data exploitation side, and demonstrated many of the reasons why this happens. Closing the semantic gap is in the best interest of both sides, but it's a very difficult mission.

One reason is that human language and thinking is rife with ambiguity, vagueness, context dependence, semantic drift, and other phenomena that make the formal and universally accepted representation of data semantics a quite difficult task. We can't do much about this, apart from continuing to research novel approaches and methods to tackle these phenomena.

A second reason, however, is that even though we already have at our disposal such methods and techniques and, no matter how effective they are, we apply them in a suboptimal way. This book has shown you how to make better use of the available technology and narrow the semantic gap to the extent that it positively impacts your data and applications, and creates fruitful results of synergy, reuse, and consistency.

The ball is now in your court.

Bibliography

[1] National Center for Biomedical Ontology. "Snomed CT Ontology" (*http://biopor tal.bioontology.org/ontologies/SNOMEDCT*). Last modified November 18, 2019.

[2] European Skills, Competences, Qualifications and Occupations (ESCO). "Occupations" (*https://ec.europa.eu/esco/portal/occupation*). 2017.

[3] AllegroGraph. "Graphs Without Semantics Are Not Enough" (*https://allegro graph.com/property-graphs-are-not-enough*). Last modified June 16, 2018.

[4] Blumauer, Andreas. "Semantic Knowledge Graphs Versus Property Graphs" (*https://www.linkedin.com/pulse/semantic-knowledge-graphs-versus-property-andreas-blumauer*). *Pulse* (blog), LinkedIn. December 11, 2018.

[5] Cagle, Kurt. "Taxonomies vs. Ontologies" (*https://www.forbes.com/sites/cognitive world/2019/03/24/taxonomies-vs-ontologies/#64e28b5a7d53*). *Forbes*. March 24, 2019.

[6] Open Data Science (ODSC). "Where Ontologies End and Knowledge Graphs Begin" (*https://medium.com/predict/where-ontologies-end-and-knowledge-graphs-begin-6fe0cdede1ed*). *Medium*. October 16, 2018.

[7] Singhal, Amit. "Introducing the Knowledge Graph: things, not strings" (*https://blog.google/products/search/introducing-knowledge-graph-things-not*). *The Keyword* (blog), Google. May 26, 2012.

[8] Panetta, Kasey. "5 Trends Emerge in the Gartner Hype Cycle for Emerging Technologies, 2018" (*https://www.gartner.com/smarterwithgartner/5-trends-emerge-in-gartner-hype-cycle-for-emerging-technologies-2018*). *Smarter With Gartner*. August 16, 2018.

[9] Amazon. "How Alexa Keeps Getting Smarter" (*https://blog.aboutamazon.com/devi ces/how-alexa-keeps-getting-smarter*). *Day One* (blog). October 10, 2018.

[10] He, Qi. "Building The LinkedIn Knowledge Graph" (*https://engineering.linkedin.com/blog/2016/10/building-the-linkedin-knowledge-graph*). *LinkedIn Engineering* (blog). October 6, 2016.

[11] Thomson Reuters. "Thomson Reuters Launches First of Its Kind Knowledge Graph Feed Allowing Financial Services Customers to Accelerate Their AI and Digital Strategies" (*https://www.thomsonreuters.com/en/press-releases/2017/october/thomson-reuters-launches-first-of-its-kind-knowledge-graph-feed.html*). Press release, October 23, 2017.

[12] Gao, Yuqing, Anant Narayanan, Alan Patterson, Jamie Taylor, and Anshu Jain. "Enterprise-Scale Knowledge Graphs" (*http://iswc2018.semanticweb.org/wp-content/uploads/2018/10/Panel-all.pdf*). Panel at the International Semantic Web Conference, Monterey, CA, October 2018.

[13] Best, Jo. "IBM Watson: The Inside Story of How the Jeopardy-Winning Supercomputer Was Born, and What It Wants to Do Next" (*https://www.techrepublic.com/article/ibm-watson-the-inside-story-of-how-the-jeopardy-winning-supercomputer-was-born-and-what-it-wants-to-do-next*). *TechRepublic*. September 9, 2013.

[14] Kalyanpur, Aditya, B.K. Boguraev, S. Patwardhan, J.W. Murdock, A. Lally, C. Welty, J.M. Prager, B. Coppola, A. Fokoue-Nkoutche, L. Zhang, Y. Pan, and Z.M. Qiu. "Structured Data and Inference in DeepQA." *IBM Journal of Research and Development* 56, no. 3/4 (May/July 2012): 10:1–10:14. *https://doi.org/10.1147/JRD.2012.2188737*.

[15] Cagle, Kurt. "The Rise of 360° Semantic Data Hubs" (*https://www.forbes.com/sites/cognitiveworld/2018/08/16/holistic-information-the-rise-of-360-semantic-data-hubs/#2db41f1c217a*). *Forbes*. August 16, 2018.

[16] Horrel, Geoffrey. "Intelligent Recommendation Engine for Financial Analysts" (*https://neo4j.com/blog/intelligent-recommendation-engine-financial-analysts*). *Neo4j* (blog). December 7, 2018. Originally presented at GraphConnect New York, October 2017.

[17] Horridge, Matthew. *A Practical Guide To Building OWL Ontologies Using Protégé 4 and CO-ODE Tools*. (*http://mowl-power.cs.man.ac.uk/protegeowltutorial/resources/ProtegeOWLTutorialP4_v1_3.pdf*) University Of Manchester, Manchester, UK, March 24, 2011.

[18] OWL Working Group. "Web Ontology Language (OWL)" (*https://www.w3.org/OWL*). World Wide Web Consortium (W3C). Last modified December 11, 2013.

[19] W3C Working Group. "SKOS Simple Knowledge Organization System Primer" (*https://www.w3.org/TR/skos-primer*). W3C. August 18, 2009.

[20] W3C. "RDF Primer" (*https://www.w3.org/TR/rdf-primer*). February 10, 2004.

[21] W3C. "RDF Schema 1.1" (*https://www.w3.org/TR/rdf-schema*). February 25, 2014

[22] Obitko, Marek. "Description Logics" (*https://www.obitko.com/tutorials/ontologies-semantic-web/description-logics.html*). 2007.

[23] American National Standards Institute/National Information Standards Organization. "Guidelines for the Construction, Format, and Management of Monolingual Controlled Vocabularies" (*https://www.niso.org/publications/ansiniso-z3919-2005-r2010*). May 13, 2010.

[24] Wikipedia. "Entity–Relationship Model" (*https://en.wikipedia.org/wiki/Entity%E2%80%93relationship_model*). Last modified July 1, 2020.

[25] Frisendal, Thomas. "Property Graphs Explained: The Universal Data Model Paradigm" (*http://graphdatamodeling.com/Graph%20Data%20Modeling/GraphData Modeling/page/PropertyGraphs.html*). 2016.

[26] Wikipedia. "Person" (*https://en.wikipedia.org/wiki/Person*). Last modified June 28, 2020.

[27] Arp, Robert and Barry Smith. "Function, Role, and Disposition in Basic Formal Ontology." *Nature Precedings* 1 (1941): 1–4.

[28] Wikipedia. "Song" (*https://en.wikipedia.org/wiki/Song*). Last modified July 14, 2020.

[29] Wikipedia. "Biology" (*https://en.wikipedia.org/wiki/Biology*). Last modified July 10, 2020.

[30] Chen, Peter Pin-Shan. "English, Chinese and ER diagrams." *Data & Knowledge Engineering* 23, no. 1 (June 1997): 5–16. *https://doi.org/10.1016/S0169-023X(97)00017-7.*

[31] Fernández-López, Mariano, Asuncion Gómez-Pérez, and Natalia Juristo. *Methontology: From Ontological Art Towards Ontological Engineering.* AAAI Technical Report SS-97-06, Madrid, Spain, March 1997: 33–40.

[32] Horrocks, Ian, Peter F. Patel-Schneider, Harold Boley, Said Tabet, Benjamin Grosof, and Mike Dean. "SWRL: A Semantic Web Rule Language Combining OWL and RuleML" (*https://www.w3.org/Submission/SWRL*). W3C. May 21, 2004.

[33] Ignatiev, Alexey, Nina Narodytska, and Joao Marques-Silva. "Abduction-Based Explanations for Machine Learning Models." *Proceedings of the Thirty-Third AAAI Conference on Artificial Intelligence (AAAI-19)* 33, no. 1 (2019): 1511–1519. *https://doi.org/10.1609/aaai.v33i01.33011511*

[34] Lucidchart. "Enhanced ER Diagram Tutorial" (*https://www.lucidchart.com/pages/enhanced-entity-relationship-diagram*). Accessed July 16, 2020.

[35] Winston, Morton E., Roger Chaffin, and Douglas Herrmann. "A Taxonomy of Part-Whole Relations." *Cognitive Science* 11, no. 4 (October/December 1987): 417–444. *https://doi.org/10.1016/S0364-0213(87)80015-0*

[36] DBpedia. "About: Machine Learning" (*http://dbpedia.org/page/Machine_learn ing*). Accessed July 16, 2020.

[37] DBpedia. "About: Apprentissage automatique" (*http://fr.dbpedia.org/page/Appren tissage_automatique*). Accessed July 16, 2020.

[38] W3C. "SKOS Mapping Vocabulary Specification" (*https://www.w3.org/2004/02/ skos/mapping/spec/2004-11-11.html*). November 11, 2004.

[39] Princeton University. "Ontology" (*http://wordnetweb.princeton.edu/perl/webwn? s=ontology&sub=Search+Word Net&o2=&o0=1&o8=1&o1=1&o7=&o5=&o9=&o6=&o3=&o4=&h=00*). WordNet. 2010

[40] Cook, Roy T. "Intensional Definition." In *A Dictionary of Philosophical Logic.* Edinburgh: Edinburgh University Press, 2009.

[41] W3C. "PROV-O: The PROV Ontology" (*https://www.w3.org/TR/prov-o*). April 30, 2013.

[42] Wikipedia. "Tripoli" (*https://en.wikipedia.org/wiki/Tripoli*). Last modified July 7, 2020.

[43] Wikipedia. "Tripoli, Lebanon" (*https://en.wikipedia.org/wiki/Tripoli,_Lebanon*). Last modified May 29, 2020.

[44] Wikipedia. "Tripoli, Greece" (*https://en.wikipedia.org/wiki/Tripoli,_Greece*). Last modified June 28, 2020.

[45] Yosef, Mohamed, Johannes Hoffart, Ilaria Bordino, Marc Spaniol, and Gerhard Weikum. "AIDA: An Online Tool for Accurate Disambiguation of Named Entities in Text and Tables." *Proceedings of the VLDB Endowment* 4, no. 12 (2011): 1450–1453. *https://doi.org/10.14778/3402755.3402793.*

[46] Hoffart, Johannes, Fabian M. Suchanek, Klaus Berberich, and Gerhard Weikum. "YAGO2: A Spatially and Temporally Enhanced Knowledge Base from Wikipedia." *Artificial Intelligence* 194 (January 2013): 28–61. *https://doi.org/10.1016/j.artint. 2012.06.001.*

[47] Princeton University. "Heap" (*http://wordnetweb.princeton.edu/perl/webwn? s=heap&sub=Search+Word Net&o2=&o0=1&o8=1&o1=1&o7=&o5=&o9=&o6=&o3=&o4=&h=00*). WordNet. 2010.

[48] Hyde, Dominic. *Vagueness, Logic and Ontology*. Ashgate New Critical Thinking in Philosophy. Abingdon, UK: Routledge, 2008.

[49] Shapiro, Stewart. *Vagueness in Context*. New York: Oxford University Press, 2006.

[50] Shotton, David and Silvio Peroni. "CiTO, the Citation Typing Ontology" (*http://purl.org/spar/cito*). February 16, 2018.

[51] Guarino, Nicola, and Chris Welty. "Ontological Analysis of Taxonomic Relationships." In *Conceptual Modeling – ER 2000*, edited by Alberto H. F. Laender, Stephen W. Liddle, and Veda C. Storey, 210–224. ER 2000. Lecture Notes in Computer Science, vol. 1920. Springer-Verlag Berlin Heidelberg, October 2000.

[52] Guarino, Nicola and Chris Welty. "Evaluating Ontological Decisions with OntoClean." *Communications of the ACM* 45, no. 2 (February 2002): 61–65. *https://doi.org/10.1145/503124.503150*.

[53] Grzega, Joachim. *Bezeichnungswandel: Wie, Warum, Wozu? Ein Beitrag zur englischen und allgemeinen Onomasiologie*. Sprachwissenschaftliche Studienbücher. Heidelberg: Universitätsverlag Winter, 2004.

[54] Bloomfield, Leonard. *Language*. New York: Holt, Rinehart and Winston, 1933.

[55] Blank, Andreas. "Why Do New Meanings Occur? A Cognitive Typology of the Motivations for Lexical Semantic Change." In *Historical Semantics and Cognition*, edited by Andreas Blank and Peter Koch, 61–90. Cognitive Linguistics Research, vol. 13 Berlin: De Gruyter Mouton, 1999. *https://doi.org/10.1515/9783110804195.61*.

[56] Wang, Shenghui, Stefan Schlobach, and Michel C. A. Klein. "Concept Drift and How to Identify It." *Journal of Web Semantics* 9, no. 3 (September 2011): 247–265. *https://doi.org/10.1016/j.websem.2011.05.003*.

[57] Stavropoulos, Thanos G., Stelios Andreadis, Efstratios Kontopoulos, Marina Riga, Panagiotis Mitzias, and Ioannis Kompatsiaris. "SemaDrift: A Protégé Plugin for Measuring Semantic Drift in Ontologies." In *Detection, Representation and Management of Concept Drift in Linked Open Data*, edited by Laura Hollink, Sándor Darányi, Albert Meroño Peñuela, and Efstratios Kontopoulo, 34–41. CEUR Workshop Proceedings, vol. 1799. Bologna, Italy, November 2016.

[58] Fokkens, Antske, Serge Ter Braake, Isa Maks, and Davide Ceolin. "On the Semantics of Concept Drift: Towards Formal Definitions of Concept Drift and Semantic Change." In *Detection, Representation and Management of Concept Drift in Linked Open Data*, edited by Laura Hollink, Sándor Darányi, Albert Meroño Peñuela, and Efstratios Kontopoulo, 10–17. CEUR Workshop Proceedings, vol. 1799. Bologna, Italy, November 2016.

[59] Recchia, Gabriel, Ewan Jones, Paul Nulty, John Regan, and Peter de Bolla. "Tracing Shifting Conceptual Vocabularies Through Time." In *Detection, Representation*

and Management of Concept Drift in Linked Open Data, edited by Laura Hollink, Sándor Darányi, Albert Meroño Peñuela, and Efstratios Kontopoulo, 2–9. CEUR Workshop Proceedings, vol. 1799. Bologna, Italy, November 2016.

[60] Jatowt, Adam and Kevin Duh. "A Framework for Analyzing Semantic Change of Words Across Time." In *JCDL '14: Proceedings of the 14th ACM/IEEE-CS Joint Conference on Digital Libraries*, 229–238. Piscataway, NJ: IEEE Press, September 2014. *https://doi.org/10.1109/JCDL.2014.6970173*.

[61] Gulla, Jon Atle, Geir Solskinnsbakk, Per Myrseth, Veronika Haderlein, and Olga Cerrato. "Semantic Drift in Ontologies." In *Proceedings of the 6th International Conference on Web Information Systems and Technologies* 2, edited by Joaquim Filipe and José Cordeiro, 13–20. Setúbal, Portugal: SciTePress, 2010. *https://doi.org/10.5220/0002788800130020*.

[62] Strasunskas, Darijus, and Stein L. Tomassen. "The Role of Ontology in Enhancing Semantic Searches: The Evoqs Framework and Its Initial Validation." *International Journal of Knowledge and Learning* 4, no. 4 (January 2008): 398–414. *https://doi.org/10.1504/IJKL.2008.022059*.

[63] Thakkar, Harsh, Kemele M. Endris, José M. Giménez-García, Jeremy Debattista, Christoph Lange, and Sören Auer. "Are Linked Datasets Fit for Open-Domain Question Answering? A Quality Assessment." In *WIMS '16: Proceedings of the 6th International Conference on Web Intelligence, Mining and Semantics*, edited by Rajendra Akerkar, Michel Plantié, Sylvie Ranwez, Sébastien Harispe, Anne Laurent, Patrice Bellot, Jacky Montmain, and François Trousset, 1–12. New York: Association for Computing Machinery, June 2016. *https://doi.org/10.1145/2912845.2912857*.

[64] DBpedia. "About: Yugoslavia" (*http://dbpedia.org/page/Yugoslavia*). Accessed July 16, 2020.

[65] DBpedia. "About: Serbia" (*http://dbpedia.org/page/Serbia*). Accessed July 16, 2020.

[66] Camacho-Collados, Jose, Claudio Delli Bovi, Luis Espinosa-Anke, Sergio Oramas, Tommaso Pasini, Enrico Santus, Vered Shwartz, Roberto Navigli, and Horacio Saggion. "SemEval-2018 Task 9: Hypernym Discovery." In *Proceedings of the 12th International Workshop on Semantic Evaluation*, edited by Marianna Apidianaki, Saif M. Mohammad, Jonathan May, Ekaterina Shutova, Steven Bethard, and Marine Carpuat, 712–724. Stroudsburg, PA: Association for Computational Linguistics, June 2018. *https://doi.org/10.18653/v1/S18-1115*.

[67] Weaver, Gabriel Barbara Strickland, and Gregory Crane. "Quantifying the Accuracy of Relational Statements in Wikipedia: a Methodology." In *JCDL '06: Proceedings of the 6th ACM/IEEE-CS Joint Conference on Digital Libraries*, 358. New York: Association for Computing Machinery, June 2006. *https://doi.org/10.1145/1141753.1141853*.

[68] Distaso, Marcia. "Measuring Public Relations Wikipedia Engagement: How Bright is the Rule?" *Public Relations Journal* 6, no. 2 (August 2012): 1–22.

[69] Wikipedia. "Vandalism on Wikipedia" (*https://en.wikipedia.org/wiki/Vandal ism_on_Wikipedia*). Last modified July 4, 2020.

[70] Acosta, Maribel, Amrapali Zaveri, Elena Simperl, Dimitris Kontokostas, Sören Auer, and Jens Lehmann. "Crowdsourcing Linked Data Quality Assessment." In *The Semantic Web—ISWC 2013*, edited by Harith Alani, Lalana Kagal, Achille Fokoue, Paul Groth, Chris Biemann, Josiane Xavier Parreira, Lora Aroyo, Natasha Noy, Chris Welty, and Krzysztof Janowicz, 260–276. ISWC 2013. Lecture Notes in Computer Science, vol. 8219. Springer-Verlag Berlin Heidelberg, 2013. *https://doi.org/ 10.1007/978-3-642-41338-4_17*.

[71] Bizer, Christian and Richard Cyganiak. "Quality-Driven Information Filtering Using the WIQA Policy Framework." *Journal of Web Semantics* 7, no. 1 (January 2009): 1–10. *https://doi.org/10.1016/j.websem.2008.02.005*.

[72] Feeney, Kevin, Declan O'Sullivan, Wei Tai, and Rob Brennan. "Improving Curated Web-Data Quality with Structured Harvesting and Assessment." *International Journal on Semantic Web and Information Systems* 10, no. 2 (April 2014): 35–62. *https://doi.org/10.4018/ijswis.2014040103*.

[73] Paulheim, Heiko and Christian Bizer. "Improving the Quality of Linked Data Using Statistical Distributions." *International Journal on Semantic Web and Information Systems* 10, no. 2 (April 2014): 63–86. *https://doi.org/10.4018/ijswis.2014040104*.

[74] Nakashole, Ndapandula, Martin Theobald, and Gerhard Weikum. "Scalable Knowledge Harvesting with High Precision and High Recall." In *Proceedings of the Fourth ACM International Conference on Web Search and Data Mining*, 227–236. New York: Association for Computing Machinery, February 2011. *https://doi.org/ 10.1145/1935826.1935869*.

[75] Carlson, Andrew, Justin Betteridge, Richard C. Wang, Estevam R. Hruschka, Jr., and Tom M. Mitchell. "Coupled Semisupervised Learning for Information Extraction." In *Proceedings of the Third ACM International Conference on Web Search and Data Mining*, 101–110. New York: Association for Computing Machinery, February 2010. *https://doi.org/10.1145/1718487.1718501*.

[76] Lehmann, Jens, and Lorenz Bühmann. "ORE—A Tool for Repairing and Enriching Knowledge Bases." In *The Semantic Web—ISWC 2010*, edited by Peter F. Patel-Schneider, Yue Pan, Pascal Hitzler, Peter Mika, Lei Zhang, Jeff Z. Pan, Ian Horrocks, and Birte Glimm, 177–193. ISWC 2010. Lecture Notes in Computer Science, vol. 6496. Springer-Verlag Berlin Heidelberg, 2010. *https://doi.org/ 10.1007/978-3-642-17749-1_12*.

[77] Census of Marine Life. "How many species on Earth? About 8.7 million, new estimate says" (*https://www.sciencedaily.com/releases/2011/08/110823180459.htm*). *ScienceDaily*. August 24, 2011.

[78] Färber, Michael, Basil Ell, Carsten Menne, Achim Rettinger, and Frederic Bartscherer. "Linked Data Quality of DBpedia, Freebase, OpenCyc, Wikidata, and YAGO." *Semantic Web* 9, no. 3 (March 2017): 1–53. *https://doi.org/10.3233/SW-170275*.

[79] Paulheim, Heiko and Christian Bizer. "Type Inference on Noisy RDF Data." In *The Semantic Web – ISWC 2013*, edited by Harith Alani, Lalana Kagal, Achille Fokoue, Paul Groth, Chris Biemann, Josiane Xavier Parreira, Lora Aroyo, Natasha Noy, Chris Welty, and Krzysztof Janowicz, 510–525. ISWC 2013. Lecture Notes in Computer Science, vol. 8218. Springer-Verlag Berlin Heidelberg, 2013. *https://doi.org/10.1007/978-3-642-41335-3_32*.

[80] Bizer, Christian. *Quality-Driven Information Filtering in the Context of Web-Based Information Systems*. Riga, Latvia: VDM Verlag Dr. Müller, 2007.

[81] Neo4j. "5.4. Constraints" (*https://neo4j.com/docs/cypher-manual/current/schema/constraints*). Accessed July 16, 2020.

[82] W3C. "OWL 2 Web Ontology Language Profiles (Second Edition)" (*https://www.w3.org/TR/owl2-profiles*). December 11, 2012.

[83] DBpedia. "About: child" (*http://dbpedia.org/ontology/child*). Accessed July 16, 2020.

[84] DBpedia. "About: children" (*http://dbpedia.org/property/children*). Accessed July 16, 2020.

[85] W3C. "The Organization Ontology – 5.3.1 Property: memberOf" (*https://www.w3.org/TR/vocab-org/#property-memberof*) January 16, 2014.

[86] W3C. "The Organization Ontology – 5.3.4 Class: Membership" (*https://www.w3.org/TR/vocab-org/#class-membership*) January 16, 2014.

[87] W3C. "Defining N-ary Relations on the Semantic Web" (*https://www.w3.org/TR/swbp-n-aryRelations*). April 12, 2006.

[88] Guha, Ramanathan, Dan Brickley, and Steve MacBeth. "Schema.org: Evolution of Structured Data on the Web." *Queue* 13, no. 9, (November 2015): 10–37. *https://doi.org/10.1145/2857274.2857276*.

[89] Zaveri, Amrapali, Dimitris Kontokostas, Mohamed A Sherif, Lorenz Bühmann, Mohamed Morsey, Sören Auer, and Jens Lehmann. "User-Driven Quality Evaluation of DBpedia." In *I-SEMANTICS '13: Proceedings of the 9th International Conference on Semantic Systems*, edited by Marta Sabou, Eva Blomqvist, Tommaso Di Noia, Harald

Sack, and Tassilo Pellegrini, 97–104. New York: Association for Computing Machinery, September 2013. *https://doi.org/10.1145/2506182.2506195.*

[90] Freire, Nuno, Valentine Charles, and Antione Isaac. "Evaluation of Schema.org for Aggregation of Cultural Heritage Metadata." In *The Semantic Web*, edited by Aldo Gangemi, Roberto Navigli, Maria-Esther Vidal, Pascal Hitzler, Raphaël Troncy, Laura Hollink, Anna Tordai, and Mehwish Alam, 225–239. ESWC 2018. Lecture Notes in Computer Science, vol. 10843. Springer-Verlag Berlin Heidelberg, 2018. *https://doi.org/10.1007/978-3-319-93417-4_15.*

[91] Source Forge. "Backups for old OpenCyc distributions" (*https://sourceforge.net/projects/opencyc-backups*). Last updated May 8, 2016.

[92] W3C. "SPARQL Query Language for RDF" (*https://www.w3.org/TR/rdf-sparql-query*). January 15, 2008.

[93] Zouaq, Amal and Roger Nkambou "A Survey of Domain Ontology Engineering: Methods and Tools." In *Advances in Intelligent Tutoring Systems*, edited by Roger Nkambou, Jacqueline Bourdeau, and Riichiro Mizoguchi, 103–119. Studies in Computational Intelligence, vol. 308. Springer-Verlag Berlin Heidelberg, 2010. *https://doi.org/10.1007/978-3-642-14363-2_6.*

[94] Ehrlinger, Lisa and Wolfram Wöß. "Towards a Definition of Knowledge Graphs." In *Posters&Demos@SEMANTiCS 2016 and SuCCESS'16 Workshop*, edited by Michael Martin, Martí Cuquet, and Erwin Folmer. CEUR Workshop Proceedings, vol. 1695. Leipzig, Germany, 2016.

[95] Bloomberg. "Bloomberg's 6 Notable Academic Contributions in Machine Learning in 2016" (*https://www.techatbloomberg.com/blog/bloombergs-top-6-academic-contributions-machine-learning-2016/*). *Tech at Bloomberg* (blog). March 17, 2017.

[96] Paulheim, Heiko. "Knowledge Graph Refinement: A Survey of Approaches and Evaluation Methods." *Semantic Web* 8, no. 3 (2017): 489–508. *https://doi.org/10.3233/SW-160218*

[97] Blumauer, Andreas. "From Taxonomies over Ontologies to Knowledge Graphs" (*https://semantic-web.com/2014/07/15/from-taxonomies-over-ontologies-to-knowledge-graphs*). Semantic Web Company. July 15, 2014.

[98] Krötzsch, Markus and Gerhard Weikum. "Web Semantics: Science, Services and Agents on the World Wide Web." *Journal of Web Semantics* 37–38 (March 2016): 53–54. *https://doi.org/10.1016/j.websem.2016.04.002.*

[99] Alexopoulos, Panos. "Building a Large Knowledge Graph for the Recruitment Domain with Textkernel's Ontology" (*https://www.textkernel.com/building-large-knowledge-graph-recruitment-domain/*). *Textkernel* (blog). Last modified December 6, 2019.

[100] Morsey, Mohamed, Jens Lehmann, Sören Auer, Claus Stadler, and Sebastian Hellmann. "DBpedia and the Live Extraction of Structured Data from Wikipedia." *Program: Electronic Library and Information Systems* 46, no. 2 (April 2012): 157–181. *https://doi.org/10.1108/00330331211221828.*

[101] European Commission. *ESCO Handbook.* (*https://ec.europa.eu/esco/portal/docu ment/en/0a89839c-098d-4e34-846c-54cbd5684d24*) 2019. *https://doi.org/ 10.2767/934956.*

[102] Borgo, Stefano and Claudio Masolo. "Ontological Foundations of DOLCE." In *Theory and Applications of Ontology: Computer Applications*, edited by Roberto Poli, Michael Healy, and Achilles Kameas, 279–295. Dordrecht: Springer, 2010. *https:// doi.org/10.1007/978-90-481-8847-5_13.*

[103] Arp, Robert, Barry Smith, and Andrew Spear. *Building Ontologies With Basic Formal Ontology*. Cambridge, MA: MIT Press, July 2015.

[104] W3C. "Pattern 1: Introducing a new class for a relation" (*https:// www.w3.org/TR/swbp-n-aryRelations/#pattern1*). April 12, 2006.

[105] Silverston, Len. *The Data Model Resource Book, Volume 1: A Library of Universal Data Models for All Enterprises*. Revised edition. New York: John Wiley & Sons, 2001.

[106] Silverston, Len. *The Data Model Resource Book, Volume 2: A Library of Data Models for Specific Industries*. Revised edition. New York: John Wiley & Sons, 2001.

[107] Silverston, Len and Paul Agnew. *The Data Model Resource Book, Volume 3: Universal Patterns for Data Modeling*. Indianapolis, IN: Wiley Publishing, 2009.

[108] Hay, David. *Data Model Patterns: Conventions of Thought*. Boston: Addison-Wesley Professional, July 2013.

[109] Swick, Ralph, Guus Schreiber, and David Wood. "Semantic Web Best Practices and Deployment Working Group" (*http://www.w3.org/2001/sw/BestPractices*). W3C. Last modified October 4, 2006.

[110] Aranguren, Mikel Egaña. "Ontology Design Patterns (ODPs) Public Catalog" (*http://www.gong.manchester.ac.uk/odp/html*). Last modified July 9, 2009.

[111] Insight Centre for Data Analytics. "The Linked Open Data Cloud" (*https://lod-cloud.net*). Last modified May 20, 2020.

[112] Ontology Engineering Group. "Linked Open Vocabularies (LOV)" (*https:// lov.linkeddata.es/dataset/lov*). Last modified July 20, 2020.

[113] Vandenbussche, Pierre-Yves, Ghislain Atemezing, María Poveda-Villalón and Bernard Vatant. "Linked Open Vocabularies (LOV): A Gateway to Reusable Semantic Vocabularies on the Web." *Semantic Web* 8 (2017): 437–452. *https://doi.org/10.3233/ SW-160213.*

[114] Ontology Engineering Group. "Music Ontology (mo)" (*https://lov.linkeddata.es/dataset/lov/vocabs/mo*). Last modified January 11, 2019.

[115] Paulheim, Heiko. "How Much Is a Triple? Estimating the Cost of Knowledge Graph Creation." In *ISWC 2018 Posters & Demonstrations, Industry and Blue Sky Ideas Tracks*, edited by Marieke van Erp, Medha Atre, Vanessa Lopez, Kavitha Srinivas, and Carolina Fortuna. CEUR Workshop Proceedings, vol. 2180. Monterey, USA, 2018.

[116] Wikipedia. "Battle of Waterloo" (*https://en.wikipedia.org/wiki/Battle_of_Waterloo*). Last modified July 14, 2020.

[117] Araúz, Pilar, Antonio San Martín, and Pamela Faber. "Pattern-based Word Sketches for the Extraction of Semantic Relations." In *Proceedings of the 5th International Workshop on Computational Terminology*, edited by Patrick Drouin, Natalia Grabar, Thierry Hamon, Kyo Kageura, and Koichi Takeuchi, 73–82. Stroudsburg, PA: Association for Computational Linguistics, 2016.

[118] Stanford Natural Language Processing Group. "Stanford Named Entity Recognizer (NER)" (*https://nlp.stanford.edu/software/CRF-NER.html*). Last modified April 19, 2020.

[119] Chinchor, Nancy and Ellen Voorhees. "MUC Data Sets" (*https://www-nlpir.nist.gov/related_projects/muc/muc_data/muc_data_index.html*). Last modified March 8, 2005.

[120] Lee, Ki-Joong, Young-Sook Hwang, and Hae-Chang Rim. "Two-Phase Biomedical NE Recognition based on SVMs." In *Proceedings of the ACL 2003 Workshop on Natural Language Processing in Biomedicine*, 33–40. Stroudsburg, PA: Association for Computational Linguistics, July 2003. *https://doi.org/10.3115/1118958.1118963*.

[121] Shalaby, Walid, Khalifeh Al Jadda, Mohammed Korayem, and Trey Grainger. "Entity Type Recognition using an Ensemble of Distributional Semantic Models to Enhance Query Understanding." In *2016 IEEE 40th Annual Computer Software and Applications Conference (COMPSAC)*, 631–636. Piscataway, NJ: IEEE Press, April 2016. *https://doi.org/10.1109/COMPSAC.2016.109*.

[122] Carnegie Mellon University. "Read the Web" (*http://rtw.ml.cmu.edu/rtw*). Accessed July 16, 2020.

[123] CMU Read the Web Project. "NELL KnowledgeBase Browser" (*http://rtw.ml.cmu.edu/rtw/kbbrowser/*). Accessed July 16, 2020.

[124] Mintz, Mike, Steven Bills, Rion Snow, and Dan Jurafsky. "Distant Supervision for Relation Extraction Without Labeled Data." In *ACL '09: Proceedings of the Joint Conference of the 47th Annual Meeting of the ACL and the 4th International Joint Conference on Natural Language Processing of the AFNLP*, vol. 2, 1003–1011. Stroudsburg,

PA: Association for Computational Linguistics, August 2009. *https://doi.org/ 10.3115/1690219.1690287.*

[125] Wikipedia. "Freebase (database)" (*https://en.wikipedia.org/wiki/Freebase_(data base)*). Last modified July 6, 2020.

[126] Hasegawa, Takaaki, Satoshi Sekine, and Ralph Grishman. "Discovering Relations Among Named Entities from Large Corpora." In *ACL '04: Proceedings of the 42nd Annual Meeting on Association for Computational Linguistics*, 415–422. Stroudsburg, PA: Association for Computational Linguistics, July 2004. *https://doi.org/ 10.3115/1218955.1219008.*

[127] Prabhakaran, Selva. "Cosine Similarity–Understanding the math and how it works (with python codes)" (*https://www.machinelearningplus.com/nlp/cosine-similarity*). *Machine Learning Plus*. Last modified April 28, 2020.

[128] Mikolov, Tomas, Ilya Sutskever, Kai Chen, Greg Corrado, and Jeffrey Dean. "Distributed Representations of Words and Phrases and their Compositionality." In *Proceedings of the 26th International Conference on Neural Information Processing Systems—Volume 2*, edited by C.J.C. Burges, L. Bottou, M. Welling, Z. Ghahramani, and K.Q. Weinberger, 3111–3119. Red Hook, NY: Curran Associates Inc., December 2013.

[129] TurkuNLP Group. "Word2Vec Demo" (*http://bionlp-www.utu.fi/wv_demo*). Last modified June 9, 2016.

[130] Etzioni, Oren, Michele Banko, Stephen Soderland, and Daniel S. Weld. "Open Information Extraction from the Web." *Communications of the ACM* 51, no. 12 (December 2008): 68–74. *https://doi.org/10.1145/1409360.1409378.*

[131] Niklaus, Christina, Matthias Cetto, André Freitas, and Siegfried Handschuh. "A Survey on Open Information Extraction." In *Proceedings of the 27th International Conference on Computational Linguistics*, edited by Emily M. Bender, Leon Derczynski, and Pierre Isabelle, 3866–3878. Stroudsburg, PA: Association for Computational Linguistics, August 2018.

[132] Yates, Alexander, Michele Banko, Matthew Broadhead, Michael Cafarella, Oren Etzioni, Stephen Soderland. "TextRunner: Open Information Extraction on the Web." In *Proceedings of Human Language Technologies: The Annual Conference of the North American Chapter of the Association for Computational Linguistics (NAACL-HLT)*, edited by Bob Carpenter, Amanda Stent, and Jason D. Williams, 25–26. Stroudsburg, PA: Association for Computational Linguistics, April 2007.

[133] Zhu, Jun, Zaiqing Nie, Xiaojiang Liu, Bo Zhang, and Ji-Rong Wen. "StatSnowball: A Statistical Approach to Extracting Entity Relationships." In *WWW '09: Proceedings of the 18th International Conference on World Wide Web*, 101–110. New York: Association for Computing Machinery, April 2009. *https://doi.org/ 10.1145/1526709.1526724.*

[134] Fader, Anthony, Stephen Soderland, and Oren Etzioni. "Identifying Relations for Open Information Extraction." In *Proceedings of the 2011 Conference on Empirical Methods in Natural Language Processing*, edited by Regina Barzilay and Mark Johnson, 1535–1545. Stroudsburg, PA: Association for Computational Linguistics, July 2011.

[135] DBpedia. "Agent" (*http://mappings.dbpedia.org/server/ontology/classes/Agent*). Accessed July 16, 2020.

[136] Schema.org. "ExerciseAction" (*https://schema.org/ExerciseAction*). Accessed July 16, 2020.

[137] Kenton, Will. "Ability to Pay" (*https://www.investopedia.com/terms/a/abilityto pay.asp*). *Investopedia*. Last modified May 9, 2019.

[138] DBpedia. "Broadcaster" (*http://mappings.dbpedia.org/server/ontology/classes/ Broadcaster*). Accessed July 16, 2020.

[139] DBpedia. "NarutoCharacter" (*http://mappings.dbpedia.org/server/ontology/ classes/NarutoCharacter*). Accessed July 16, 2020.

[140] International Press Telecommunications Council. "NewsCodes Concept: subj: 04001002" (*http://cv.iptc.org/newscodes/subjectcode/04001002*). *Information Technology for News*. Last modified December 15, 2010.

[141] International Press Telecommunications Council. "NewsCodes Concept: subj: 17004000" (*http://cv.iptc.org/newscodes/subjectcode/17004000*). *Information Technology for News*. Last modified December 15, 2010.

[142] International Press Telecommunications Council. "NewsCodes Concept: subj: 01010002" (*http://cv.iptc.org/newscodes/subjectcode/01010002*). *Information Technology for News*. Last modified December 15, 2010.

[143] DBpedia. "About: Poetry" (*http://dbpedia.org/page/Poetry*). Accessed July 16, 2020.

[144] Princeton University. "Democracy" (*http://wordnetweb.princeton.edu/perl/ webwn?s=democracy&sub=Search+Word Net&o2=&o0=1&o8=1&o1=1&o7=&o5=&o9=&o6=&o3=&o4=&h=000*). WordNet. 2010.

[145] Hayes, Adam. "Elasticity" (*https://www.investopedia.com/terms/e/elasticity.asp*). *Investopedia*. Last modified July 1, 2020.

[146] Navigli, Roberto and Paola Velardi. "Learning Word-Class Lattices for Definition and Hypernym Extraction." In *Proceedings of the 48th Annual Meeting of the Association for Computational Linguistics*, edited by Jan Hajič, Sandra Carberry, Stephen Clark, and Joakim Nivre, 1318–1327. Stroudsburg, PA: Association for Computational Linguistics, July 2010.

[147] Velardi, Paola, Roberto Navigli, and Pierluigi D'Amadio. "Mining the Web to Create Specialized Glossaries." *IEEE Intelligent Systems* 23, no. 5 (September/October 2008): 18–25. *https://doi.org/10.1109/MIS.2008.88.*

[148] Espinosa-Anke, Luis and Horacio Saggion. "Applying Dependency Relations to Definition Extraction." In *Natural Language Processing and Information Systems*, edited by Elisabeth Métais, Mathieu Roche, and Maguelonne Teisseire, 63–74. NLDB 2014. Lecture Notes in Computer Science, vol. 8455. Cham, Switzerland: Springer, 2014. *https://doi.org/10.1007/978-3-319-07983-7_10.*

[149] Jin, Yiping, Min-Yen Kan, Jun-Ping Ng, and Xiangnan He. "Mining Scientific Terms and their Definitions: A Study of the ACL Anthology." In *Proceedings of the 2013 Conference on Empirical Methods in Natural Language Processing*, editbed by David Yarowsky, Timothy Baldwin, Anna Korhonen, Karen Livescu, and Steven Bethard, 780–790. Stroudsburg, PA: Association for Computational Linguistics, October 2013.

[150] Zhang, Chunxia and Peng Jiang. "Automatic Extraction of Definitions." In *Proceedings of 2nd IEEE International Conference on Computer Science and Information Technology*, 364–368. 2009. *https://doi.org/10.1109/ICCSIT.2009.5234687.*

[151] Fahmi, Ismail and Gosse Bouma. "Learning to Identify Definitions Using Syntactic Features." In *Proceedings of the EACL 2006 workshop on Learning Structured Information in Natural Language Applications*, 64–71. 2006.

[152] Westerhout, Eline. "Definition Extraction using Linguistic and Structural Features." In *Proceedings of the 1st Workshop on Definition Extraction*, edited by Gerardo Sierra, Maria Pozzi, and Juan-Manuel Torres, 61–67. Stroudsburg, PA: Association for Computational Linguistics, September 2009.

[153] Androutsopoulos, Ion, Gerasimos Lampouras, and Dimitrios Galanis. "Generating Natural Language Descriptions from OWL Ontologies: A Detailed Presentation of the NaturalOWL System." Preprint, submitted December 2012.

[154] Filipowska, Agata, Martin Hepp, Monika Kaczmarek, and Ivan Markovic. "Organisational Ontology Framework for Semantic Business Process Management." In *Business Information Systems*, edited by, Witold Abramowicz, 1–12. BIS 2009. Lecture Notes in Business Information Processing, vol. 21. Springer-Verlag Berlin Heidelberg, 2009. *https://doi.org/10.1007/978-3-642-01190-0_1.*

[155] Alexopoulos, Panos and John Pavlopoulos. "A Vague Sense Classifier for Detecting Vague Definitions in Ontologies". In *Proceedings of the 14th Conference of the European Chapter of the Association for Computational Linguistics*, vol. 2, edited by Shuly Wintner, Stefan Riezler, and Sharon Goldwater, 33–37. Stroudsburg, PA: Association for Computational Linguistics, 2014.

[156] Glen, Stephanie. "Cohen's Kappa Statistic" (*https://www.statisticshowto.datascien cecentral.com/cohens-kappa-statistic*). *Statistics How To*. December 8, 2014.

[157] Wilson, Theresa, Paul Hoffmann, Swapna Somasundaran, Jason Kessler, Janyce Wiebe, Yejin Choi, Claire Cardie, Ellen Riloff, Siddharth Patwardhan. "Opinion-Finder: A System for Subjectivity Analysis." In *Proceedings of HLT/EMNLP 2005 Interactive Demonstrations*, edited by Donna Byron, Anand Venkataraman, and Dell Zhang, 34–35. Stroudsburg, PA: Association for Computational Linguistics, October 2005. *https://doi.org/10.3115/1225733.1225751*.

[158] Alexopoulos, Panos and José-Manuel Gómez-Pérez. "Dealing with Vagueness in Semantic Business Process Management through Fuzzy Ontologies." Paper presented at the 7th International Workshop on Semantic Business Process Management, Heraclion, Greece, May 2012.

[159] Pahn, Michael. "Meet Michael Pahn: The Fiddle and The Violin are Identical Twins (that Separated at Birth)" (*https://www.smithsonianmag.com/smithsonian-institution/meet-michael-pahn-the-fiddle-and-the-violin-are-identical-twins-that-separated-at-birth-86121430*). *Smithsonian Magazine*. September 21, 2011.

[160] DBpedia. "About: Paris" (*http://dbpedia.org/page/Paris*). Accessed July 16, 2020.

[161] Stadler, Claus. "OSM Example Queries" (*http://linkedgeodata.org/OSM*). *Linked GeoData*. Last modified September 14, 2016.

[162] Halpin, Harry, Ivan Herman, and Patrick J. Hayes. "When owl:sameAs isn't the Same: An Analysis of Identity Links on the Semantic Web." Paper presented at the RDF Next Steps Workshop, Palo Alto, CA, June 2010.

[163] Baxter, David. Email message to W3C. (*https://lists.w3.org/Archives/Public/public-lod/2009Feb/0186.html*) February 23, 2009.

[164] KBpedia. "Reference Concepts" (*https://github.com/Cognonto/kbpedia/raw/master/versions/2.50/kbpedia_reference_concepts.zip*). Accessed August 10, 2020.

[165] Noy, Natalya and Deborah L. McGuinness. *Ontology Development 101: A Guide to Creating Your First Ontology*. Stanford Knowledge Systems Laboratory Technical Report KSL-01-05, March 2001.

[166] W3C. "Simple part-whole relations in OWL Ontologies" (*https://www.w3.org/2001/sw/BestPractices/OEP/SimplePartWhole*). August 11, 2005.

[167] Aitken, J. Stuart, Bonnie L. Webber, and Jonathan Bard. "Part-of Relations in Anatomy Ontologies: A Proposal for RDFS and OWL Formalisations." Paper presented at the 9th Pacific Symposium on Biocomputing, Hawaii, USA, January 2004. *https://doi.org/10.1142/9789812704856_0017*.

[168] Altowayan, A. Aziz and Lixin Tao. "Simplified Approach for Representing Part-Whole Relations in OWL-DL Ontologies." In *2015 IEEE 17th International Confer-*

ence on High Performance Computing and Communications, 2015 IEEE 7th International Symposium on Cyberspace Safety and Security, and 2015 IEEE 12th International Conference on Embedded Software and Systems, 1399–1405. Piscataway, NJ: IEEE Press, August 2015. *https://doi.org/10.1109/HPCC-CSS-ICESS.2015.147*.

[169] W3C. "SKOS Simple Knowledge Organization System Primer: 2.3.2 Associative Relationships" (*https://www.w3.org/TR/skos-primer/#secassociative*). August 18, 2009.

[170] Tessler, Michael H. and Michael Franke. "Not Unreasonable: Carving Vague Dimensions with Contraries and Contradictions." Paper presented at the 40th Annual Conference of the Cognitive Science Society, Madison, Wisconsin, July 2018.

[171] W3C. "Shapes Constraint Language (SHACL)" (*https://www.w3.org/TR/shacl*). July 20, 2017.

[172] Aroyo, Lora and Chris Welty. "Truth Is a Lie: Crowd Truth and the Seven Myths of Human Annotation." *AI Magazine* 36, no. 1 (Spring 2015): 15–24. *https://doi.org/10.1609/aimag.v36i1.2564*.

[173] Hoffart, James, Mohamed Amir Yosef, Ilaria Bordino, Hagen Fürstenau, Manfred Pinkal, Marc Spaniol, Bilyana Taneva, Stefan Thater, and Gerhard Weikum. "Robust Disambiguation of Named Entities in Text." In *Proceedings of the 2011 Conference on Empirical Methods in Natural Language Processing*, edited by Regina Barzilay and Mark Johnson, 782–792, Stroudsburg, PA: Association for Computational Linguistics, July 2011.

[174] Mendes, Pablo N., Max Jakob, Andrés García-Silva, and Christian Bizer. "DBpedia Spotlight: Shedding Light on the Web of Documents." In *Proceedings of the 7th International Conference on Semantic Systems*, edited by Chiara Ghidini, Axel-Cyrille Ngonga Ngomo, Stefanie Lindstaedt, and Tassilo Pellegrini, 1–8. New York: Association for Computing Machinery, September 2011. *https://doi.org/10.1145/2063518.2063519*,

[175] Usbeck, Ricardo, Axel-Cyrille Ngonga Ngomo, Michael Röder, Daniel Gerber, Sandro Athaide Coelho, Sören Auer, and Andreas Both. "AGDISTIS—Graph-Based Disambiguation of Named Entities Using Linked Data." In *The Semantic Web – ISWC 2014*, edited by Peter Mika, Tania Tudorache, Abraham Bernstein, Chris Welty, Craig Knoblock, Denny Vrandečić, Paul Groth, Natasha NoyKrzysztof Janowicz, and Carole Goble, 457–471. ISWC 2014. Lecture Notes in Computer Science, vol. 8796. Cham, Switzerland: Springer, 2014. *https://doi.org/10.1007/978-3-319-11964-9_29*.

[176] Milne, David and Ian H. Witten. "Learning to Link with Wikipedia." In *Proceedings of the 17th ACM Conference on Information and Knowledge Management*, 509–518. New York: Association for Computing Machinery, October 2008. *https://doi.org/10.1145/1458082.1458150*.

[177] Kulkarni, Sayali, Amit Singh, Ganesh Ramakrishnan, and Soumen Chakrabarti. "Collective Annotation of Wikipedia Entities in Web Text." In *Proceedings of the 15th ACM SIGKDD International Conference on Knowledge Discovery and Data Mining*, 457–466. New York: Association for Computing Machinery, June 2009. *https://doi.org/10.1145/1557019.1557073*.

[178] Buonocore, Tommaso. "Man is to Doctor as Woman is to Nurse: The Gender Bias of Word Embeddings" (*https://towardsdatascience.com/gender-bias-word-embeddings-76d9806a0e17*). *Towards Data Science*. March 8, 2019.

[179] Gangemi, Aldo, Valentina Presutti, Diego Reforgiato Recupero, Andrea Giovanni Nuzzolese, Francesco Draicchio, and Misael Mongiovì. "Semantic Web Machine Reading with FRED." *Semantic Web* 8, no. 6 (2017): 873–893.

[180] "Tf-idf: A Single-Page Tutorial" (*http://www.tfidf.com*) Accessed July 16, 2020.

[181] Tiddi, Ilaria, Nesrine Ben Mustapha, Yves Vanrompay, and Marie-Aude Aufaure. "Ontology Learning from Open Linked Data and Web Snippets." In *On the Move to Meaningful Internet Systems: OTM 2012 Workshops*, edited by Pilar Herrero, Hervé Panetto, Robert Meersman, and Tharam Dillon, 434–443. OTM 2012. Lecture Notes in Computer Science, vol. 7567. Springer-Verlag Berlin Heidelberg, 2012. *https://doi.org/10.1007/978-3-642-33618-8_59*.

[182] Zaveri, Amrapali, Anisa Rula, Andrea Maurino, Ricardo Pietrobon, Jens Lehmann, and Sören Auer. "Quality Assessment for Linked Data: A Survey." *Semantic Web* 7, no. 1 (2016): 63–93.

[183] Tartir, Samir and I. Budak Arpinar. "Ontology Evaluation and Ranking using OntoQA." In *ICSC '07: Proceedings of the International Conference on Semantic Computing*, 185–192. Washington, DC: IEEE Computer Society, September 2007. *https://doi.org/10.1109/ICSC.2007.65*.

[184] Duque-Ramos, Astrid, Jesualdo Tomás Fernández-Breis, Robert Stevens, and Nathalie Aussenac-Gilles. "OQuaRE: A SQuaRE-based Approach for Evaluating the Quality of Ontologies." *Journal of Research and Practice in Information Technology* 43, no. 2 (May 2011): 159–176.

[185] DBpedia. "About: Steel" (*http://dbpedia.org/resource/Steel*). Accessed July 16, 2020.

[186] DBpedia. "About: Spawn (comics)" (*http://dbpedia.org/resource/Spawn_(comics)*). Accessed July 16, 2020.

[187] DBpedia. "About: Spawn (biology)" (*http://dbpedia.org/resource/Spawn_(biology)*). Accessed July 16, 2020.

[188] Miller, George A. and Walter G. Charles. "Contextual Correlates of Semantic Similarity." *Language & Cognitive Processes* 6, no. 1 (1991): 1–28. *https://doi.org/10.1080/01690969108406936*.

[189] Ferragina, Paolo and Ugo Scaiella. "TAGME: On-the-fly Annotation of Short Text Fragments (by Wikipedia Entities)." In *Proceedings of the 19th ACM International Conference on Information and Knowledge Management*, 1625–1628. New York: Association for Computing Machinery, October 2010. *https://doi.org/10.1145/1871437.1871689*.

[190] DBpedia. "About: starring" (*http://dbpedia.org/ontology/starring*). Accessed July 16, 2020.

[191] DBpedia. "About: Roger Moore (computer scientist)" (*http://dbpedia.org/resource/Roger_Moore_(computer_scientist)*). Accessed July 16, 2020.

[192] Papandrea, Simone, Alessandro Raganato, and Claudio Delli Bovi. "SupWSD: A Flexible Toolkit for Supervised Word Sense Disambiguation." IN *Proceedings of the 2017 Conference on Empirical Methods in Natural Language Processing: System Demonstrations*, 103–108. Stroudsburg, PA: Association for Computational Linguistics, September 2017. *https://doi.org/10.18653/v1/D17-2018*.

[193] Sharma, Pawan, Rashmi Tripathi, and R.C. Tripathi. "Finding Similar Patents Through Semantic Query Expansion." *Procedia Computer Science* 54. (2015): 390–395. *https://doi.org/10.1016/j.procs.2015.06.045*.

[194] Lord, P.W., R.D. Stevens, A. Brass and C. Goble. "Investigating Semantic Similarity Measures Across the Gene Ontology: The Relationship Between Sequence and Annotation." *Bioinformatics* 19, no. 10 (July 2003): 1275–1283. *https://doi.org/10.1093/bioinformatics/btg153*.

[195] Caviedes, Jorge E. and James J. Cimino. "Towards the Development of a Conceptual Distance Metric for the UMLS." *Journal of Biomedical Informatics* 37, no. 2 (April 2004): 77–85. *https://doi.org/10.1016/j.jbi.2004.02.001*.

[196] Princeton University. "Banal" (*http://wordnetweb.princeton.edu/perl/webwn?o2=&o0=1&o8=1&o1=1&o7=&o5=&o9=&o6=&o3=&o4=&s=banal&i=1&h=1000#c*). WordNet. 2010.

[197] Publications Office of the European Union. "Civil law" (*https://publications.europa.eu/en/web/eu-vocabularies/th-concept/-/resource/eurovoc/523*). *EU Vocabularies*. Accessed July 16, 2020.

[198] Gan, Mingxin, Xue Dou, and Rui Jiang. "From Ontology to Semantic Similarity: Calculation of Ontology-Based Semantic Similarity." *Scientific World Journal* (2013): 1–11. *https://doi.org/10.1155/2013/793091*.

[199] Slimani, Thabet. "Description and Evaluation of Semantic Similarity Measures Approaches." *International Journal of Computer Applications* 80, no. 10 (2013): 25–33. *https://doi.org/10.5120/13897-1851.*

[200] Althobaiti, Ahmad Fayez S. "Comparison of Ontology-Based Semantic-Similarity Measures in the Biomedical Text." *Journal of Computer and Communication* 5, no. 2 (February 2017): 17–27. *https://doi.org/10.4236/jcc.2017.52003.*

[201] Rada, R., H. Mili, E. Bicknell, and M. Blettner. "Development and Application of a Metric on Semantic Nets." *IEEE Transactions on Systems, Man, and Cybernetics* 19, no. 1 (January/February 1989): 17–30. *https://doi.org/10.1109/21.24528*

[202] Jiang, Rui, Mingxin Gan, and Peng He. "Constructing a Gene Semantic Similarity Network for the Inference of Disease Genes." *BMC Systems Biology* 5, S2 (2011). *https://doi.org/10.1186/1752-0509-5-S2-S2.*

[203] Al Jadda, Khalifeh, Mohammed Korayem, Camilo Ortiz, Chris Russell, David Bernal, Lamar Payson, Scott Brown, and Trey Grainger. "Augmenting Recommendation Systems Using a Model of Semantically Related Terms Extracted from User Behavior." Preprint, submitted September 2014.

[204] Škvorc, Bruno. "Knowledge Graph Quickstart" (*https://docs.diffbot.com/docs/en/dql-quickstart*). *Diffbot.* Accessed July 16, 2020.

[205] Wikipedia. "Wikipedia: Consensus" (*https://en.wikipedia.org/wiki/Wikipedia:Consensus*). Last modified June 22, 2020.

[206] Financial Industry Business Ontology (FIBO). "Contributor Covenant Code of Conduct" (*https://github.com/edmcouncil/fibo/blob/master/CODE_OF_CONDUCT.md*). Last modified December 19, 2019.

[207] Wikipedia. "Assassin's Creed Odyssey" (*https://en.wikipedia.org/wiki/Assassin%27s_Creed_Odyssey*). Last modified July 15, 2020.

[208] W3C Working Group. "Representing Classes As Property Values on the Semantic Web" (*https://www.w3.org/TR/2005/NOTE-swbp-classes-as-values-20050405*) April 5, 2005.

[209] Uschold, Michael. *Demystifying OWL for the Enterprise.* San Rafael, CA: Morgan & Claypool, 2018.

[210] DBpedia. "OntologyProperty:originalLanguage" (*http://mappings.dbpedia.org/index.php/OntologyProperty:OriginalLanguage*). Accessed July 16, 2020.

[211] DBpedia. "Language" (*http://mappings.dbpedia.org/server/ontology/classes/Language*). Accessed July 16, 2020.

[212] DBpedia. "OntologyProperty:filmColourType" (*http://mappings.dbpedia.org/index.php/OntologyProperty:FilmColourType*). Accessed July 16, 2020.

[213] DBpedia. "About: 0 (number)" (*http://dbpedia.org/page/0_(number)*). Accessed July 31, 2020.

[214] DBpedia. "About: 15 (number)" (*http://dbpedia.org/page/15_(number)*). Accessed July 31, 2020.

[215] Zadeh, Lotfi A. "Fuzzy Sets." *Information and Control* 8, no. 3 (June 1965): 338–353. *https://doi.org/10.1016/S0019-9958(65)90241-X.*

[216] Alonso, Sanjay Krishnankutty. "Fuzzy operators" (*http://www.dma.fi.upm.es/recursos/aplicaciones/logica_borrosa/web/fuzzy_inferencia/fuzzyop_en.htm*). *eMath-Teacher: Mamdani's Fuzzy Inference Method.* Accessed July 16, 2020.

[217] Ahmad, Khurshid and Andrea Mesiarova-Zemankova. (2007). "Choosing t-Norms and t-Conorms for Fuzzy Controllers." In *Fourth International Conference on Fuzzy Systems and Knowledge Discovery*, 641–646. Piscataway, NJ: IEEE Press, 2007. *https://doi.org/10.1109/FSKD.2007.216.*

[218] Farahbod, Fahimeh and Mahdi Eftekhari. "Comparison of Different T-Norm Operators in Classification Problems." *International Journal of Fuzzy Logic Systems* 2, no. 3 (July 2012): 33–39. *https://doi.org/10.5121/ijfls.2012.2303.*

[219] Hong, Tzung-Pei and Chai-Ying Lee. "Induction of Fuzzy Rules and Membership Functions from Training Examples." *Fuzzy Sets and Systems* 84, no. 1 (November 1996): 33–47. *https://doi.org/10.1016/0165-0114(95)00305-3.*

[220] Medasani, Swarup, Jaeseok Kim, and Raghu Krishnapuram. "An Overview of Membership Function Generation Techniques for Pattern Recognition." *International Journal of Approximate Reasoning* 19, no. 3/4 (October/November 1998): 391–417. *https://doi.org/10.1016/S0888-613X(98)10017-8.*

[221] Bilgiç, Taner and I. Burhan Türkşen. "Measurement of Membership Functions: Theoretical and Empirical Work." *Fundamentals of Fuzzy Sets*, edited by Didier Dubois and Henri Prade, 195–227. The Handbook of Fuzzy Sets Series, vol. 7. Boston: Springer, 2000. *https://doi.org/10.1007/978-1-4615-4429-6_4.*

[222] Zwick, Rami, Edward Carlstein, and David V. Budescu. "Measures of Similarity Among Fuzzy Concepts: A Comparative Analysis." *International Journal of Approximate Reasoning* 1, no. 2 (April 1987): 221–242. *https://doi.org/10.1016/0888-613X(87)90015-6.*

[223] Bednář, Josef. "Fuzzy Distances." *Kybernetika* 41, no. 3 (2005): 375–388.

[224] Stoilos, Giorgos, Giorgos Stamou and Jeff Z. Pan. "Fuzzy Extensions of OWL: Logical Properties and Reduction to Fuzzy Description Logics." *International Journal of Approximate Reasoning* 51, no. 6 (July 2010): 656–679. *https://doi.org/10.1016/j.ijar.2010.01.005.*

[225] Bobillo, Fernando and Umberto Straccia. "Fuzzy Ontology Representation Using OWL 2." *International Journal of Approximate Reasoning* 52, no. 7 (October 2011): 1073–1094. *https://doi.org/10.1016/j.ijar.2011.05.003.*

[226] Bobillo, Fernando and Umberto Straccia. "The Fuzzy Ontology Reasoner FuzzyDL." *Knowledge-Based Systems* 95 (March 2016): 12–34. *https://doi.org/10.1016/j.knosys.2015.11.017.*

[227] Galindo, José, Angelica Urrutia, and Mario Piattini. *Fuzzy Databases: Modeling, Design and Implementation.* Hershey, PA: Idea Group Publishing, 2006.

[228] Ranganathan, Priya, C.S. Pramesh, and Rakesh Aggarwal. "Common Pitfalls in Statistical Analysis: Measures of Agreement." *Perspectives in Clinical Research* 8, no. 4 (October/December 2017): 187–191. *https://doi.org/10.4103/picr.PICR-123-17.*

[229] Alexopoulos, Panos and Manolis Wallace. "Improving Automatic Semantic Tag Recommendation through Fuzzy Ontologies." In *Proceedings of the 7th International Workshop on Semantic and Social Media Adaptation and Personalization,* 37–41. Washington, DC: IEEE Computer Society, December 2012. *https://doi.org/10.1109/SMAP.2012.28.*

[230] Amplayo, Reinald Kim, Seung-won Hwang, and Min Song. "AutoSense Model for Word Sense Induction." In *AAAI-19, IAAI-19, EAAI-20,* 6212-6219. Proceedings of the AAAI Conference on Artificial Intelligence, vol. 33, no. 1. Palo Alto, CA: AAAI Press, 2019.

[231] Bartunov, Sergey, Dmitry Kondrashkin, Anton Osokin, and Dmitry Vetrov. "Breaking Sticks and Ambiguities with Adaptive Skip-gram." *Proceedings of Machine Learning Research* 51 (2016): 130–138.

[232] Navigli, Roberto. "A Quick Tour of Word Sense Disambiguation, Induction and Related Approaches." In *SOFSEM 2012: Theory and Practice of Computer Science,* edited by Mária Bieliková, Gerhard Friedrich, Georg Gottlob, and Stefan Katzenbeisser, 115–129. Lecture Notes in Computer Science, vol. 7147. Springer-Verlag Berlin Heidelberg, January 2012. *https://doi.org/10.1007/978-3-642-27660-6_10.*

[233] Jurgens, David and Ioannis Klapaftis. "SemEval-2013 Task 13: Word Sense Induction for Graded and Non-Graded Senses." In *Second Joint Conference on Lexical and Computational Semantics (*SEM), Volume 2: Proceedings of the Seventh International Workshop on Semantic Evaluation (SemEval 2013),* edited by Suresh Manandhar and Deniz Yuret, 290–299. Stroudsburg, PA: Association for Computational Linguistics, June 2013.

[234] Guru99. "Software Engineer vs Software Developer: What's The Difference?" (*https://www.guru99.com/difference-software-engineer-developer.html*) Last modified July 13, 2020.

[235] Princeton University. "Analysis" (*http://wordnetweb.princeton.edu/perl/webwn?o2=&o0=1&o8=1&o1=1&o7=&o5=&o9=&o6=&o3=&o4=&s=analysis&h=000000&j=1#c*). WordNet. 2010.

[236] Princeton University. "Engineer" (*http://wordnetweb.princeton.edu/perl/webwn?o2=&o0=1&o8=1&o1=1&o7=&o5=&o9=&o6=&o3=&o4=&s=Engineer&i=0&h=0000#c*). WordNet. 2010.

[237] Stevens, Robert, Phillip Lord, James Malone, and Nicolas Matentzoglu. "Measuring Expert Performance at Manually Classifying Domain Entities Under Upper Ontology Classes." *Journal of Web Semantics* 57, (August 2019): 100469. *https://doi.org/10.1016/j.websem.2018.08.004*.

[238] Wikidata. "Bertrand Russell" (*https://www.wikidata.org/wiki/Q33760*). Last modified July 11, 2020.

[239] DBpedia. "About: Data science" (*http://dbpedia.org/resource/Data_science*). Accessed July 17, 2020.

[240] Berners-Lee, Tim. "Linked Data" (*https://www.w3.org/DesignIssues/LinkedData*). Last modified June 18, 2009.

[241] Emsi Data. "FAQs: How often does the classification change?" (*https://skills.emsidata.com/faqs#changes*) Accessed July 17, 2020.

[242] EDM Council. "FIBO Release Notes: 2019 Q4" (*https://spec.edmcouncil.org/fibo/FIBO-Release-Notes#2019Q4*). Accessed July 17, 2020.

[243] European Commission. "The European Qualifications Framework for Lifelong Learning (EQF)" (*http://ecompetences.eu/wp-content/uploads/2013/11/EQF_broch_2008_en.pdf*). 2008.

[244] Glen, Stephanie. "Kendall's Tau (Kendall Rank Correlation Coefficient)" (*https://www.statisticshowto.com/kendalls-tau*). *Statistics How To*. April 26, 2016.

[245] Shirky, Clay. "The Semantic Web, Syllogism, and Worldview" (*https://www.karmak.org/archive/2004/06/semantic_syllogism.html*). First published November 7, 2003 on the "Networks, Economics, and Culture" mailing list.

[246] Verborgh, Ruben and Miel Vander Sande. "The Semantic Web Identity Crisis: In Search of the Trivialities That Never Were" (*https://ruben.verborgh.org/articles/the-semantic-web-identity-crisis*). Special issue, *Semantic Web* 11, no. 1 (2020): 19–27. *https://doi.org/10.3233/SW-190372*.

Glossary

Abductive reasoning
Tries to infer the premises that led to a conclusion by reverse-engineering known deduction rules.

Accuracy
The degree to which the semantic assertions of a model are accepted to be true.

Ambiguity
The situation in which a piece of information can be interpreted in more than one plausible way.

Class
Abstract entity that represents a kind of thing in the world and may serve as the semantic type of other entities.

Class dependence
A class C1 is dependent on a class C2 if for every instance of C1 an instance of C2 must exist.

Class subsumption
Meaning inclusion applied to classes.

Closed-world assumption
If for a given statement we don't know whether it's true or not in our model, then we can infer that it's false.

Completeness
The degree to which elements that should be contained in the model are indeed there.

Conciseness
The degree to which a model does not contain redundant elements.

Consistency
The degree to which the model is free of logical or semantic contradictions.

Contextualization
The explicit representation of all the contexts in which a model's statements are considered true.

Deductive reasoning
Reasoning from one or more statements (premises) to reach a logically certain conclusion.

Design pattern
Reusable, well-proven solution to recurring modeling/design problems or scenarios.

Entity
Something that may exist concretely or abstractly, outside, or within one's mind.

Entity attribute
A characteristic of an entity that we cannot (or choose not to) represent as a relation with another entity, and instead we use literal values.

Entity extraction
The task of automatically extracting from a given data source terms that denote enti-

ties of some particular entity type, such as persons, organizations, locations, or other.

Epistemic uncertainty

The phenomenon when a statement's truth cannot be determined due to complete or partial lack of required knowledge.

Evolution

The process of adapting the model to arisen changes in the corresponding domain.

Fuzzification

The assignment of a real number to a vague statement, within a range from 0 to 1, indicating the degree to which the statement is considered to be true.

Governance

The mechanisms by which decisions about the model and its development, application, and evolution are made and executed.

Hierarchical relation

Indicates that one element is in some way more general ("broader") than the other ("narrower"). This usually includes three different relation types, namely instantiation, meaning inclusion, and part-whole relations.

Identity

The problem of determining whether or not two entities are the same.

Individual

An entity that is an instance of one or more classes.

Inductive reasoning

Takes a premise and a conclusion and attempts to infer the rules by which the former leads to the latter.

Instantiation

Relates an entity to one or more classes it is an instance of.

Interlinking

Also known as mapping, the process of linking elements that belong to different semantic models.

Inverse relation

A relation R1 is the inverse of a relation R2 if for every entity A related to entity B through R1 we can infer that B is related to A via R2.

Knowledge acquisition

The generation of entities, relations, and other model elements from appropriate sources.

Lexicalization

Links a semantic model element to one or more terms that can be used to express it in natural language.

Meaning inclusion

The meaning of a modeling element is included in the meaning of another.

Model mining

Knowledge acquisition from data, with limited human effort.

Open-World assumption

If for a given statement we don't know whether it's true or not in our model, then we cannot draw any conclusion about its validity.

Relation

Expresses a particular way two or more entities can be related to one another.

Relation extraction

The task of automatically extracting from a given data source relations that hold between different entities and/or other elements.

Relation subsumption

Meaning inclusion applied to relations.

Relevancy

The degree to which the structure and content of the model are useful and important for a given task or application.

Rigid class

A class that is essential for all its instances, i.e., the instances could not exist if they were not an instance of that class.

Semantic change

Also known as semantic drift, the phenomenon where a word's meaning and usage change over time, often in such a way that its new meaning is radically different from the initial one.

Semantic data modeling

The development of descriptions and representations of data in such a way that the latter's meaning is explicit, accurate, and commonly understood by both humans and computer systems.

Semantic relatedness

Indicates that the meanings of two model elements are somehow related, without specifying the exact nature of this relation.

Semantic web

A collaborative effort to enable the publishing of semantic machine-readable and shareable data on the web.

Standard model

A generally agreed-upon model that is widely applied in some domain, industry, or community.

Strategy

The definition of the model's goals, the high-level approach to achieve these goals, and the decision-making mechanisms to execute this approach.

Symmetric relation

When an entity A is related to entity B via a symmetric relation R, then we can infer that B is related to A via the same relation.

Synonyms

Two terms with the same or nearly the same meaning.

Term

A string of characters (word or phrase) that can be used to lexically describe an entity, a relation, an attribute, or any other semantic modeling element.

Terminology extraction

The task of automatically extracting from a given data source (usually a corpus) terms that are relevant and important for a domain.

Timeliness

The degree to which the model contains elements that reflect the current version of the world.

Transitive relation

When a relation R is transitive, then if R links entity A to entity B, and entity B to entity C, then it also links A to C.

Trustworthiness

The perception and confidence in the quality of the model by its users.

Understandability

The ease with which human consumers can understand and utilize the model's elements, without misunderstanding or doubting their meaning.

Unity

Tells us whether and under what conditions instances of a class are considered whole entities or not.

Upper ontology

Also known as top-level or foundational ontology, describes very general concepts and relations that are independent of any particular problem or domain.

Vagueness

The phenomenon when a predicate admits borderline cases.

Index

A

abductive reasoning, 291

ABSA (see aspect-based sentiment analysis, semantic model for)

abstract entities, 15
    determining if they are classes, 18
    modeling, difficulty of, 15
    wrong classes in DBpedia, 137

accuracy, 156, 291
    (see also semantic accuracy)

AIDA named entity resolution system, 141

ambiguity, 35-37
    lexicalizations and, 228
    measuring in entity resolution system, 173, 178
        metric values for companies case, 180
    subclasses and, 211
    vagueness versus, 40

anaphoric ambiguity, 36

annotators of training data, 134

ANSI/NISO Z39-19 or ISO 25964 standards, 25
    Broader term (instance) or Narrower term (instance), 25
    hierarchical relations in ANSI/NISO, 27
    part-whole relationships, 26
    semantic relatedness in ANSI/NISO, 28

anti-rigid classes, 41

antiphrasis, 45

antonyms and behaviors of vague gradable predicates, 122

AP (Average Population), 162

applicability of a semantic model, 108

application effectiveness, improvement with semantic model, 129

application-centered quality, 49, 70
    failure to specify knowledge graph in tandem with application, 127
    relevance to different applications, 157

application-neutral quality, 49

applications that will use a semantic model, identifying, 128

applications, mistakes in applying semantic models to, 169-187
    bad entity resolution, 169
        entity resolution stories, 178-180
        how entity resolution systems use semantic models, 170
        how to select disambiguation-useful knowledge, 172-178
        when knowledge can hurt you, 171
    bad semantic relatedness, 181-186
        getting the semantic relatedness you really need, 183
        why semantic relatedness is tricky, 182

aspect-based sentiment analysis (ABSA), semantic model for, 146-152
    model population, 149
    model specification and design, 146
    population process evaluation, 151

aspect-evaluation-polarity ontology, 147

associatives, 28

assumptions
    closed- and open-world, 43
    failure to document in semantic models, 107-108

attitudes to avoid on semantic model teams, 198

attribute values, vagueness in, 40

bad, 133-146
  using wrong knowledge sources, 134
  when data is wrong, 135
  when people are wrong, 137
  wrong acquisition methods and tools,
    140-146
mechanisms and processes for, 69
specification and knowledge acquisition
  story, 146-152
knowledge graphs
  building using Neo4j, 264
  differing definitions of, 64
  misunderstanding of pain points it's sup-
    posed to treat, 127
  quality signals disguised as metrics, 164
Knowledge Tagger, 178, 223

L

labels, lexical, 25
legacy and history for semantic data models
  ignoring, problems with, 127
  understanding before developing new
    model, 129
LEILA, 152
lexical ambiguity, 36, 173
lexical databases, 14
lexicalization, 24-25, 292
  changes in, semantic drift and, 252
  controversial, insulting, or discriminatory,
    avoiding, 230
  deciding what lexicalizations to have,
    227-230
    lexicalizations you can omit, 231
    reasons fo lexicalizations, 227
  importance in semantic models, 25
  interlinking and, 240
  lexical variants vs. synonyms, 24
  measuring drift in, 253
linguistics
  meronymy/holonymy, 26
linked data
  bad interlinking, 113
  mapping and interlinking relations, 28
Linked Open Data (LOD)
  datasets available as, 74
  overview in 2011, 75
Linked Open Vocabularies, 75
location relations, extracting, 80

M

machine learning
  classes in, 19
  concept drift, 46
  distant supervision methods, 82
  semi-supervised methods, 81
  supervised methods, 80
  symbolic knowledge representation versus,
    265
  training a model with vague features and
    data, 99
map is not the territory, 261
mapping relations, 28
  bad mapping, 113
Maslow's hammer, 141
meaning
  semantics as study of, 4
  under- and over-specification in semantic
    models, 10
meaning inclusion, 26
meiosis, 45
member-collection, 27, 120
mention-level IE, 77
meronymy/holonymy, 26
metaphor, 44
metonymy, 44
metrics
  ambiguity metric values for companies case,
    180
  ambiguity metric values for soccer case, 178
  improving disambiguation capability, metric
    values and actions, 177
  measuring drift, 253
  measuring prevalence of graph's contextual
    evidence in input texts, 175
  for semantic model richness, 174
metrics for semantic model quality, bad practices with, 160-167
  equating model quality with information
    extraction quality, 166
  measuring accuracy of vague assertions in
    crisp way, 165
  using metrics that are quality signals, 164
  using metrics with arbitrary value thresh-
    olds, 162
  using metrics with little comparative value,
    162
  using metrics with misleading interpreta-
    tions, 160

vocabularies, patterns, and exemplary models, 71-75
    public models and datasets, 74
    standard and reference models, 74
    upper ontologies, 71

W

W3C Semantic Web Best Practices and Deployment Working Group, 74
Wikipedia, inaccurate data in, 50

word embeddings, 83
word sense induction (WSI), 229
Word2Vec, 83
    source of gender stereotypes in machine learning models, 142
    synonym extraction and, 140
WordNet
    lexicalization relations, 25
    use in semantic relatedness study, 181

About the Author

Panos Alexopoulos has been working since 2006 at the intersection of data, semantics, and software, contributing to building intelligent systems that deliver value to business and society. Born and raised in Athens, Greece, he currently works as Head of Ontology at Textkernel BV, in Amsterdam, Netherlands, leading a team of data professionals in developing and delivering a large cross-lingual Knowledge Graph in the HR and Recruitment domain.

Panos has obtained a PhD in Knowledge Engineering and Management from National Technical University of Athens, and has published several research papers at international conferences, in addition to journals, and books. He is a regular speaker and trainer in both academic and industry venues, striving to bridge the gap between academia and industry so that they can benefit from each other.

Colophon

The animal on the cover of *Semantic Modeling for Data* is a glossy ibis (*Plegadis falcinellus*). It is the most widely distributed species of ibis and can be found in many tropical and temperate climates around the world, including parts of Africa, Eurasia, Australia, North America, and the Caribbean. These birds typically live in coastal regions or near shallow wetlands like marshes, rice fields, estuaries, and swamps.

The glossy ibis is a wading bird with a compact body, long neck and legs, and a thin, curved bill. Adults have deep maroon feathers around the head and neck, and metallic green and violet wings. These birds are nomadic and their breeding territories are wide-ranging; some of the populations in the northern hemisphere are at least partially migratory and head further south for the winter. They feed by lowering their bills into the shallow water or mud and foraging for aquatic insects, larvae, worms, mollusks, crustaceans, tadpoles, fish, frogs, and whatever else they can find. Glossy ibises breed during the local spring or rainy season and often nest alongside other ibis, heron, egret, or spoonbill pairs in mixed-species colonies. They are highly gregarious and feed and rest in flocks throughout their lives. Both parents build and defend the nests, typically raising three to four offspring at a time.

Glossy ibises have been known to travel great lengths—some birds that were tagged in Spain have managed to cross the Atlantic and turn up as far away as Barbados! The oldest recorded glossy ibis lived in Virginia between 1971 and 1992, and was at least 21 years old. The glossy ibis is considered a species of "Least Concern" by the IUCN; their population size and range have been declining in Eurasia/Africa, but increasing in Western Europe and North America. Many of the animals on O'Reilly covers are endangered; all of them are important to the world.

The cover illustration is by Karen Montgomery, based on a black and white engraving from *Shaw's Zoology*. The cover fonts are Gilroy Semibold and Guardian Sans. The text font is Adobe Minion Pro; the heading font is Adobe Myriad Condensed; and the code font is Dalton Maag's Ubuntu Mono.

O'REILLY®

There's much more where this came from.

Experience books, videos, live online training courses, and more from O'Reilly and our 200+ partners—all in one place.

Learn more at oreilly.com/online-learning